**Eve-Ann Prentic...** ...d has written exte... ...st fifteen years. She ... ...ook, her first, when her interpreter was killed in May 1999 as a result of a NATO attack on Kosovo. Eve-Ann Prentice continues to be a committed correspondent in the Balkans and a vital witness to the human complexities of war.

***What the critics said***:

'A powerful and important book.'

Harold Pinter

'Excellent … an invaluable corrective to the spin doctors of Nato HQ.'

Mark Almond, *Literary Review*

'*One Woman's War*, spurred by the death of the author's Serb interpreter during the Nato bombing of Kosovo, is an unselfconscious, intensely human and exceptionally honest reflection of the past ten years of conflict.'

Allan Mallinson, *The Times*

'In the best tradition of a rare kind of eyewitness war reporting, the sort that is highly readable, but does nothing to make the military theatre an inviting destination.'

Elaine Lafferty, *Irish Times*

# ONE WOMAN'S WAR

# One Woman's War

### Eve-Ann Prentice

**Duckbacks**

First published in 2000 by
Duckworth Literary Entertainments Ltd.
61 Frith Street, London W1D 3JL
Tel: 020 7434 4242
Fax: 020 7434 4420
email: DuckEd@duckworth-publishers.co.uk
www.ducknet.co.uk

Published in 2001 by Duckbacks, a paperback imprint of
Duckworth Media Group

A CIP catalogue record for this title is available
from the British Library.

ISBN 0 7156 3104 7

Typeset by Derek Doyle & Associates, Liverpool
Printed in Great Britain by
BOOKMARQUE Ltd, Croydon, Surrey

# Contents

'A love of one's land is a terrible thing
It banishes fear with the speed of a flame
And makes you part of the patriot game'

The Publishers would like to thank the following for permission to reproduce copyright material. While every effort has been made to trace and acknowledge all copyright holders, we would like to apologise in advance should there have been any errors or omissions.

'The Patriot Game' by Dominic Behan. Reprinted by permission of Onward Music Ltd, 11 Uxbridge Street, London W8 7TQ

'My Generation' by Pete Townshend. Copyright Fabulous Music Ltd. 1965. Reprinted by permission of Fabulous Music Ltd, Suite 2.07, Plaza 535 Kings Road, London SW10 0SZ

BURY MY HEART AT WOUNDED KNEE by Dee Brown. First published in the US by Henry Holt and Company and in Great Britain by Random House UK Ltd. Copyright Dee Brown 1970. Reprinted by permission of Henry Holt & Co., LLC and The Peters, Fraser & Dunlop Group Ltd.

FIGHTING FOR PEACE by Michael Rose. First published in Great Britain in 1998 by The Harvill Press. Copyright The Rose Partnership 1998. Reprinted by permission of The Harvill Press.

YUGOSLAVIA: AN AVOIDABLE WAR by Nora Beloff. Reprinted by permission of New European Publications Ltd.

*Los Angeles Times* Article by Paul Watson published 28 March, 1999. Copyright, 1999, *Los Angeles Times*. Reprinted by permission.

*The Spectator* Article by Kirsten Sellars published 28 August, 1999. Copyright, 1999, *The Spectator*. Reprinted by permission.

*Cankao Xiaoxi* Article by Shao Yunhuan published 27 April, 1999. Copyright, 1999, *Cankao Xiaoxi*.

# Acknowledgements

Thanks to the following whose support and inspiration were invaluable in countless ways: Goran Zdravkovic for helping me to survive at all; Dessa Trevisan; my former husband Pat Prentice; my father, Lord Whaddon; my stepmother, Angela, Lady Whaddon; Sandra Parsons; and the unsung heroes of *The Times* and other newspapers, the sub-editors who guard against so many unintended mistakes. Thanks also to Ed Victor, my agent, his assistant Lizzy Kremer, and to Tom Hedley and Sarah Such at Duckworth for giving me the opportunity to write this book in the first place. Last but not least all my friends and colleagues in Serbia, especially Marija Ilic, Srdjan Stojanovic, Toma and Dusica, Nenad Golubovic and Nebojsa Radojevic, our translator who was killed at 3.30 p.m. on Sunday, 30 May 1999; as well as those government, opposition and other officials who must remain nameless but whose understanding has been much appreciated.

# The Former Yugoslavia, 1999

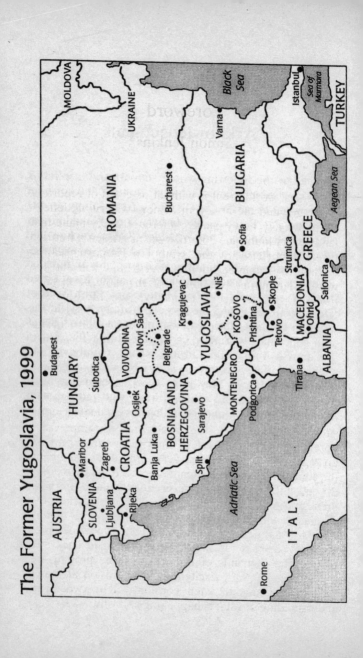

# Foreword

## Simon Jenkins

No critical world event is without its cloud of reporters, buzzing round the honeypot of news. Every battlefield, every atrocity, every peace conference, every plane that lands, every limousine door that opens attracts a frenzied pack. Reporters are the symbol of importance, the medium of communication between the event and the world. Clamouring, questioning, often hostile, never satisfied, the pack represents humanity's appetite for news. No amount of technology seems able to supplant it. No shield can ever protect a public figure from its furious attention. The pack is more than the poor bloody infantry of a free press. It is the first eye-witness of history.

Through most of the 1990s, Eve-Ann Prentice watched the unfolding of the latest tragedy to afflict what was once Europe's frontier with the East, the Balkans. The progressive dismemberment of Tito's Yugoslavia was a saga of inhumanity, intolerance and incompetence. Foreign, particularly Western, intervention in the break-up of Yugoslavia was intense yet confused. Disentangling the motives of the participants meant not just reading events on the ground but interpreting the minds of those orchestrating them far away. Ms Prentice watched the drama in one theatre after another, from the bloody streets of Sarajevo to the smooth conference rooms of Geneva. She was rarely given time to stand back and reflect. The demands of reporting on the ground are today's 'fog of war'. Excitement or revulsion at man's inhumanity to man threatens constantly to overwhelm an understanding of what is happening and why.

This book meets these challenges. It is a testament to the physical courage of the modern reporter, often working in conditions as unsafe as those of a soldier. It is also a testament to Ms Prentice's intellectual courage. Few conflicts have been so subject to 'spin', to state-sponsored mendacity, as those in which Nato became involved in both Bosnia and Kosovo. The reporter depends on a measure of access to those shaping events, yet must know to treat that access with scepticism. It is one thing to seek answers to questions, another to question the answers. This is a book full of answers being questioned. Its independence of view challenges official bias. It holds up to the light the cruelty and stupidity that can be displayed even by those who profess liberal values.

Eve-Ann Prentice writes in the fine tradition of reporters of global conflict. She offers events for what they are, not what someone would like them to be. She is her own woman. Her witness is indispensable.

# Part I
# Taking Sides

# Chapter One

# The Bombing: 30 May 1999

The engine tone of the aircraft above us had changed; the drone had become a dive. Carlos and I looked at one another as, wide-eyed but wordless, we realised we were about to be bombed. We scrambled across the rubble on the track in front of us, desperately seeking some sort of cover from the unpromising choices of a towering rock face on our right and the steep ravine dropping sharply to a river below us on our left.

The deep, menacing and thunderous boom of the bomb exploding came seconds after I crouched against the rock face at the mouth of a road tunnel. The monstrous explosion ricocheted around the surrounding canyons and gorges. Inside the tunnel, which was heaped high with rubble from an earlier bombing, I could see Carlos Julio, a fellow journalist from Portugal, and Nenad our bodyguard trying to shield Elsa, a petite young reporter from Portuguese television who was pleading, 'Don't leave me, don't leave me.' I was struck then by the stark terror which normally only ever occurs in nightmares, just as you are jolted awake on the brink of what you think will be certain death. Only this time, there was no awakening.

As one aircraft was climbing away, I could hear through blast-dulled ears a second jet homing in for a new bombing run. 'Come in here!' Nenad shouted at me from the back of the tunnel. 'It is safer here.' I could not believe him, much as I wanted to, for it seemed obvious that this tunnel and a second so-far-untouched tunnel a few yards away were the targets of the gleaming warplanes and their deadly cargoes.

We were on a mountain road in southern Kosovo in late May 1999, at a time when Nato was intensifying its bombing campaign against the southern Serbian province. It was more than two months after the start of the Nato campaign and the Alliance had flown thousands of sorties. I had witnessed scores of dead and wounded across Serbia but – until now – I had believed that I could stay in one piece.

'Oh my God, oh my God, what a fucking nightmare,' I heard myself shouting, as my mind went into hyperdrive in search of safety. I was horrified by the thought of being buried under tons of rock and began pleading with Carlos, Nenad and Elsa to come with me out of the tunnel. I could not see where the rest of our group had scattered when the first explosion hit. The unmistakable *zheeee* sound of a second bomb hurtling to earth robbed me of more time to think. Instinctively I ran from the tunnel mouth – and, inadvertently, directly towards the missile as it slammed to the ground about twenty yards away.

This time the deep, rumbling roar of the explosion was accompanied by a pulse of awesome energy, which hit me like a wave. I was sure it would be my last moment of consciousness on earth. Stark terror jolted my brain, making the moment seem to pass like minutes. I cursed the Fates which were ending my life on this rubble-strewn mountain road which reeked of danger, and prayed that the end would be swift and clean. Shameful to say, I did not think of my family, but of how I was being robbed of the chance to use my last breath to draw on the comfort of a cigarette.

The next sensation was amazement that I was still breathing, albeit flat on my face in a pall of chokingly thick asbestos-coloured dust thrown up by the explosion. It was like being caught in a monumental soot-fall. I hardly dared believe that I was alive, let alone unmutilated, and wondered for a split second whether I had been so horribly injured that the pain would come only later. Realising that I was still in one piece, I scrambled shakily to my feet as the impenetrable fug cleared to a haze, and saw, in the shade of the second tunnel, one of the two cars we had been using. The last time I had seen it, the gleaming Toyota Carina had been a head-turning marvel of Western technology on the tank- and tractor-rutted roads of Kosovo. Now it looked like a drinks can, crumpled and discarded.

Five hours before, Nenad's friend and our translator, Nebojsa Radojevic, had been in the car, guarding it and our belongings after we were forced to abandon the vehicles and walk into Prizren because the road had been blocked by the earlier bombing. Was he still inside? There was no sign of the second car, a Volkswagen Golf, so I leapt to the optimistic conclusion that Nebojsa had had time to pull away in it when he heard the unmistakable approach of the first bomb, and had gone for help.

About a minute passed as I staggered like a drunk among the dust-strewn rubble, looking for my shoulder bag which had been ripped from my grasp in the second blast. It contained my passport, accreditation papers, reading-glasses and those vital cigarettes and lighter. Carlos emerged from behind me through the haze: 'Come quick, come quick, we must get away,' he gasped, pulling at my arm as we heard yet again the whine of a swooping jet engine. There was no going back towards Prizren, as the rubble blocking our path that way was so high and wide that, even in panic, it would have taken several minutes to climb back over. So the two of us staggered towards the other tunnel, which sheltered the twisted wreckage of the Toyota. As we ran past it, I paused for a second to try to see if I could see Nebojsa inside, but the vehicle had been so flattened that only a few inches of window space remained, and it seemed in that brief moment that the car was empty.

We slithered and stumbled on through the tunnel and

out, through to the other side. We were on our own now, with no idea where the rest of the group was or whether they were alive or dead. My eyes swept the road ahead as, once more at super-speed, my brain tried to calculate the safest place to shelter. A couple of caves were rejected for fear that the next bomb would hit the rocky overhangs and bury us in the rubble. To our left, the steep drop to the river, about twenty feet below, seemed suicidal. Then Carlos made the miraculous discovery of a culvert, about eight feet in diameter, which carried rainwater from the road to the river. The mouth of the culvert was hidden in greenery and the mountain did not overhang it. With seconds to spare before the next bomb exploded, we half-fell into the massive water pipe.

Until then, it had been hard to grasp the obvious – that someone was trying to kill myself, Carlos, Nenad, Elsa and four others on this mountain road about three miles from the picturesque medieval town of Prizren in southwest Kosovo. The villains were not Serb soldiers or Albanian snipers – hidden somewhere in the towering mountains all around us – but people from 'our' side, from Nato. The anger was to come later; for the moment I was galvanised by a fierce desire to survive. It did fleetingly cross my mind that the bombs were being aimed by someone with a clipped RAF accent, who would go home for tea afterwards; or one of our American cousins with an overdeveloped sense of Top Gunmanship.

Three more bombs pounded the area around the road tunnels in the following fifteen minutes. The towering mountains provided perfect acoustics and amplification for the menacing sound. Carlos and I shouted for the others in our party during the lulls between the explosions, but our calls went unanswered. Carlos, a forty-two-year-old newspaper reporter, tried to reassure me that we were safest where we were. During each of the hammer-blow blasts, I clung to him, literally for dear life, as he stroked my face. The helplessness of the situation was stultifying. I alternated between wanting to move on, so as to feel as if I had some control, and a yearning to give in and abandon myself to fate. Carlos was growing more agitated at the thought that we were the only ones to have survived. He thought he had seen one of our group, Renzo Cianfanelli, a seasoned Italian war correspondent, take the full force of the first explosion.

Eventually, the relentless drone and dive of what seemed to be two aircraft started to fade but not before I grabbed at Carlos in a new surge of panic, having heard yet another roaring, rumbling noise – slightly different in tenor to the recent sounds of war.

'Don't be afraid, it is just the river,' he said.

The culvert sloped steeply down to the river and was too deep for me to climb from, unaided. I cowered near the upper end, praying that the bombing raid had ended, and wondering how we were going to get away from this isolated, dangerous place.

It was 3.30 in the afternoon on Sunday, 30 May 1999 when the first bomb struck, and I had been in a Yugoslavia at war for almost six weeks. Our small group of journalists had first arrived at the road tunnels near Prizren soon after nine that morning. The plan had been to leave Kosovo and travel back to the Serbian capital, Belgrade, in our two cars later that day. First we wanted to try to visit the medieval town of Prizren to report on the war situation there and visit survivors from the Nato shelling of more than two hundred ethnic Albanians at the nearby village of Korisa a few days earlier. Serbian police at several checkpoints en route from the Kosovo capital, Pristina, had warned us that we might not be able to get through to Prizren, and we should have been doubly on the alert when we reached the two tunnels, just a few yards apart, and found one of them blocked. We did not know that this stretch of road had until that morning been one of the last passable roads near the front line of the battles raging between the Yugoslav Army and the Kosovo Liberation Army. The decision to carry on by

foot was one of those moves where group responsibility
in reality made us irresponsible; no one wanted to hinder
our party's progress into Prizren by voicing doubts about
the safety of the venture. Later, I would curse my failure
to speak out.

There were eight of us: Nenad Golubovic, the karate-
practising bodyguard who had driven one of the cars
around Kosovo, his automatic pistol ever ready; Nebojsa,
the other driver, who also acted as our translator; Carlos
Julio; Elsa Marujo, twenty-nine; her cameraman – also
called Carlos – Pinota, twenty-seven, from Portuguese
television; Renzo Cianfanelli from the Italian newspaper,
*Corriere della Sera*; myself; and Daniel Schiffer, a self-
proclaimed Franco-Italian humanist and philosopher
who organised occasional visits to Kosovo for journalists
based in Belgrade during the Nato bombing campaign on
Yugoslavia.

When we had arrived that morning, we should have
read the danger signals. I had felt more uneasy than at
any time since arriving in the southern Serbian province,
especially after hearing the drone of aircraft and looking
skywards. Two pinpricks in the blue expanse visible
between the towering peaks directly above us had been
weaving a vapour trail figure of eight, and it had
occurred to me that they could be reconnaissance
aircraft taking photographs to aid a bombing run later in
the day.

Reaching the path on the Prizren side of the tunnel, I
had seen a burnt-out bulldozer, still smouldering, and an
incinerated Serbian armoured personnel carrier lying on
its side on the edge of the ravine leading to the river.
Jagged remains of an olive green shell-case, about fifteen
inches in diameter and about three feet long, lay near a
newly-made bomb crater. Yugoslav Army soldiers
referred to these 500-pound missiles as *krmace* or 'sows'.
I looked at my watch: it was 9.30 a.m., an hour which
would later come back to haunt me. Just ahead of us, a
group of about twelve civilians had also manoeuvred

themselves across the rubble, apparently on their way to church and the Sunday market in Prizren. They were elderly men, women and children.

Elsa had almost opted to stay behind with Nebojsa rather than make the three-mile walk in blazing heat down into Prizren, and the debate about who would and would not go on by foot delayed us for about twenty minutes. When all of us but Nebojsa were finally under way, I had been relieved. Rarely had I been in a place which was hung so heavily with an atmosphere of peril. My edginess increased when we began to find Serbian-language leaflets dropped by Nato lying by the roadside, warning the Yugoslav Army to leave Kosovo or face 'certain death'.

Now, more than six hours later, Carlos and I were shaking with fear in the culvert. I began to wonder why Nato felt it had to bomb a road clearly used by civilians at 3.30 in the afternoon, instead of attacking it at 3.30 in the morning if the Alliance felt it was strategically important to block the route.

'I am pretty sure Renzo was killed,' Carlos said again, fifteen minutes after the boom of the fifth shell-blast reverberated between the peaks on all sides. 'I saw a shell burst just where he was standing.' I wanted to try to climb out of the water conduit and get away from this Nato target area. 'We must wait at least half an hour,' said Carlos.

Within seconds, we heard the sound of a car approaching on the unseen road above us. Huge relief pulsed through me; it was the first time I dared to hope there was a real chance of escaping alive. Nebojsa had come to the rescue, I assumed.

Carlos and I called out as we heard the car stop somewhere close by, followed by the banging of a car door and footfalls brushing through the undergrowth and moving towards us. At any moment, Nebojsa's face would appear over the edge of the culvert. Instead, there were two seemingly enormous Yugoslav Army soldiers, beaming and stretching their hands down towards us. Effortlessly, one of them scooped me from our hiding place and enfolded me in his arms. I felt like a lost child who had just found her father.

In seconds we were bundled towards a small civilian car; squashed together in the back were Daniel Schiffer, Elsa and a very-much-alive Renzo. The Italian had a round, crinkled, well-lived-in face which sat oddly atop a strangely boyish body kept thin by regular sessions in the gym. With Carlos and myself now to be accommodated, we rearranged ourselves in the car; the bob-haired Elsa sat on my knee as one of the soldiers drove hell for leather from the bomb site and into the village of Rekane a couple of miles away. En route, we tried to account for everyone. Where was Nenad? He was OK, said Schiffer, for he had been with him until seconds before we were picked up. No one knew the fate of either Nebojsa or Carlos Pinota, the Portuguese cameraman. Renzo had seen the cameraman jump or fall into the river near the beginning of the raid; but no one had seen Nebojsa. Tears were pouring down Elsa's face as she sat, pleading to get away faster and still shaking with fear. 'Make her be calm,' someone in the back said exasperatedly. I stroked her face, close to weeping and wailing myself but just about managing restraint – for the moment. Panic was to clamp its cold hand more firmly on my brain as the next twenty-four hours unfolded.

When we reached the tiny village of Rekane, men, women and children swarmed onto the street and urgent, concerned faces pressed around us. Chairs and sweetened water were brought onto the pavement and we were all urged to sit. Most of the villagers seemed to be of Turkish descent and appeared surprisingly at ease with the Serbian soldiers. Like almost every civilian from all ethnic backgrounds in Kosovo, they were the personification of kindness. They said they saw us as people willing to share their fate in this time of war rather than as representatives of the countries which were bombing them.

But what should have felt a place of blessed safety suddenly became a deathtrap in my eyes. The name Rekane means Little Rivers in English and the chairs had been arranged next to a small stone bridge crossing one of the streams – and bridge equalled Nato target. 'I can't stay here, none of us can stay here,' I said, jumping to my feet and running deeper into the village away from the bridge. The rest ambled along behind and we all gathered in a huddle behind a house in a street set back from the river.

Most of us had suffered cuts and bruises but seemed otherwise miraculously unscathed. Although the taste and smell of bomb-blasted dust was in my nose and mouth, I craved a cigarette and a villager eagerly obliged. Then I began to take stock: my black jeans and jacket were smothered in ash-like debris and one shoe was hanging askew from my left foot which was bleeding. Both feet were almost bare as shredded tights now provided merely a cobweb of cover. Most of my fingernails were torn, whether in the blast which had thrown me to the ground or in the mad scramble for cover afterwards, I did not know. My right leg felt bruised beneath my jeans and I had a burgeoning bump on my forehead.

Elsa had a deep cut on her left leg and grazes to her forehead, Carlos Julio looked dusty, battered and bruised but insisted he was unhurt. Daniel Schiffer said he thought he had broken his arm and we could see a cut on the bridge of his nose. (Nenad later said that Schiffer was injured when he had pushed him to the ground when one of the bombs fell.) Nenad's main concern was the dust on his normally immaculately-polished black shoes; he spent the next twenty-four hours grabbing any piece of cloth or paper he could find to try to restore their pristine appearance. Renzo insisted he was unhurt and seemed to be becoming ever more agitated and angry because he could not immediately file a report to his newspaper. I don't think it occurred to any of us to dwell too deeply on our astonishingly light injuries – at that moment most of us were ecstatic just to be alive and away from immediate danger. We had also seen too many dead and badly wounded bomb victims in the previous weeks to consider ourselves anything other than lucky.

Nevertheless, one of the two saviour soldiers explained he was a doctor and insisted on driving us higher up the mountain, to a village where he said he had a small clinic. The settlement transpired to be the Turkish-dominated village of Lokvica, perched high on the mountain, which served as a base for several dozen Yugoslav Army troops. The village looked like a scene from a nineteenth-century Austro-Hungarian oil painting. Trees, heavy with the foliage of late May, overhung many of the buildings, shading them from the heat of the sun and from the eyes of Nato, while women in Turkish-style pantaloons and exotic headscarves led a lazy procession of cows through the dusty, dung-spattered main square. The soldiers had made camp in what seemed to be a disused farmhouse and the adjoining outbuildings. There was no electricity or water, although the soldiers did have a small generator which they used for cooking and presumably powering radio and other communications equipment.

The doctor's name was Goran Zdravkovic and he tended our cuts and grazes in the clean but spartan room which served as an army clinic, and which had witnessed far more serious injuries than ours. It fleetingly occurred to me that we might be arrested; after all, we were a group of journalists from 'aggressor' countries who could easily pass on information about the whereabouts and conditions of this Yugoslav Army position if allowed to go free. Instead, we were treated with the utmost care, by the troops and by the Turkish villagers. This was partly because we were with Daniel Schiffer, who was seen as a staunch ally by many Serb soldiers, who had often seen him speak out against the Nato action on state-controlled Serbian television. As for the villagers, like country folk the world over, they were endowed with an innate generosity of spirit which would seem alien – even idiotic

– to city slickers in London or New York. In the end, no one from Nato ever contacted me about the bombing or the army base where we were taken, and the soldiers did their utmost to get us swiftly and safely back to the Kosovo capital, Pristina.

Many weeks later, I was to learn that we owed our deliverance to a shepherd boy on the mountain near the tunnels, who had seen our predicament when the bombing began and had run to Rekane to raise the alarm, telling a Yugoslav soldier there that he thought some people were trapped. The news was radioed to Lokvica, where Dr Zdravkovic and his commander had decided to drive down to see if anyone needed help. They did not ask for volunteers to join them, Dr Zdravkovic later said, 'since this mission looked like certain death'. Instead they just made the Orthodox sign of the cross and set out.

Weeks later, in July, I was also told that Slobodan Milosevic, the Yugoslav President, had personally intervened on our behalf. Dr Zdravkovic and his commander had argued about what to do with us. The commander had wanted us to be shipped immediately down the mountain despite the risk of us finding ourselves caught in yet another bombing raid or falling prey to ethnic Albanian terrorist snipers. But Dr Zdravkovic had argued that Elsa and I were too traumatised to run the gauntlet of more bombs. He was apparently about to be overruled when Milosevic contacted the commander by radio to ask how we were. The Yugoslav leader, indicted war criminal and bête noire of the West, was probably not acting merely for humanitarian reasons, since our plight was rich fodder for his propaganda machine. Indeed, the first contact we were to have with the outside world, apart from one satellite telephone call made by Renzo, was to be greeted in the nearby ski resort of Brezovica next day by a television crew and Reuters correspondent despatched from the Yugoslav Government-controlled press centre in Pristina. Nonetheless, Milosevic's intervention that evening meant that the doctor had his way and we were allowed to stay in the relative safety of the army camp rather than face the Nato bombs which pounded the tunnel road and Prizren almost incessantly through the night.

That evening, as Elsa, myself, Carlos Julio, Schiffer and Renzo were offered plates of roast meat, salad, cheese and bread in the disused farmhouse kitchen, we were told that Nebojsa was dead. The first bomb that afternoon had struck an almost direct hit beneath the car where he was sleeping. He had spent the hours while we were in Prizren socialising with villagers in Rekane before returning to the road tunnel to wait for us. The power of the bomb had lifted the car and smashed it against the roof of the tunnel where it was parked, killing Nebojsa instantly. As with any sudden death of someone you know, my first reaction was disbelief. How could anyone so large and full of life exist no more? His presence had played a large part in my life for the previous two weeks as we had worked, eaten, laughed and occasionally grown irritable. He had told us that he was divorced, doted on his ten-year-old son and that his ambition was to run a travel agency when the war was over.

A small group of troops set out with Nenad as dusk was falling, to return to the scene of the bombing and retrieve the translator's body. They also wanted to gather our belongings, which had been in the boot of the pulverised car. I was horrified by the prospect of yet more people being killed in any new bombing for the sake of our luggage – and no one could help Nebojsa now. Elsa and I pleaded with them not to go; we could hear aircraft droning overhead, en route to release yet more deadly shells, and we felt there was a very real risk that those setting out for Nebojsa would not survive. To me, it seemed inconceivable that anyone would voluntarily return to that hellish road.

I fleetingly wondered whether their willingness to put their lives at risk illustrated a deep-rooted difference between men and women. Having spent thirty years working in a predominantly male environment, I am usually not aware of my gender. I never regard myself as a Woman Journalist, a feminist, or even one of the boys. I just do the job to the best of my ability. But now I could see that Elsa and I seemed to be far more acutely aware of the danger than the men. It was impossible to say whether this was due to bravado on their part, an unwillingness to show fear to other men, or whether they truly were less concerned. Watching them set off for Nebojsa's body as night fell on the mountains made me think of the boys and men who had climbed out of First World War trenches into the teeth of cannon fire.

Later that evening, news came that the missing Portuguese television cameraman had been traced to Prizren. Soldiers in our camp were told by radio that he had been found hammering on the door of a monastery, dripping wet and still clutching his camera, after being washed downstream in the river. His ordeal was by far the worst of those of us who had survived. After being cut and bruised by boulders in the fast-flowing river, he had managed to grab a branch and haul himself from the numbingly cold mountain water. Initially, the monks and police had suspected him of being a downed Nato pilot and after being provided with some ill-fitting but dry clothes, he had been taken to the police station in Prizren for questioning. After enduring a night of almost constant bombardment in a building which must have been high on Nato's wish list, he then had to face a high-risk car drive through sniper territory before being reunited with the rest of our party the following afternoon. Driving along remote mountain roads in KLA territory on the far side of the mountain, his car was shot at several times by suspected Albanian gunmen.

The rest of us, meanwhile, were being settled for the night in the army encampment. Villagers offered us clean clothes and the use of their bathrooms while Dr Zdravkovic even came up with a pair of pristine white sports socks for me. 'You MUST put on socks,' he insisted, 'to keep wound clean.' Periodically, I was racked by uncontrollable trembling, especially when the sound of Nato jets sounded unhealthily close as they arced over the mountain. 'Don't be 'FRAID,' he repeatedly admonished. 'They are your planes, why you 'FRAID?' He was about thirty years old and compensated for his lack of English by staring intensely into our faces as he spoke. Elsa was also terrified and the doctor several times offered both of us an injection of Valium. Instead, we accepted the other soldiers' offer of copious amounts of home-brewed liquor.

For hour after hour we sat by candlelight in a tiny courtyard next to the farmhouse, drinking and talking to the soldiers and one another. The drone of Nato jets en route to pulverise Prizren and the surrounding area continued intermittently. Nebojsa's body had now been brought back to Lokvica and lay in the tiny, picturesque Orthodox chapel perched on a hummock on the edge of the village. The group which had made the perilous journey had barely escaped alive themselves, since a fresh bombing raid began at the tunnels just as they had arrived. At the farmhouse, Nenad frequently brushed tears away from moist eyes whenever the talk turned to Nebojsa, and we all joined him and the villagers to light candles for the dead man in the church. An Orthodox church has two tiers of candles set in sand, one at waist height for the living, and one at ground level for the dead.

Most of the soldiers based in and around the dilapidated farmhouse were curious but friendly towards us. Few of them could speak English and none from our group but Schiffer and Nenad spoke more than a few words of Serbian. All the Yugoslav Army troops constantly tried to make us more comfortable. They put army jackets around Elsa and me when the night became chilly and six of them vacated their beds, insisting that we sleep in them. A crude wooden stairway with no banisters led to two bedrooms where simple but surprisingly clean beds were strewn with army clothes. About half a dozen Kalashnikov rifles were leaning against the walls. The scene reminded me of council house bedrooms I had seen in the fens of Lincolnshire nearly thirty years before, where shotguns were stacked in place of the Kalashnikovs here.

Eventually, at about four in the morning, the Nato flights and bombardment ceased and Elsa and I fell into an exhausted sleep for a couple of hours. Nenad heeded Elsa's pleas and slept on a mattress on the floor between us, though even his massive karate-honed body could have done nothing to counter a Nato shell. His presence was just a huge psychological comfort. If he looked calm, we could feel less panicky. I have always marvelled at war correspondents who regularly and voluntarily put themselves in the line of fire. I have occasionally found myself on the fringes of battle over the years; in Gdansk during martial law in Poland, in Romania during the revolution there, Croatia and very briefly in Sarajevo. But I have become more, not less jumpy with the passage of time. I had long known that I was not the stuff of which war correspondents are made; I was drawn to Eastern Europe and the Balkans by a fascination with the politics of the region – where tectonic plates of capitalism, Communism, Roman Catholicism, Eastern Orthodoxy and Islam clashed against one another. War correspondents, on the other hand, roam the world looking for trouble. They usually want to concentrate on the effects rather than the causes of conflict. Some genuinely seem to get an adrenalin high, living on the edge of existence. I have to be honest and say that my instinct for self-preservation tends to override all other sensations in times of danger.

Next morning, while being urged to eat an omelette which would have done the Savoy Grill proud, a small explosion somewhere outside sent me involuntarily scurrying for cover. One second I was at the table in the main living room, the next I was crouching near the sink in the kitchen as a Yugoslav soldier flung his arms protectively around me, laughing not unkindly. I began to think about the hundreds of thousands of men, women and children across Serbia, who had by this time spent weeks enduring nightly bombings close to their homes because they happened to live near what Nato described as a 'legitimate target'. How did they stay sane?

We washed at a standpipe in the little courtyard while soldiers brought us treacle-thick black coffee. Despite the enormous amounts of liquor sipped in the night, I had not the slightest hangover. Instead, I had discovered a large bump on my right knee, which now felt as if it was badly sprained, and I had a jabbing pain in my side. My holdall from the smashed car had been riddled with shrapnel and the clothes inside had been knitted together by shards of metal, still warm fifteen hours on.

The Serbian soldiers decided that we should all be taken to Brezovica, a ski resort about ten miles east of Prizren, and if possible back to Pristina later in the day. This was a time when the KLA had made great inroads back into Kosovo and large swathes of the province were no-go areas for Serbs, who were fearful of sniper attacks. At the beginning of the Nato campaign on 24 March, the Yugoslavian Army, police and special forces had already swept the KLA – and vast numbers of innocent ethnic Albanian civilians along with them – from at least two thirds of Kosovo. Even ten days before the road tunnel bombing, I had seen Serbs travelling relatively freely in the eastern half of the region. But now, on 31 May, twelve days before Nato was to enter the province, the situation was radically different.

Better armed and trained, and working in at least covert co-operation with Nato, the KLA held sway in many areas. The road from Pristina to the outskirts of Prizren had been eerily deserted; village after village stood in silent testimony to the Serbian reign of terror which had driven the innocent and guilty from their homes. Occasionally, smoke rose from the blackened ruins of one or two houses.

A few weeks later, I was to learn much more about how

these Kosovo battles had been planned and executed. The picture which was to emerge during many discussions with disaffected, demobilised troops from the towns in southern Serbia, and with human rights lawyers and monitors, would be far more subtle than the image projected by Jamie Shea, the Nato spokesman, and his cohorts in Brussels. At the time we were bombed, much of the world believed that an essentially innocent ethnic Albanian community had been forced at gunpoint to leave Kosovo simply because they were not Serbs. In reality, a civil war had raged for decades and extremists among the ethnic Albanians, as well as among the Serbs, had fuelled the conflict. Many of the aircraft used in the Alliance campaign flew extremely high to avoid anti-aircraft fire; so high that most of the time they were heard but not seen by those of us on the ground, even on those cloudless sun-splashed days which seemed to make a mockery of the death and mayhem on the ground. By the end of May, however, the Yugoslav Army had little if any anti-aircraft cover left in Kosovo and the airmen who attacked us had flown low enough for us to see their aircraft. I hold a pilot's licence and I am almost certain that the Nato airmen would have clearly seen us and the other people travelling along that stretch of road.

I gained my private pilot's licence in 1997. While there can be no comparison between the skill needed to pilot a modern fighter or bomber and that needed to become a recreational flyer, all pilots have to start learning to fly in single-engined aircraft. I knew, therefore, that most pilots were extremely disciplined and many were courageous. Until now, my idea of a wartime pilot had been the likes of John Jordan, a Second World War veteran who performed aerobatics in his venerable Steerman from a grass strip airfield at Little Gransden in Bedfordshire until he was well over seventy. During the war, he had swooped down into enemy territory in Eastern Europe to pluck an important Polish general, Bor Komarowski, and his family from a field as the Nazis closed in.

I qualified as a private pilot in an attempt to conquer a fear of flying which was threatening to cramp my love of travel to distant places. I was lucky when a colleague and old friend at *The Times*, Alan Copps, offered me the chance of a free course at Oxford Air Training School. The school, one of the finest in the world, wanted to publicise its work.

My flying phobia had its roots in the convent school in Wales where I spent most of my secondary education. My father, a keen private pilot, decided to rent a light aircraft and fly from Cambridge to an airfield near Chester to pick me up at the start of the summer holidays when I was twelve. The headmistress and another nun had driven me to Howarden airfield on the Wales-Cheshire border, where the paternal aeroplane was due to land. A kind enough gesture – except that they spent almost the entire journey in a litany of prayer to 'save me from the eternal flames of hell-fire' should the plane crash on the way home.

This eventuality, which had barely crossed my mind when we set out from Brigidine, had become a virtually pre-ordained certainty by the time we reached Howarden. To make matters worse, my father and the fellow-pilot he had brought along to share the workload decided to run one of the two fuel tanks dry to maximise the available fuel. They did not enlighten me about their plan. Sitting alone in the rear of the aircraft, with a freshly-ingrained nervousness about the feasibility of flight, I was less than reassured when the engine suddenly spluttered and fell silent. The propeller, a blurred disc of speed, slowed to the point where its outline was clearly visible. It was only a matter of seconds before my father switched to the other fuel tank and the engine began to screw the propeller through the air once more, but the damage had been done.

Over the next few years, I convinced myself that all aircraft were perpetually on the brink of plummeting to earth. For years I avoided all air travel and journeyed as far as possible across Europe by train. The yearning to see distant continents eventually dragged me unwillingly to board giant jets to Australia and the Far East, but it was always a torture. I tried hypnotism, relaxation tapes, sleeping tablets and copious amounts of whisky, but the panic was so severe on each trip that I could only stare rigidly at the seat back in front of me and try to will the jet to stay aloft. Wild horses could not have persuaded me to look out of the window.

The only thing which worked was the flying lessons. I knew I had cracked the phobia on the day I flew my first solo, and gazed in awe at the airfield below me and the Cotswold countryside stretching away to the distance. By then, I had learned to love the sound of aircraft engines and to thrill at the sight of wings lifting skyward at the moment of take-off. But after a few weeks' experience of Nato's air strikes, I had begun to loathe and dread the drone of jet engines once more. It was also hard to equate the mentality of the men and women who had taught me to fly with the Top Gun psychology which must be needed to target bridges, post offices and tower blocks, knowing they had to be used by civilians.

After news of the attack on our journalists' group near Prizren filtered out, Jamie Shea – known as the 'Barrow Boy' among educated Serbs because of his wide-boy London accent – initially denied that the Alliance had launched an attack at the time and place we were bombed. Since we had obviously been hit by something highly explosive, the unspoken suggestion by Brussels would seem to have been that we were the victims of Serbian shellfire.

As we had travelled towards Prizren that Sunday morning, it was clear that a dread of ethnic Albanian snipers gripped most Serb civilians. The rare Serbian cars we passed were driving at breakneck speed to minimise the risk of any sniper taking aim. Beads of sweat had formed on Nenad's brow and upper lip as he careered

along the narrow byways, sweeping through any
unmanned road-blocks. These barriers, often of tyres,
were a favoured KLA trap to try to force Serbs to slow
down or stop, whereupon the snipers would appear and
open fire.

The day after the tunnel bombing, we knew we would
have to run the risk of these gunmen again, since we had
to travel in Serb vehicles. Early in the afternoon, we all
assembled in Lokvica's packed-dirt main square to take
our leave. Many of the soldiers shook our hands and one
or two embraced us as we climbed into two civilian cars
driven by two of the troops. Three of the soldiers who
stayed behind insisted on exchanging home addresses
and telephone numbers, as if we had all become friends
on holiday rather than hostages to a situation beyond all
our control. The soldiers said it was too risky for us to use
the remaining undamaged car in which we had originally
driven from Pristina, because it might be tracked by the
KLA who were bound to have heard of our plight and
who had the noted Serb-supporting Schiffer high on their
wanted list. Instead, we were to change cars en route to
try to outfox any KLA ambush plans.

The only uneasy moments during our drive to
Brezovica came when the driver of one car in which I
travelled decided to do a spot of socialising and shopping
en route while the other vehicle sped ahead and soon
disappeared from view. Our man, who did not speak
English and therefore could not explain what he was
doing, ambled along the country lanes at an easy pace
and periodically stopped to disappear mysteriously into
houses, reappearing several minutes later protectively
clutching plastic bags containing unknown plunder. Or he
would spot a group of Serbian police smoking and lolling
under a roadside tree, and pull over to chat.

After reaching the ski resort hotel in Brezovica, we
were met by Radovan Orusevic, head of the government-
controlled press centre in Pristina, accompanied by a
Serbian reporter from Reuters news agency and a

cameraman. Until now, we had all felt immensely isolated from the outside world. We were not even sure if our friends, families and colleagues were aware of what had happened to us. Now we were given access to Reuters' satellite telephone, and were interviewed in front of a television camera. We were also reunited with Carlos Pinota, who was brought to Brezovica wearing the clothes donated by the monks at the monastery where he had clambered ashore the previous day: jeans which were too short and which he could not fasten at the waist, a lurid lumberjack-check shirt, and humble monk-like sandals.

Daniel Schiffer, meanwhile, had insisted on seeing another doctor. Back in the army encampment, Dr Zdravkovic had put Schiffer's arm in a small sling and applied sticking plaster to grazes on his forehead. After disappearing to a bedroom at the ski resort hotel, the Franco-Italian emerged an hour or so later with his left arm in plaster and his head swathed in bandages. 'If he carries on like this, he will look like an Egyptian mummy by the time we reach Pristina,' said Renzo in evident scepticism about the seriousness of his injuries.

Soon we were off again, with yet another set of cars, making our way through a Kosovo landscape ravaged by Nato shells and cluster bombs, as well as by the mortars and guns used by Serbs and ethnic Albanians against one another.

That night, back in the Grand Hotel in Pristina, Nato made sure some of us had yet another sleepless night. The Alliance bombing was intensifying in what turned out to be the closing stages of the campaign. Several massive blasts on the outskirts of the town rocked the hotel. I eventually passed most of the night sheltering near the lift shaft on the fourth floor of the eleven-storey hotel, along with Elsa, her cameraman, and Sherif, a brave young woman who worked for Turkish television and who stayed in Kosovo for the duration of the bombing campaign. She made us coffee in her room and passed round biscuits. Most of the rooms at the Grand Hotel were high-ceilinged monuments to communistic discomfort and dreariness, often in darkness during those nights of bombing. Sherif had added Turkish rugs, knick-knacks and coffee-making equipment to try to brighten what had been her home for the past three months.

I was mentally and physically exhausted, but still too edgy to sleep. Sherif coaxed me to lie down on her bed, but barely had I curled up when an approaching droning noise in the eerie blackness outside sent me diving to the floor. The almond-eyed, raven-haired Sherif rushed to the window to peer into the night – it was just a car speeding down the long, straight road outside the hotel. Then, at around midnight, two thundering explosions rattled the windows in the massive hotel. Sherif threw her arms round me, stroked my hair and kept telling me 'It's all right, Baby.'

In the morning, Elsa, her cameraman and I decided to leave Kosovo by the fastest possible route, to Macedonia, a forty-five-minute drive away. Renzo, Carlos Julio, Daniel Schiffer and Nenad were to brave the ever-intensifying Nato bombing and drive back to Belgrade. It was to take them nearly two days dodging the bullets and bombs. We all posed for a football-team style photograph on the fore-court outside the sardonically-named Grand Hotel in Pristina before going our separate ways. I apologised to the Italian Renzo, whose calm during the bombing had seemed impenetrable, for being so panicky at times over the previous two days. His parting shot was the ultimate in chivalry: 'Were you? I deedn't notice.'

# Chapter Two

# Goran's Story: 1968–1999

Two days after escaping the might of Nato bombs, I stood at the border between Kosovo and Macedonia. Limping and sore, I was leaving the war zone, despite the blandishments of more war-hardened colleagues that I should stay. White plumes of smoke puffed from distant mountain ridges on the chain of mountains strung along the southern Kosovo border and on towards Prizren, as the Alliance continued its attacks on Serbian positions. The sound of Nato jets was low, menacing and constant as they droned back and forth on their missions.

I waited for the anticipated surge of relief at feeling safe. Instead, all I felt was guilt; it was easy for Elsa, her cameraman and me to leave. But what about those staying behind, such as the cheerful driver who had driven us to the frontier? He was now in no man's land, buying black market petrol from a Macedonian before making the uncertain trek back to Pristina. And what of the humble apartment dwellers living near the often-blasted Jugopetrol dump on the outskirts of the Kosovo capital? How had they not gone mad with the terror of it all? Or maybe they had, for how were we to know?

It was 1 June, a blisteringly hot and humid day. It was hard to imagine that, for weeks, this border had been a shrine for crisis-craving television cameras, ravenous for interviews with weeping, limping men, women and children as they poured across from Kosovo. The reporters had given up by now, many spending frustrated days in the Macedonian capital, Skopje, yearning for a ground invasion and trying to win promises of a lift on the first

tank to roll into the province. At the very least, they
would be there come the glorious day when the ethnic
Albanians were returned to their homes, as many then
thought, in peace and harmony.

A few hundred yards inside Macedonia, we saw our
first sign of the refugees – what looked like the car park
at Wembley on Cup Final day. On open ground to our
right, countless thousands of Yugos, Zastavas, rusty
Volkswagens, vans, tractors and trailers were parked in
tidy row upon row in the middle of the wilderness. A
short distance further, on the opposite side of the road,
were the tents, tens of thousands of them, also in neat
rows but with a sense of growing settlement with washing
strung outside and kitchen equipment ranged around
packed dirt areas.

Few of the refugees were to be seen, perhaps because
they were sheltering from the intense heat inside their
canvas city. A handful ambled aimlessly from tent to tent.
We debated stopping to try to talk to them but the driver
who had travelled from Skopje to pick us up at the frontier was reluctant to dally, whether pressed by lack of
time or dearth of empathy with the homeless Albanians
it was impossible to say.

We turned for a last glimpse of Kosovo and I felt I was
watching a beautiful but cursed landscape. I also
wondered if I would be able to return to try to find the
shepherd boy who had raised the alarm when our group
was bombed or the villager who had given us cigarettes
and water. My narrow escape from death made me feel as
if I was born again in Kosovo, that I had been given a new
chance of life there. I consequently felt very close to
those who had helped me and I wanted to see them again
one day and know that they, too, were safe.

Ten days after I left Kosovo, Nato troops arrived.
Before the month was out, I met the intense young
conscripted army doctor once again; by the end of June
1999, he and his family were refugees living in a high-rise

tenement block in the industrial town of Pancevo, near Belgrade. I had returned to the Serbian capital after spending ten days in London, just long enough to gain a new visa.

Goran Zdravkovic was demobilised on 12 June. He came down from his mountain stronghold in Lokvica and reported, as ordered, to the hospital director at the Prizren Medical Centre, where he had been working before being called up at the beginning of the Nato campaign. The young army doctor finally took off his camouflage fatigues a few hours before German Nato troops began their triumphal entrance to Prizren, accompanied by crowds of cheering, gun-waving Albanians. On Monday morning, 14 June, Goran made his way to the hospital, only to find dozens of Albanians in the yard outside. Looking up at the windows, he saw a sea of Albanian faces peering from inside, their noses pressed against the windows. 'It was the most dangerous moment for me of the entire war because in seconds I was surrounded,' he said. Many of the flag-waving crowd looked as if they were from Albania proper rather than from Prizren, where he knew many members of the ethnic Albanian community, having treated them in the past. Some had the sunburnt, shaven-haired look of guerrilla fighters. 'To save my life, I decided to join in their singing and dancing, chanting Albanian slogans, and I managed to get away.'

He, his elfin-faced wife and two young children decided to leave immediately, joining a five-kilometre convoy which snaked out behind the retreating Yugoslav Army. All they managed to salvage from their home was a camera which Goran's father had given him as a graduation present, the perennial refugee requisite of family photograph albums to remind them of a life they had once had, clothes and a few toys for the children, plus a few hundred Deutschmarks.

It was hard to equate the scenes he described with the Prizren which I had visited the morning before we were bombed, a few weeks earlier at the end of May. Then, most ethnic Albanians had been living on one side of the almost toy-sized stone bridge which crossed the river in the centre, and most Serbs on the other, near the Serbian Orthodox church. The streets had been tense, with Albanians seeming reluctant to talk to journalists in the company of the Serbophile Daniel Schiffer and his body-guard. I had managed, however, to lose my chaperones for a while and talked to some English-speaking Albanians sitting on the steps of their home, down a secluded side-street.

Few Albanians had left Prizren, they had said, but they were sure that people from a nearby village had been forced to leave on buses a couple of days earlier. How did they feel about the intensifying Nato bombing in the area? 'Very happy, come on Nato,' they had cheered, spreading their arms and looking skyward. Market stalls on both sides of town had been laden with fruit and vegetables, although people from both the communities had complained about the prices, which had been nearly double those charged for similar foods in Belgrade. Nenad had bought a large bag of cherries which we had all shared, washing them in a drinking fountain.

There had been few police or troops visible on the streets and knots of Serbian men sat drinking coffee and beer in the sunshine outside whitewashed bars. The cream-robed nuns in an Italian-run Roman Catholic convent on the edge of the town had said that they feared Nato bombs more than the Serbian security forces in the region. The sisters had heard, though, that ethnic Albanian villagers a few miles away had been forced to abandon their homes. Outside the Orthodox church, middle-aged Serb women had tears spilling down their cheeks as they explained that they had just been praying for soldier sons who had disappeared, believed to have been kidnapped by the KLA.

Prizren had been tense that Sunday morning; nonetheless it had not felt like a town in a state of high terror. An old man drinking coffee with his friends near the little stone bridge had beckoned me over and given me a red rose. Apart from the sounds of occasional Nato bombs exploding in the middle distance, there had been no mayhem of unrestrained gunfire, such as Goran said he had experienced when Nato came to his town. Before fleeing, the young doctor had seen two drunken Serbs drive into the town centre, singing Serb songs as they leant from the car windows. They were shot dead, he said, as German Nato troops looked on.

Goran, whose name means 'Man from the Mountains', laid his life story before me. The last time we had met he had not only been my saviour, he had also been in control. Now, a month later, he, his wife, Sonja, and two young children, Radosav, six, and Bojana, three, were living near-penniless in the high-rise apartment in Pancevo. They did not even have a change of clothes.

As he recounted his story, his ice-blue eyes – usually found among Slovenes – were aflame with the same indignation he had shown in the army encampment, when he had berated Nato for the bombing. Although his account cannot be independently verified, much of it tallies with reports from other Kosovo Serbs, my own impressions during several visits to Kosovo in the 1980s and early 1990s, and other independent sources. Perhaps most importantly, Goran's tale provides a rare insight into the mentality of Serbs from the province. It indicates that Serbs for years felt that they were being swamped by a mushrooming Albanian community. They often knew and even respected individual ethnic Albanians, but as a nation, Albanians were regarded as uneducated, shifty and bent on taking Kosovo for themselves. The young doctor described his early years in the village overlooking Prizren where he and his forebears were born but which he may well never see again.

Churchill said that the Balkans produced more history than the region could digest. By the time Goran was born in 1968, the area had been convulsed by dozens of wars,

stretching back hundreds of years as Serbs, Albanians
and Turks wrestled for control. Nonetheless, Kosovo was
relatively tranquil in the late 1960s, largely thanks to the
policies of Marshal Josip Broz Tito, the Communist who
became leader of the new Socialist Federal Republic of
Yugoslavia which emerged at the end of the Second
World War.

Britain and the other Allies had initially backed
royalist forces in the fight against Hitler's Fascism, but
towards the end of the war they switched their support to
Tito and his Partisans. The man who was to rule
Yugoslavia for the next thirty-five years was a Croat by
birth and he understood only too well the old rivalries
between various groups which made up the new country,
especially between Serbs, Croats, Bosnian Muslims and
ethnic Albanians. The new Yugoslavia was made up of six
republics and Tito managed to keep potentially
dangerous nationalism in check by creating republican
borders which cut through areas dominated by a given
group, thereby forcing them to live together.

Serbs were still too dominant for Tito's liking,
however, so he also created two autonomous provinces
within Serbia – Vojvodina in the north and Kosovo to the
south. During and just after the war, Tito also maintained
close links with the emerging Stalinist state of Albania.
After 1945, the whole of the Balkans – Yugoslavia,
Bulgaria, Albania and Romania – was united by
Communist ideology. The system kept nationalism in
check, but it could not eliminate ancient antagonisms in
the region which continued to fester beneath the surface.

Although Goran grew up in this relatively tranquil
post-war period, he soon came face to face with the old
Serb-Albanian rivalries which had plagued previous
generations in Kosovo. 'The first time I met an Albanian
was when I was seven years old and had just started
primary school,' he said. 'Until then, I had only heard
about the Albanian-Serbian divide or seen Albanians
coming to my village to trade cattle.' Relations between

Goran and ethnic Albanians were sour from the start.
After beginning primary school, he noticed that some
boys were stealing shoes and books and he wanted to
tackle them. Older Serb boys told him not to fight them
'because they were Albanian and dangerous,' he said. 'At
break-time there was always a fight between Albanian
and Serb children – every day, every day'; he shook his
head in exasperation at the memory. Teenaged ethnic
Albanians used to send children as young as two years
old to taunt Goran and his friends, he said. 'If we retaliated, then a group of much older Albanians would come
and beat us up. By the time I was eleven, I had learned
to avoid the Albanians; they were always looking for a
fight.'

As Goran grew up, he realised that Serb families
usually had one or two children, while the ethnic
Albanians had eight or more. This trend was seen by the
Serbs as proof that the ethnic Albanians wanted to take
over Kosovo. Goran and his contemporaries were told
that only two children from each ethnic Albanian family
went to school; 'the rest were left illiterate,' he said.
'Usually, only one or two of the children were born in
hospital and had their names registered. The rest were
born at home in remote villages and were not registered;
it was as if they were living in another state.'

In 1981, when Goran was thirteen, a national census in
Yugoslavia showed that the ethnic Albanian population
in Kosovo had ballooned from 350,000 in 1945, to
1,700,000 – an annual population growth of 45,000. The
Serb population throughout these years was around
200,000. Tito had offered to be godfather to the eleventh
child of any Yugoslav citizen and he had sponsored many
more ethnic Albanian than Serb children by the time he
died in May 1980.

In 1981, the same year as the census, most Serbs were
horrified when ethnic Albanian students organised large
demonstrations in Prizren and Pristina, chanting
demands for a 'Kosovo Republic'. It was March, less than

one year after the death of Tito, and the Kosovo Serbs
were not sure how the country would survive and prosper
without him. By April 1981, the ethnic Albanian protests
demanding independence had spread and a state of
emergency was declared in the province. The Federal
Yugoslav Government also announced the formation of
a special military police force, the MIAs, under the
Ministry of Internal Affairs.

It was a huge turning-point in relations between
Kosovo's Serbs and ethnic Albanians; what had been a
mutual unease and distrust between the communities
turned to outright hostility. 'The Albanian demonstrations created the first big gap between us and them,' said
Goran. 'They destroyed Serbian monuments and beat up
some Serbs; it completely ruined our mutual life.
Suddenly, some of my very good Albanian friends didn't
want to know me any more. Nothing was ever the same
again.'

From 1981, ethnic Albanians in Kosovo began leading
increasingly separate lives; many ceased to pay taxes or
for state-supplied electricity, and they increasingly began
to run their own, unofficial, police and education systems.
Rumours and counter-rumours thrived in this increasingly two-tier society. 'In one village we heard about an
Albanian son who killed his father with an axe, but the
neighbours would not even let the Serb police approach
the village,' said Goran. After 1981, most Serb youngsters
were expected to be indoors by 8 p.m. 'I was thirteen and
was just beginning to want to go out in the evening, but it
was too dangerous. We had to escort Serb girls in groups
everywhere, and my father taught me to drive. It was
illegal, but he felt I was safer if I went out in the car.'

In the next few years, large numbers of Serbs left
Kosovo, further tipping the ethnic balance in favour of
the Albanians. The exodus accelerated when ethnic
Albanians began offering inflated prices for Serb-owned
houses and land, a strategy which was seen by Serbs as
more proof that the ethnic Albanians were determined to

take over Kosovo. The Zdravkovic family stayed put and got on with their lives.

In the West, few people cared or had even heard of Kosovo. In Britain, only the comparatively small readerships of broadsheet newspapers and serious magazines, or listeners to the BBC World Service, were likely to have been even vaguely aware of tensions in the province in the late 1980s. Even some broadsheet foreign editors had for years regarded the subject as worthy but dull. For the vast majority of the population, Margaret Thatcher's third term in power, pop singer Boy George, and a new television soap called *EastEnders* were among the main fixations.

The eighteen-year-old Goran was preparing to leave school and undertake his one-year compulsory military service before starting to read medicine at university in Pristina. At the same time, more than seven thousand ethnic Albanians were registering for places at the new unofficial and illegal university in Pristina organised by the Democratic League of Kosovo, which was led by the moderate Albanian, Dr Ibrahim Rugova. All classes at the parallel university were in Albanian. Unlike most in the West, the future doctor was fully aware of the history, causes and effects of the tensions in his homeland.

In the mid-1980s, Serbs in Kosovo began to hear about a rising new politician in Belgrade. By 1987, the ambitious Slobodan Milosevic was reaching towards the pinnacle of power. As head of the Serbian League of Communists, and encouraged by his wife, Mira Markovic, he decided to make Kosovo his proving ground. Unlike Tito, who had always striven to quell nationalistic sentiments, Milosevic decided to exploit them. He was playing with fire.

Slobodan Milosevic had been born amid the turmoil and savagery of the Second World War, on 20 August 1941. He married Mira, the daughter of a noted Communist family, after they met at high school in their

home town of Pozarevac, thirty miles south-east of
Belgrade. The two of them may have been initially drawn
together because they each came from disturbed families.
Milosevic was from an old Montenegrin family of the
Vasojevic tribe, with roots which went back to Kosovo in
medieval times. He was the second son of two teachers
and had an unhappy childhood. As well as coping with
the upheaval of the Balkans at war, his father was a
manic depressive who deserted the family when
Slobodan and his elder brother, Bora, were children.
Both parents went on to commit suicide, their father in
1962 and their mother eleven years later. The future
political star was later said to suffer from depression
himself.

Mira's childhood was equally tragic. Her mother, a
leading Partisan called Vera Miletic, had been dragged
from her home and executed by fellow Partisans after she
was accused of betraying her comrades. Milosevic's
future wife was just a few months old when her mother
was arrested by anti-Communist special police in 1943
and tortured. Soon after her release, almost all Belgrade's
underground Partisan leaders were seized and the finger
of suspicion pointed to Vera Miletic. Just before being
taken to her death, Mira's mother had brought flowers
into the house and this is said to be why Milosevic's wife
to this day wears a pink bloom tucked behind her ear.

The young Mira and Slobodan may also have been
attracted to one another by a common dislike of their
fathers. Milosevic never forgave his father, Svetozar, for
leaving his mother just after the end of the Second World
War and going off to live alone in Montenegro in a fit of
depression. Mira, meanwhile, was illegitimate and she
always harboured a grudge against her father, Moma
Markovic, for not aknowledging her as his child.

Slobodan Milosevic joined the Communist Party in
1959 when he was nineteen, but for several years led a
relatively low-key life. From 1978 until 1983, he was
director of Belgrade's national Beobank bank. Then, in

1984, Ivan Stambolic, head of the Serbian Communist Party, put him in charge of the party's Belgrade organisation. Two years later, in 1986, Milosevic was given control of the party throughout Serbia. The promotion caused a huge family row when Mira Markovic's uncle, Draza Markovic, declared that Milosevic was the wrong man for the job, accusing him of being too arrogant, self-opinionated and unwilling to compromise. Then, in May 1989, Milosevic seized his moment and ousted his former mentor, Ivan Stambolic, to became President of Serbia.

Slavoljub Djukic, a key biographer of Milosevic, quotes a former schoolfriend of Milosevic as saying: 'When we were children, I could imagine him as a future railway station-master or a pedantic clerk.' The young Milosevic was portrayed as a withdrawn, industrious boy who did not like sport and who avoided school excursions. He dressed in old-fashioned clothes, with a white shirt and tie.

Milosevic grew up to be 'stubborn, intelligent, hard-working, lonely and suspicious,' according to Djukic. Nowadays 'he regularly changes his private telephone number and lets only those currently in favour know how to contact him. He has a small number of close friends, all people with limited political ambitions. Only one person is forever, only one to whom he opens his soul and shows endless love and confidence – and that is Mira Markovic,' Djukic says. Milosevic is said occasionally to show tolerance to people who have criticised him, but never forgives those who offend his wife. The couple set great store by their home life and are said to dislike war films, but to adore soap operas.

Back in 1987, little of this was known when Milosevic was sent to Kosovo to try to pacify Serbs who increasingly complained about the pressure they felt they were under from ethnic Albanians. Milosevic addressed a huge gathering of Serbs who wanted to complain about what they saw as aggressive Albanian nationalism. Outside the town hall at Kosovo Polje, a couple of miles west of

Pristina, near the site of the medieval Battle of Kosovo where Serbs were defeated by Turks in 1389, Mr Milosevic uttered the words which were taken as a sea change in Belgrade's attitude to Kosovo: 'No one shall dare to beat you again.' Milosevic returned to the Yugoslav capital a changed man, according to Ivan Stambolic. 'Before that visit, he was a communicative, sociable, fun-loving person – witty, reliable, a political fighter, but loyal,' Stambolic said of his old protégé. 'Milosevic had this feeling of nationhood and this is why I sent him to Kosovo in April 1987, knowing he would see that the Serbs had a problem there. When he uttered "none will dare to beat you", it just came out of him in reply to shouts from the crowd. After he returned he convened a Party meeting and used phrases such as "fatherland in peril" and "Serb uprising"; he was pale, trembling and emotional.' Stambolic said he had called in vain for cool heads.

Back in Kosovo, as he grew to manhood, Goran Zdravkovic was regaled with stories about his maternal grandfather. Milivoje Bajkic had come into the world the same year, 1914, that a young Serb, Gavrilo Princip, fired the shot which killed the Austro-Hungarian Archduke Franz Ferdinand in the Bosnian capital, Sarajevo, lighting the powder keg which exploded into the Great War. Bajkic eventually became a lifelong and passionate advocate of Communism, at one time teaching the young future Albanian leader, Enver Hoxha, the tenets of Marx and Engels, according to Goran. How could he have imagined that, more than half a century later, Hoxha's fellow Albanians would come close to murdering his grandson after rolling into the family's home town of Prizren as allies alongside the historically-hated Germans?

Bajkic had been a leading and early member of Tito's Partisans, but he had 'loved Stalin more than Tito', the young doctor said. Bajkic's own father had sought his fortune in America at the turn of the century, helping to build the skyscrapers that today adorn the US urban skyline. The property developer had returned to his homeland only every four or five years, leaving behind a pregnant wife each time he ventured back to America.

When Bajkic was old enough, he travelled to America to work with his father but his already-forming passion for Communism had quickly made him a wanted man by the FBI. He had been horrified by the sight of wealthy industrialists taking their pick of just two or three workers from huge crowds of job-starved men, jostling for employment. The experience had spurred him to join shadowy Communist syndicates in the USA and, because he was physically large and fit, he tried to earn a living as a boxer. After attracting the unwelcome attention of the US regime, the young man returned to the Balkans and soon found himself caught up in the Second World War. Goran is proud that his grandfather distinguished himself as a Partisan officer at the Battle of Drenicka in 1944, between Albanian Fascist forces and Tito's Communist Partisans. He says that his grandfather was tortured by Albanian Fascists, who prised off his toenails at an inter-rogation centre in Prizren. He escaped with his life only because his family had bribed the jailers. The building later housed the school attended by young Goran, and one of the future doctor's earliest memories was seeing the basement where his grandfather had been disfigured for life.

Goran's grandfather died in 1984. 'He understood that he had made mistakes in his life,' says Goran. 'His way of thinking, his ideas, had led to disaster among his own people. But despite everything, he believed that all people were equal and should have equal rights.'

By the end of the 1980s, Tito had been dead for nearly a decade and many Kosovo Serbs were itching for a fight. They felt besieged by the massive rise in the ethnic Albanian population and growing ethnic Albanian

demands for full independence. In March 1989, Milosevic
scrapped the region's special autonomous status and
installed a heavy military presence. He began to suppress
Albanian-language media and schools and, in 1990, he
abolished Kosovo's Parliament. The clampdown heart-
ened the Kosovo Serbs, but predictably hardened ethnic
Albanian separatist aspirations and drove hardliners
underground. Antagonism between the two groups only
increased as the 1990s advanced.

   Goran was growing up. Before 1987, many of the police
in Kosovo were Albanian and the young doctor claimed
that, until then, there was 'no violent organised response
to the Albanian terrorists'. After Milosevic's visit to
Kosovo, Serbs began a wholesale crackdown against the
ethnic Albanian community; Goran says he began to feel
as if he were living in his own country again. The leader of
the ethnic Albanians at this time was Ibrahim Rugova, a
moderate who had studied at the Sorbonne in Paris and
who advocated a campaign of passive resistance. He was
to be sidelined by the embryonic hardline Kosovo
Liberation Army after 1996. Back in the late 1980s, Dr
Rugova responded to Milosevic's tough stance against
ethnic Albanians by urging them to leave state jobs and
intensify a strategy of withholding state taxes and
payment for water and electricity.

   This situation, where ethnic Albanians failed to pay
their way for state-provided services, continued for years.
When I asked the Serbian authorities in the province why
they had not simply cut the Albanians off, I was told that
water and power were supplied in a way which made it
almost impossible to isolate individual homes. If the
services were cut to one flat or village homestead, the
entire block or village would have suffered, and this may
well have included some Serbs, they said.

   Goran had a friend who was an Albanian girl and, as
the two grew to adolescence, he claims she fell in love
with him. 'She used to come everywhere with me,' he
said, 'but she never ever allowed me to kiss her or let

anything happen between us. She was very beautiful. We had to go to cafés secretly and we couldn't hold hands in public because she said her uncles would have killed her for being with a Serb.' Goran was flattered by her adolescent devotion and his family was not upset by the liaison, believing it to be a passing fancy. The pair did indeed drift apart but a couple of years later, in 1991, Goran was a student at Pristina University when he happened to see the beautiful young Albanian on a street in the Kosovo capital. Their past attachment was to count for nothing when Goran saw that she was leading a large group of Albanian separatists. 'I called out to her *"Et tu, Brute,"* but she pretended not to hear. I think she was also studying medicine.'

The separate Serbian and ethnic Albanian education systems only increased the growing resentment felt by Goran and his classmates at university. During examinations, the Serbs were tested by a professor from Belgrade who passed just five out of twenty, he says, while the ethnic Albanians insisted on their own examiner. All the Albanians were successful, said Goran. After finally qualifying as a junior doctor, however, his relationship with most Albanians improved. Professional people from both communities maintained far friendlier relations than the bulk of the working classes. 'It was easy for me to say that the Albanian people were good, because the Albanians needed me as a doctor. But the poor Serbian man working in a factory lived in a foreign country from the day he was born,' he said.

During the winter of 1991 Milosevic's campaign against the ethnic Albanians intensified; many Albanians were dismissed from state jobs in Kosovo and all others were pressed by Rugova to strike or resign in sympathy. 'I had Albanian neighbours and they were effectively ordered to leave well-paid jobs. That family became so poor that the wife used to come to our apartment for food. It was all done in secret because her husband would have been angry,' he said. 'When we asked why she and her husband had left their jobs, she said it was better to be without bread than to be killed.' The family was also asked to send their two sons to fight with the Albanian separatists, Goran said. 'We agreed to hide one of her boys. We stayed good friends and she is trying to protect my apartment in Prizren today.'

Goran's story made me ponder previous visits I had made to Kosovo. Since I have never aspired to be a war correspondent, I also began to ponder how life sometimes took me to some of the most dangerous places on Earth. After all, most people do not just wake up one morning and say to themselves, 'I think I'll set out for a war zone today.'

For me, the reasons were rooted in my upbringing. Most of my secondary education was undertaken at a convent boarding school run by Irish nuns who regarded Communism as akin to sin. However, their view did not sit comfortably with the stories I heard from my father, who frequently travelled to Warsaw Pact countries on business. He seemed to think that there was good and bad on both sides of the Iron Curtain. I was no more than fourteen when I determined to try to find out for myself.

# Chapter Three

# Talking 'bout My Generation: The 1960s

I was once told that I had no sense of history. This sweeping utterance came from a senior journalist whose protégés included an Oxford graduate who believed that the Second World War ended in 1943 – she telephoned her mother to check the date when less glitteringly educated sub-editors had the temerity to query her insistence that the conflict came to an end two years earlier than generally accepted. While I may not have a professional historian's *knowledge* of the past, I definitely have a *sense* of history. We all have our own perception of history and our places in it, and I believe we are all products to a great extent of the generation to which we belong. The two graduates who caused me to pause and ponder this were less than ten years younger than me, yet light-years distant in temperament and outlook. I have always felt that I could never quite step out of the shadow of the Second World War, while my two fellow journalists seemed to regard the conflict as so distant that it happened in another age.

Born in 1952, my earliest memories are of my mother, father and maternal grandmother constantly chiding me for wasting food when I did not clear my plate. When filling the butter dish, my mother and grandmother, who lived with us, would fanatically scrape the wrapper until the greaseproof paper was flat and shining, in case the minutest particle was left behind and subsequently thrown away. They would unpick tea packets (no tea bags then) to ensure that every single tea-leaf was emptied from folds and crevices into the caddy. Food rationing had done all this to them.

My father was seventeen and my mother eighteen when the war ended, and they vividly remembered VE Day. When I was born, the war was closer in time to them than the fall of the Berlin Wall is to the rest of us today. As a small child on Sunday afternoons – the one day when my younger brother, Keir, and I were likely to see my father – we would listen to *Round the Horne* or the *Goon Show* on the Bakelite wireless while my mother and grandmother cooked the roast. We did not have a television until about 1960, and conversation among the adults would often turn to the Manchester Blitz. We lived in Lancashire and Cheshire until I was five and I would be told of my father's penchant for ignoring the air raid sirens to watch German bombers flying overhead en route to do their worst, or of his subsequent evacuation. I can remember seeing the ruins of bombed buildings in the centre of Manchester, and the talk from time to time of unexploded wartime bombs being found, as the painful process of rebuilding progressed in the Fifties.

This discovery of unexploded shells used to fascinate me and I think I became slightly paranoid about it. When I was about seven, I went through a phase of peering down wells and gingerly pulling aside undergrowth at our new home in rural Essex, or scouring tumbledown barns and sheds, convinced an unexploded shell lay hidden there. I was also dimly aware of the growing hostility between America and the Soviet Union, and of adult fears of a new, more terrible war involving the dreaded atom bomb. I genuinely believed that one day sirens might sound, heralding this cataclysm. This residue of war lasted for years. As late as 1961, when we moved to a village near Cambridge, the old vicarage which was to be our first long-term home had ugly, thick dark green blinds at all the windows – a hangover from the Second World War blackout.

Even the First World War impinged on our lives. My

maternal grandfather and his brother had been so shell-shocked in the trenches that I suspect they were never mentally well-balanced again. My great-uncle had a leg blown away during the conflict and he seemed, understandably, to be in a perpetually bad temper. His brother, my grandfather, died before I was born, but he had by all accounts made my grandmother's life such a misery that she carried the burden even after his demise. He was noted, among other things, for putting the family's pet cat in the oven and roasting it alive while in one of his many black moods, according to one of the anecdotes which made up our family lore.

This was the atmosphere in which most of us who were to go on to become the Sixties Generation grew up. It was a world of Enid Blyton, *Beano* comics, and Harold Macmillan, who had been Prime Minister forever. Toilet paper was just that; shiny, perforated sheets of scratchy paper. Almost everyone of my generation had their tonsils out at the first hint of a bad cold. But by the dawning of the 1960s, we were on the cusp of a new era; the word 'teenager' became synonymous with mischief and a young Russian Air Force officer was in training to become the first man in space.

We began to tire of all the talk of war memories and started to believe that there really would be peace in our time. As my generation reached puberty the Beatles, the Who and the Rolling Stones kidnapped our imaginations and stole us away from our parents. Whereas my mother and father had dressed as replicas of their parents as they reached adulthood, we wanted our own clothes and hair-styles, even our own vocabulary. 'Don't try to dig what we all say,' the Who told our parents. A Communist guerrilla by the name of Che Guevara became our hero and we felt as if we were rebelling like no one had rebelled before. The sensation separates us to this day from those who came before or after.

Being part of this madcap, iconoclastic, inventive, kind and generous generation – born on the edge of war and

determined never to go that way again – was to give me
an edge in later life as I grappled to understand the
people living in Communist countries. For they also
remembered the Second World War and they, too, were
determined to rebel.

Another spur to my interest in things Communist was
Mother Dolores. Never was a woman more aptly named
than the headmistress at the Irish-run convent where I
spent most of my life between the ages of twelve and
seventeen. A whirling dervish of sexual and intellectual
frustration, she was able to distribute misery in quantities
which belied her tiny stature and extended far beyond
her lifespan.

The convent, in the foothills of a mountain in North
Wales, provided an environment which would have
made North Korea seem hedonistic. Those of us who
were full-time boarders had only fleeting glimpses of
the great events in the world outside. There was no
access to newspapers, post was rigorously and – literally
– religiously censored, and about the only television
allowed was a weekly dose of the *Val Doonican Show*.
Once a week, on Saturdays, we were allowed to take our
new-fangled transistor radios from Mother Dolores's
office to listen to pop music while washing our hair.
Only sixth formers were allowed to visit the nearby
town of Denbigh, and then only once a week to buy
shampoo, stationery or hair grips for the younger girls.
The rest of us were trapped firmly behind the high flintstone walls.

The contrast with a normal existence at home during
the holidays made it feel as if you were watching life on
a video which is repeatedly put on fast-forward mode;
normal viewing during the Christmas, Easter and
summer breaks, but unwatchable when whizzing by
outside the convent's time-vacuum. You would return to
school having just caught up with the world's main
events, but then lose track in the black hole of masses,
classes, rosaries and benedictions. I even failed to catch

up with some political earthquakes, such as the 1967 Arab-Israeli conflict, until years later.

The story ran that Mother Dolores had been in love with a young man in her native Ireland who had been badly injured in a road accident. As a good Catholic (there are no bad Catholics in Ireland), she had made the sort of nonsensical pact with God for which logic-bending believers are renowned: if he lived, she would become a nun. Never mind that the young man in question might be devastated at losing his beloved, or that she would spend the rest of her life persuading herself and all those around her that men were good for just one thing, procreating more little Catholic babies.

It was not even that Brigidine provided a sound education. I was always fascinated by evolution and astronomy – both subjects which do not sit easily with the sort of literal interpretation of the Bible to which we were subjected. I was too young to realise this, so had no compunction in asking the general science teacher – a nun by the name of Mother Scolastica who always looked on the verge of a nervous breakdown – about the relatively newly discovered planet of Pluto. How did astronomers know what was and what was not a planet, and how far away was it? 'All the heavenly moving bodies have been created by a loving God,' she said, as if I had implied that planets were an instrument of the devil. It made you wonder what would have become of Newton under her instruction. 'If you spent more time learning the curriculum, you would not be asking such eejit questions.' A sharp jab of nun's knuckle below my collar bone. End of subject.

Worse was to come after my father finally managed to get himself elected as Labour MP for King's Lynn in North Norfolk at the time of Harold Wilson's 1964 election triumph. His name in those days was Derek Page, he had dark hair and seemed always to be in a tearing hurry. He was something of a stranger to my younger brother and me. Nowadays, the hair that remains is grey and he goes by the name of Lord Whaddon, after being vaulted to the Upper House by James Callaghan in 1979. He was not encouraged to call himself Lord Page, because that was deemed a contradiction in terms by the man whose name is law in such matters, the Garter King of Arms. Instead, he took his title from the village near Cambridge where the family home has been since 1961.

When we were home, Dad seemed forever to be just leaving for, or returning from, a gathering of about twenty soul mates in some godforsaken village hall in the fens. Or he was arriving back from a visit to then strange sounding places such as Warsaw and Prague. He had set up his own pharmaceuticals import-export company, dealing with Poland and Czechoslovakia, and he came back laden with exotically-dressed dolls and stories of life under Communism during those dark days of the Cold War.

At first, I could never understand why he used to say he had been to Prague, when the labels on his luggage clearly said Praha. He always came back smiling and excited, which seemed odd when the nuns at Brigidine clearly gave the impressions that life under Communism was akin to being in hell.

During one summer holiday in the early 1960s, Dad had a visit from a man from Russia who came accompanied by his daughter. She was about my age, twelve, and it was my first meeting with someone from these exotic countries where God was outlawed. It was like being able to examine an extra-terrestrial at close quarters – and it was all very disappointing. The Russian's daughter and I were consigned to the garden while the adults did whatever adults were supposed to do at these times.

The little girl was dressed in a pretty blue print dress with the sort of swirling, petticoated skirt that my friends all possessed but which I was not allowed to have. My convent uniform, with a vast array of clothes for all eventualities, had been extremely expensive and I was constantly pressed against my will to wear at least some of it during the holidays. The Russian girl also spoke

English, with an accent I found beguiling and a vocabulary which seemed to exceed even my own. This must mean that school in the anti-Christ countries was horrifically hard work, I thought, trying to make the nuns' picture of Communism fit at least in part. Wrong. Not only did she positively enjoy her lessons but she, along with all other Russians, had not been sent to school until she was seven years old. I suddenly felt cheated out of two years of freedom and was overwhelmed with envy.

One day, when I was about fourteen, my father came back from Cuba with a poster of Fidel Castro and copies of the Cuban state newspaper, *Granma*, both of which I innocently took back to the convent with me after the summer holidays. These were the days when possession of a Che Guevara poster was the essence of cool, but a photograph of the bearded, cigar-toting Fidel would surely count for something. We pupils were not even supposed to bring a copy of *Bunty* magazine, let alone what I now realise to have been regarded as subversive literature.

Mother Dolores and her de facto chief warden, Sister Elizabeth – a former pupil with large bones and a flat and polished Irish farm girl's face, who taught art – periodically made surprise swoops on our dormitories and desks to inspect lockers and prise open our small secrets. Pathetic little illicit scraps of comfort, such as half-eaten sweets or a letter which had evaded the system, were energetically elicited from beneath hard mattresses, the corner of a pencil box, or the recesses of a pyjama case. These were terrifying encounters which often took place late at night or on a Saturday afternoon. The nuns wore full-length black habits, tied at the waist with a leather belt from which hung a large rosary. The beads would rattle, announcing the approach of a nun, but Mother Dolores and Sister Elizabeth had learned to silence this giveaway signal by wrapping their rosary beads around their hands as they approached with a stealth which would have done the SAS proud.

The raids were terrifying because punishment was often swift and harsh. Mother Dolores was, I now realise, a sado-masochist. She kept a cane in her office which was so well used that the hitting end was held together with sticky tape because it was so frayed. The physically diminutive nun suffered from phlebitis, which caused what seemed to be excruciating pain in her right leg. Many times, we saw her lift her habit and hit herself over-zealously on her calf with the cane, ostensibly to rap out time to music at a pantomime rehearsal, or when trying to beat irregular French verbs into our brains.

The cane was used even more energetically on us. The headmistress's tactics were not so different from those I later saw used to crush dissent in Communist countries. Be brutal with one, and the rest should buckle. One girl from Essex was discovered to have a comic in her desk and we were all lined up, late at night, to witness the corporal punishment. The cane was ceremoniously carried from the office to the cold and echoing hall where we stood, trembling, in lines. Mother Dolores had ensured that the guilty girl was placed at the head of the first tier, the insinuation being that we would all be beaten. The swish of the cane and the sharp sound as it repeatedly bit into the fourteen-year-old's palm was almost like watching an eighteenth-century press-ganged sailor being subjected to the cat-o'-nine-tails. Tears oozed from the girl's eyes, but she failed to utter a sound, a reaction which seemed to drive Mother Dolores into an ever-increasing frenzy as she wielded the cane. Another caning victim, a year or so before, had been so badly cut by the Sellotaped stick that, hours later, drops of blood fell from her hand into a milk jug as she reached for bread at tea time.

All these images leapt to my mind when the inevitable discovery was made of my Castro poster and the copies of *Granma*. To my enormous relief, I was not caned. Instead, I was taken to one side by Sister Elizabeth, who spent about two hours trying to cajole me into telling her how much I knew about Communism. More importantly, what did my father think about these anti-Christs with whom he did business? Did I know, she eventually asked, that Communism was a sin, and that tampering with such ideas would blot my soul, like cigarette tar blackening the lungs?

The upshot of these experiences was, predictably, the opposite from that intended by the nuns. The convent spawned such a craving for information that, by the time I was fourteen, I was determined to become a journalist. I was also desperate to investigate the mysteries of sex at the earliest opportunity, was agnostic bordering on atheist – and I wanted to know as much as possible about Communism and Communist countries. I did manage to glean something of life in these lands, which were ideologically light-years away from Planet Brigidine, from the books and records which my father accumulated during his business trips. But they were isolated, disjointed atoms of knowledge.

It was to take the best part of a decade, working on local newspapers in Lincolnshire and Bristol, before I began to achieve my ambition to work abroad as a journalist. By 1977, I was working for the *Guardian* and over the next nine years spent some months in China and made several working visits to Poland, Hungary and Romania. My job was as a desk-bound sub-editor in the foreign department, so I had had to make many of these reporting trips in my own time.

In 1981 I visited Poland during a winter of martial law, and it had felt dark, dismal and sinister. The Solidarity movement under Lech Walesa had won the hearts and minds of many in his campaign to shake off the oppressive hand of the Kremlin, but it was a slow and painful process. The President, General Vojciech Jaruzelski, was above all a patriotic Pole. He knew that too fast a change would bring a Soviet invasion, something from which he wanted to protect his nation. I had been able to spend

weeks covering the Polish upheaval only because the
*Guardian's* doyenne of Eastern Europe, Hella Pick, had
been unable to get a visa. I succeeded in acquiring this
magic document because my father intervened with the
Polish Government on my behalf. Hella was furious,
especially when I gained instant access to the Polish
ministers she had spent years cultivating. I managed to
gain a similar entrée into the opposition's world because
a secretary at the *Guardian* hailed from Gdansk,
Solidarity's heartland. She had put me in touch with her
friends and family in the Hanseatic port, all of whom
were active in the movement to overthrow Communism.

It was during this time that I learned a lesson which
would prove invaluable in my later dealings with
Yugoslavia. I accompanied my father to a week of business meetings with senior officials from the Polish
state-owned pharmaceutical company, Ciech. These men
and women were crucial planks in the Communist
*nomenklatura* and I had expected them to be interested
more in power and privilege than in the teachings of
Marx and Engels. What had amazed me was that many of
the Ciech directors held a deep and abiding faith in
Communism. In most cases this was because they saw it
as an antidote to Fascism in a country which had suffered
so brutally under the Nazis during the Second World
War. A quarter of the population had perished and much
of the old city of Warsaw was razed.

Appreciating the depth of this hatred of Fascism was
to prove vital when trying to understand the Serb
mentality a few years later. I also learnt that the quality
of life for most ordinary citizens in Poland was not as dire
as the West had wanted us all to believe. In many ways it
was just different. Almost everyone had access to cheap
housing, heating and food; unemployment was rare. The
big problem for ordinary people, as distinct from dissi-
dents who felt the fury of the state, was a lack of choice.
Everyone wore similar outdated clothes, ate similar food,
and read the same reports in state-controlled news-

papers. However, this uniformity also meant that those living under Communism were protected from the stress endemic in the West, where people felt they were failures if they did not possess the latest car, lawnmower or action doll as shown on TV.

In late autumn, 1985 I visited Romania, here to see an already unwell Harold Wilson address a gathering attended by Nicolae and Elena Ceausescu. The former British Prime Minister was part of a UK trade delegation, organised partly by my father, which was visiting Romania. After endless, tedious protestations of mutual co-operation and respect, Lord Wilson rose to speak. His interpreter looked apoplectic as the grand old man intoned in an almost Mike Yarwoodesque parody of himself, 'Yorkshire born and Yorkshire bred; strong in th' arm and weak in th' 'ead.'

Although my knowledge of Romanian was akin to my understanding of Icelandic, I am sure that the frightened translator swerved from the reality, for it seemed to be peppered with words such as 'cooperatul' and 'multumesc', or 'thanks'. It was nonetheless clear from the stony faces that many on the Romanian side had understood the spirit, if not the exact content, of the homily. The hilarity of the moment was tinged with sadness for me; Harold Wilson had been my hero. Apart from having been photographed in his heyday with my adolescent gurus, the Beatles, he had instigated the opening of the Open University.

I had left school at the earliest opportunity to take up a job offer as a trainee reporter with the *Lincolnshire Free Press* and *Spalding Guardian*, and my lack of a university education had made itself felt over the ensuing years. At the *Guardian*, as elsewhere in Fleet Street, Oxford degrees abounded. I subsequently took an Open University course in basic science and physics and it proved to be one of the biggest joys of my life.

Two weeks after the trade delegation visit, in December 1985, I returned to Romania. This time I was alone, travelling on a tourist visa and hoping to see something of the life of ordinary people. The first heavy snows of the winter had foiled my original plan of flying from Bucharest to Suceava in the north, because the runway there was blocked by deep drifts. Undeterred, I travelled by train, keenly anticipating the chance to speak to Romanians outside the confines of the senior party officials who had chaperoned the trade delegation. As the train pulled in after an eight-hour journey from Bucharest, I leapt onto what I thought was a snow-dusted platform – and found myself chest-high in a snowdrift.

To my horror, a group of Romanian musicians dressed in folk costumes approached me as I scrambled clumsily onto the real platform next to the drift. They were accompanied by the Communist Party official who had helped ensure the trade delegation's comforts two weeks earlier. By his side was a waiter carrying a tray containing glasses of *vin fierte*, the Romanian equivalent of mulled wine. 'We are here to welcome you and to make your stay as pleasant as possible,' said the official, smiling knowingly.

## Chapter Four

# First Impressions: 1986–1993

I first visited Yugoslavia in May 1986, just days after catastrophe at the Chernobyl nuclear power plant in the Ukraine had provided a potent symbol of the impending political meltdown throughout the Soviet bloc. Welsh farmers were worrying about the dangers of radioactive contamination of their sheep on the far side of Europe. The citizens of Belgrade barely seemed to give the Chernobyl disaster a second's thought.

I was one of a group of British journalists being fêted, wined, and dined as part of a regular public relations exercise by the Belgrade regime. Yugoslavia seemed a haven of prosperity compared with the ill-lit streets of Warsaw, and the depressing towns and villages of Nicolae Ceausescu's Romania. Knez Mihailova, the main shopping street in the capital, was a cornucopia of stores selling Italian designer suits and shoes, fine wines, and restaurants selling food from around the world. On the Montenegrin coast, sunseekers from all over Europe were relaxing in the resorts of Budva and Sveti Stefan, the latter a subsequent favourite of Bruce Springsteen. Sveti Stefan is a seriously up-market hotel on a tiny island linked to the mainland by a bridge. One of the workers there told me that Rambo actor Sylvester Stallone had been so particular about his food that he had insisted on inspecting the kitchens. 'He was not so big,' the typically towering Montenegrin worker said. In Warsaw and Bucharest, Communist leaders had sat po-faced and reserved at official functions; in Belgrade many party officials seemed to want to share a joke and a drink as much as they wanted to pass on their Socialist philosophies.

Yugoslavia was like no other Socialist country I had seen. We in the press group were taken to a delightful garden restaurant where the junior Information Minister, sitting opposite, refrained from delivering a home-grown history monologue. The director of the state-owned Tanjug news agency – a powerful person in any Socialist society – plied us all with plum brandy and jokes. It was so much more Western than similar junkets organised by Warsaw Pact countries. Everywhere we looked, as we travelled from Belgrade to Dubrovnik and Sveti Stefan, there seemed to be sunshine by day, bright lights by night, music, theatres, art galleries, writers and poets. We all knew, of course, that we were meant to see just the icing on Yugoslavia's cake; nonetheless, the contrast with other Communist societies was enormous.

Beneath the surface, though, the seeds of conflict were germinating. In January 1986, a mere four months before we all caroused our way round Yugoslavia, more than two thousand citizens of Kosovo Polje had signed a petition carried by the *Knjizevne Novine* literary newspaper, denouncing Albanian separatism. It was the first organised protest in modern history by Kosovo Serbs against ethnic Albanians. A month later, on 26 February 1986, about one hundred Kosovo Serbs arrived in Belgrade to demand protection from ethnic Albanians in the province. It was to be the first of many such protests, which drew sympathy inside Serbia but aroused suspicion in other parts of the Yugoslav federation. Slovenes called these demonstrations 'the nationalism trains'.

All this was hidden from the Western journalists during my first visit. Instead, I was captivated by the physical beauty of Yugoslavia, ranging from the flatlands and breadbasket of Vojvodina to the dramatic mountains which pushed skywards along the Dalmatian coast, and the medieval towns and cities buzzing with people who seemed so much more alive than the television-watching, armchair-huggers at home. There was also something so Irish about their love of music, drinking and vigorous political and religious debate.

Subsequent visits over the next few years only made it harder to believe that many of the Serbs I came across were the demons portrayed in the West as the Balkan wars began to unfold. Once, in 1993, I seemed to be the only woman on board a train crammed with hundreds of fatigue-clad soldiers. They lolled in carriages and corridors as the train began to snake its way through the Montenegrin mountains at the start of a twelve-hour journey from the coastal port of Bar to Belgrade. Some of the soldiers began singing Serbian nationalist Chetnik songs and making the three-fingered Serb salute. These were the people who much of the world by now believed were mass rapists and murderers. I was about to learn a lesson in the importance of questioning perceived wisdom.

While Kosovo tensions were simmering gently in 1993, the Bosnian conflict had already boiled over, demanding the urgent attention of diplomats, politicians and television crews. Far braver colleagues than I risked daily bombardment from Serbian artillery and bullets from gunmen in Sniper's Alley, the road running outside the Holiday Inn in Sarajevo.

I had flown from Belgrade to Tivat in Montenegro to investigate the political situation in the only republic, alongside Serbia, which by this time made up the rump Yugoslavia. Swingeing international sanctions were being imposed against the Serbs in an effort to press the Yugoslavs to force some sort of settlement on the Bosnian Serbs. The sanctions seemed to have absolutely no effect on the progress of the war but they did cause hyper-inflation in Yugoslavia, and a widespread fuel shortage.

After interviewing several leading Montenegrin government and opposition members, it was time to head back to Belgrade. Trying to dictate reports by telephone from the grim hotel in Podgorica to *The Times* back in London had been futile – the lines from the Montenegrin capital were non-existent. Of course, I had been unaware of this during the early hours of the morning, as I had plied the switchboard operator with whisky, money and cigarettes while he played a telecommunications version of charades. It must have been an interesting diversion for a man probably used to dreary solitude through the night-time hours. Lap-top computers and mobile phones were not yet standard and the cheap, plastic telephone in my room, with its frayed cord, was little more use than a toy, since it was barely capable of making a connection with the reception desk downstairs.

After joining a local businessman for a hearty break-fast of slivovic and black coffee, I was offered a lift to Tivat airport by the entrepreneur and his friend, a doctor. They were overwhelmingly helpful, trying to find a work-able fax machine en route, for me to send my story. They were also worried that flights might have been cancelled because of the fuel shortage and wanted to be on hand in case I was stranded. I was unconcerned, still in that stage of innocence when possession of an airline ticket meant you got where you wanted to go.

Tivat airport was unusually quiet when we arrived, despite swarms of people milling confusedly around the low departures terminal building. It took a while for it to dawn on me that the lack of noise associated with airports was because no aircraft were arriving or departing. There is only one thing for Yugoslavs to do in such circumstances – we all sat down and drank slivovic and coffee while we pondered our next move. The doctor had disappeared for about an hour, reappearing with a beaming smile and a railway ticket from the port of Bar, an hour or so's drive away, to Belgrade.

My two new friends looked a little uneasy as they hoisted my luggage up from the low platform onto the train. The soldiers were everywhere, probably returning from Serb-held areas in Bosnia, said my two helpers. No one mentioned the fact that the world had been outraged a few weeks previously, when a group of Muslims travelling on this same railway route had been reportedly rounded up, forced off the train when it reached the Sandjak region on the border between Serbia and Montenegro, and shot dead.

I was a little nervous when the soldiers cast coldly curious glances at me as I sandwiched myself in a corner seat near the corridor. The only civilian I could see was a Muslim edging slowly through the mass of troops, selling bitter-tasting but hot coffee in paper cups. The soldiers stared indifferently as I tried to lift my holdall onto a net luggage rack already chock-a-block with olive green military bags. All the men were wearing camouflage fatigues, with the exception of a large, early middle-aged bear of a soldier sitting opposite me, who was clad in an olive green uniform resplendent with the Bosnian Serb Republic insignia, and a peaked cap adorned with a magnificent heavy silver badge. He failed to move his large black-booted feet, which were sprawled across my path, as I smiled and made a mute appeal with my eyes while trying to find space for my own legs. Dark eyes briefly met mine and he shuffled his feet a few inches nearer to his side of the carriage. It was early afternoon and the train left the station and began twisting its way through some of the most dramatic mountain scenery on earth.

I closed my eyes to try to doze while two soldiers near the window played cards and others, squeezing down the crowded corridor, periodically pulled open the door to our compartment in the vain hope of finding a seat, then slammed it closed before moving on.

I could tell that the troops near the window were talking about me, the *stranac* or foreigner. Their tone was none too friendly, and I could not help thinking about the many Western reports of Serb forces engaging in rape and shooting sprees as they rampaged across many parts of Bosnia-Herzegovina. Perhaps it had been an unwise decision to travel alone.

Even as early as 1993, the world had already come to see the Bosnian conflict as essentially black and white, bad Serbs against good Muslims. Hundreds of Serbian soldiers, wearily and drunkenly making their way back from the front line in Bosnia, would not seem to be the ideal travelling companions for a British Imperialist lackey journalist. But I felt I had little choice as I had to reach Belgrade ready for an onward journey to London the following day.

The officer sitting opposite me was obviously being pressed to try to discover my identity. 'You Amerikanski? Angleski?' he eventually asked. Since America and England were the least loved nations in the hearts of Bosnian Serb soldiers, I lied. 'Irish,' I replied – after all, my mother's family was from Mayo while my paternal ancestors were from Tipperary. The atmosphere in the carriage instantly changed; the huge officer beamed and the seemingly hostile soldiers next to the window raised their eyebrows in approval. We were several hours into the journey and most of the bottles of bitter-sweet smelling home-brew alcohol which the soldiers had brought for the journey were now empty.

I decided to capitalise on the nascent sense of cama-raderie by offering round the bottle of whisky I had in my holdall. It lasted just half an hour or so, but at least the spell had been broken. The officer's name was Dragan, and he spoke about as much English as I spoke Serbian – a few words. Nonetheless, it was enough for him to question me more and the lie about my origins grew larger. Why was I here alone? Was I with the United Nations? Tricky one, that, since the UN mission to the former Yugoslavia, Unprofor, would be no more popular with the soldiers than British and American journalists. So, desperate to portray myself as totally apolitical, I explained that I was a nurse, attached to the UN but not really part of the organisation.

The soldiers were ecstatic beyond all imaginings. I felt slightly guilty about capitalising on the hard work and dedication of real nurses, but no harm had been done and possibly some good in that the ice had been thawed. Then, to my horror, the officer began insisting that I accompany him down the train. There were wounded colleagues in a carriage near the back and he wanted them to see me. My entreaties to stay put were threatening to destroy the new atmosphere of bonhomie, so I reluctantly relented.

Then, as we pushed our way towards the rear of the train, I could hear someone nearer the front barking a demand to see identity papers. My mouth went dry. If I were forced to show my passport, my real identity as a British journalist would be revealed and I would be in a far more vulnerable position than merely tolerating an unfriendly atmosphere. There was little time to think as I was eagerly shepherded to a carriage where about four soldiers were lying on bunks. The officer, Dragan, was babbling something incomprehensible and the prone soldiers began excitedly unbuttoning jackets, pulling up vests and drawing down trousers to reveal lurid scars on abdomens, groins and backs. Officer Dragan was urging me to come close to examine the wounds and seemed to be asking whether I thought that their own medical staff had done a good job in stitching them up. 'Excellent – *dobro, vrlo dobro*,' I said, trying to look professionally competent to judge. The men kept asking where I had been stationed with the UN in Bosnia, I kept pretending not to understand while trying to formulate a way to escape showing my passport as the calls for identity papers loomed slowly but surely closer.

In sheer desperation, but faint-hearted about the chances of success, I made another smiling assurance about the wonderful state of the soldiers' wounds and fled to the toilet. The cubicle, almost opposite the casualties' compartment, made a public lavatory at King's Cross seem like an advert for *House and Home* bathrooms. The stench was so overpowering that the prospect of discovery by the identity-papers men seemed almost preferable. After living briefly in China, however, I had learned to cope with the unbelievably vile toilets there by breathing through my mouth and staring at the ceiling. A few minutes later, imperative banging on the door announced the arrival of the officials demanding to see identity cards or passports. Then came Dragan's voice, apparently talking to the men hovering outside. A brief but robust discussion seemed to take place between them and then, miraculously, the voices died away as the group apparently moved off. Maybe the army officer had vouched for what he assumed to be the Irish UN nurse. It was a few more minutes before I dared to emerge back into the throng of uniforms and camouflage fatigues, but not before I had taken my passport from my handbag and shoved it down the back of my jeans, between my tights and knickers. I was worried that any subsequent search of bags might reveal the damning document. If this happened, I would pretend to have lost it, calculating that the situation would have to be exceedingly serious for anyone to discover its new hiding place.

I need not have worried. After getting back to my seat, the officer, Dragan, was all smiles and chivalry. The other soldiers in the carriage had acquired more bottles of liquor from somewhere and the Chetnik songs had become became louder and more boisterous. One of the soldiers kept pointing at himself, then at me and then sticking his stomach forward in mimicry of a pregnant woman. I had by now managed to maintain some sort of basic dialogue and eye-contact with their officer. Although he laughed heartily at their japes, he also mercifully began to ask me if I could help him. Did I have pencil and paper, because there was something very important I could do for all of them. What did they most want, these people renowned the world over for their aptitude for rape and pillage? They yearned to learn the words of Paul McCartney's *Yesterday*.

I gladly obliged, while all in the compartment began Serbian renditions of Beatles songs. We were still singing these hits of thirty years before when we reached

Belgrade in the early hours of the morning. Just before we reached the sanctions-strapped city, the army officer had taken the heavy silver Republika Srpska badge from his peaked cap and insisted on giving it to me in exchange for the words of *Yesterday*. He was very keen that we meet the following evening and pressed me to exchange telephone numbers with him. As we parted on the dimly-lit platform, he bowed low as he took my hand in his and kissed it. I felt not a little churlish as I sped away in a taxi, knowing that I had given him a false number and that, anyway, I hoped to be in Budapest the following evening before flying back to London.

# Chapter Five

# Demonisation: 1992–1999

During the Nato bombing campaign in 1999, Serbs repeatedly referred to the plight of American Indians as an example of US hypocrisy. The Serbs were consistently demonised, they said, yet the antecedents of today's Pentagon planners had indulged in a campaign of ethnic cleansing of their own which made Kosovo pale by comparison.

In the book, *Bury My Heart at Wounded Knee*, Dee Brown writes that by the second half of the nineteenth century the Indians' 'musical names remained forever fixed on the American land, but their bones were forgotten in a thousand burned villages or lost in forests fast disappearing before the axes of twenty million invaders.' All nations have dark secrets, including those at the helm of Nato – today's self-appointed world policemen, the Serbs protested. The West's claims that sanctions and missiles have been aimed solely at the Belgrade regime and not at the Serbian people, are laughed to scorn. Most of them take it personally when their homes and workplaces are bombed, their fields turned to minefields by unexploded cluster bombs, and the southern part of their country is turned into a virtual no-go area patrolled by foreign troops.

Reading the American Indians' plaintive cries about their treatment at the hands of the Europeans, it is hard not to feel an echo down the years. 'The white man made us many promises, more than I can remember, but they never kept but one; they promised to take our land and they took it,' said Chief Red Cloud of the Oglala Teton

Sioux tribe as the nineteenth century drew to a close. Chief Tecumseh of the Shawnees asked, 'Where are the many once powerful tribes of our people? They have vanished before the avarice and oppression of the White Man, as snow before a summer sun.'

So what lies behind the West's apparent demonisation of the Serbs? The Yugoslav President's ability to whip up Serb nationalism to a battle-ready fervour is part of the reason but he could not have done this without realising that there is something in the Serb psyche which never flinches from a fight, at the same time revelling in the role of victim. What other country would make a national virtue out of a catastrophic defeat? The Serbs, under King Lazar, were vanquished by Turks at the Battle of Kosovo in 1389, yet the clash is hailed as a shining moment in the nation's history.

In the twentieth century alone, the Serbs have fought in seven conflicts: the First and Second Balkan Wars, the First and Second World Wars, Croatia, Bosnia-Herzegovina and, now, Kosovo. Like the Irish, the Serbs can be fierce fighters and drinkers – as well as poets, songsters and lifelong friends after just a few minutes' acquaintance. They can also be deeply superstitious and have a tendency to paranoia, both traits which make them all the more malleable in the hands of Slobodan Milosevic.

During and after the 1999 bombing campaign, rumours grew fat on the state's manipulation and control of information. Even among the educated classes in Belgrade, who probably enjoy the best access in Serbia to satellite television beamed in from America, Britain, Germany, Italy and Greece, the daftest stories took root. Many were convinced, for example, that President Bill Clinton's daughter, Chelsea, had converted to Islam, hence the US President's support for Muslims in Bosnia and Kosovo. Others believed that Nato flights over Serbia were causing catastrophic climate changes. This story grew especially strong when a series of dramatic summer storms swept the country in the weeks immediately after the bombing ceased, leaving floods and mayhem in their wake.

'What do you think about these jets, do you really think they are affecting the weather?' asked Marija, my earnest-faced interpreter as we sheltered from yet another lashing by rain, thunder and lightning. The young graduate looked genuinely worried as we sat over coffee after taking refuge in the government media centre in Belgrade one day in July. Bomb-raw nerves had been set on edge once more by the sights and sounds of thunder and lightning which bore an uncanny resemblance to the explosions of a month before. That day's Belgrade newspapers carried a report by a Serbian scientist, complete with 'statistics' indicating that the chemical composition of the atmosphere had been altered by the exhaust particles from the aircraft. My first instinct had been to laugh, but Marija looked so concerned that instead, I said: 'Look, huge jets often take off from Heathrow in London every two minutes, hour after hour. People living nearby hate the noise and pollution but they do not think it makes them ill. And that has been going on for years, not a few weeks as here.' Marija's anxious face relaxed. 'Of course,' she said. 'I hadn't thought of that. You have made me feel much better.'

A deeply superstitious streak runs through the Serbian heart: soldiers who would not flinch at the thought of storming into battle outnumbered by an enemy, blanch at the idea of losing their 'lucky' belts. Every soldier deems his uniform belt to be his personal lucky charm, the power of which grows with every new skirmish. The highly-educated Goran told me of a friend who had misplaced his own belt and asked to borrow Goran's when the soldier-doctor was off duty. 'I said to him, "Are you MAD? This belt will only protect me, not you," ' said Goran as if explaining a rational treatise on military strategy. 'In the end, my friend could not find his belt and had to go to fight without it. He was killed,' he added with an air of sad inevitability.

There is still a latent belief in the power of witchcraft in some country areas. Even Belgrade citizens, who consider themselves far more sophisticated than 'primitives' from the countryside, often display deep-seated superstitiousness.

The nation's tendency to embrace catastrophe as if it were a shining opportunity came home to me a few weeks later. Djule Djukic, leader of one of Serbia's most famous rock bands, Van Gogh, was being filmed in a café in a side-street off Belgrade's 29 November Street, for a weekly pop music programme broadcast by TV Pink. The station is run by the United Yugoslav Left, or Jul, Party led by Slobodan Milosevic's wife, Mira Markovic. Between sessions in front of the camera, he came to sit at my table. 'Were you afraid of the bombs?' he asked. 'Yes, very, they terrified me,' I said. 'How about you?'

'I thought they were wonderful,' he said in all seriousness. 'I used to watch the explosions around Belgrade. You could hear the missiles, *zheeee*, and then a split second of complete silence before the explosion.' Djule had become so captivated by the symphony of war that he had begun to record the blasts. 'I am going to make an album using the sounds of the bombs in place of drums,' he said. This is a man who also professes to enjoy the sensation and sound of a dentist's drill at work in his mouth.

The rock star went on to ask what I thought of Tony Blair, and came back with his own opinion of the British Prime Minister. 'He is a dishonest liar, whereas Milosevic is an honest liar,' he said, in a good example of the sort of Serbian pseudo-logic that has had many Western politicians tearing their hair out over the past decade.

One man who became hollow-eyed with fatigue and frustration trying to apply his ideals and logic on a people who can bend rationality and truth in this way was David Owen. As Bosnian peace negotiator at a myriad futile negotiations in Brussels and Geneva in the mid-1990s, Lord Owen seemed to be transformed from a pull-your-

socks-up and take-your-medicine-like-a-man broker, to a
disillusioned, sleep-deprived wreck. This was partly
because of the phenomenal workload, but also because
he was slowly undermined by the bare-faced lying to
which he was subjected by all sides – Serbs, Croats and
Muslims. Owen definitely seemed a humbler as well as
wiser man by the time the Bosnian war ended.

One of the first peace negotiations was hosted by Lord
Carrington and took place in the unlikely surroundings
of Christie's, the auctioneers, early in 1992. Antique guns
were exhibited like jewels in glass cases lining the walls
near a staircase leading to the rooms where the protagonists were to meet. The weapons seemed a poignant
reminder of two faces of war. In London, with its polished
corridors of power and genteel rules of diplomatic
engagement, even guns – produced with the aim of killing
people – could look charming and fighting was something
of an academic exercise. The reality of guns and mortar
fire in Bosnia could barely impinge on the plush
surroundings in which the leaders of the warring sides
now found themselves. The leaders emerged from
Christie's to address press conferences with assurances
that peace was imminent, when in reality the war had
barely begun. Judy Dempsey, a *Financial Times* journalist, and I were standing on a street corner when we
saw Bosnian Serb leader, Radovan Karadzic climbing
into a taxi a few yards away. Dempsey had met Karadzic
before and she jogged across to speak to him. 'Climb in,'
he had told her, and seconds later she had found space
for me, too.

While dozens of other newspaper and television journalists pressed for interviews with the bodyguard- and
limousine-protected Bosnian Muslim and Croat delegations, the three of us slipped away unnoticed in the black
cab. Karadzic, thick, wavy grey hair falling in an unruly
mop over his eyes, seemed more like a wayward Irish
playwright than a future indicted war criminal. Back in

his hotel suite, where his wife was waiting, Karadzic produced a bottle of malt whisky and poured four generous measures before settling down to answer our questions. The former psychology professor from Sarajevo University spoke good English and refrained from the usual Balkan trait of narrating at least three centuries of Balkan history before deigning to address present-day problems. Was there going to be peace as a result of these talks, we wanted to know. Karadzic poured more whisky as he proceeded to forecast – accurately – the timing and progress of the fighting still to come.

There followed countless futile peace conferences in Brussels and Geneva between 1992 and 1995, where David Owen and Thorvald Stoltenberg, the peace negotiators for the European Community and the UN, took on mission impossible. It rapidly became clear that the war would end only when all sides had grabbed as much land as they knew they could physically take and had fought themselves to a standstill.

Throughout the war, the West blamed Serbs for the fighting while effectively minimising the impact of battles launched by Croats and, occasionally, Muslims. The Serbs were undoubtedly better armed and battle-ready, so were better equipped to pursue their war aims. But their goal was the same as that pursued by the Croats and Muslims – to control as much territory for their people as they could. It was clear to all that the old multicultural society imposed by Tito, largely as a way to neutralise Serb power, would no longer be able to exist after Yugoslavia broke apart. Therefore, battles to create individual areas for Serbs, Croats and Muslims were almost inevitable. It was also misleading to label the Serbs' campaigns as 'ethnic cleansing'. Serbs, Croats and Muslims in Bosnia are ethnically identical. They are all Slavs, the Muslims having converted from Christianity to Islam while the region was under Ottoman rule to gain economic advantages from their rulers. The fighting in Bosnia was vicious and the international community was bound to intervene.

Humanitarian aid was desperately needed and attempts
had to be made to bring the warring parties to a negoti-
ated settlement but, by consistently portraying the Serbs
as the guilty party, the West was taking sides.

The Croats had powerful allies in Germany and the
Vatican, and the Muslims won the support of America by
default – any enemy of the communistic Serbs was
Washington's friend. It was a bad precedent, for the same
principle was applied in Kosovo and America now finds
itself as bedfellow with an Albanian organisation largely
funded by drug- and gun-running and which is proving
increasingly uncontrollable.

By the time the Kosovo crisis reached meltdown in
1999, there was almost no difference in many people's
minds between Slobodan Milosevic, the Yugoslav Army
and the Serbian people. When more than two hundred
thousand Serbs and Roma gypsies were forced to flee
Kosovo after Nato entered the province with its KLA
protégés, there was barely a whimper of protest in the
West. Almost the entire Serbian population of Kosovo
left the province in the two months following Nato's
arrival in mid-June, proportionately far more than the
ethnic Albanians whose exodus sparked the bombing
campaign. Yet the attitude in the West was that the Serbs
somehow deserved it and many from Kosovo must have
at least known of the atrocities against the Albanian
population. The fact that at least half the Kosovo Serb
refugees were children, according to the United Nations
High Commissioner for Refugees, seemed to make no
difference. This was an annoying statistic which merely
muddied the waters.

Nonetheless, it was during the Bosnian war that the
Western-fostered imagery of good against evil was fine-
tuned. Back in the mid-1990s in Geneva, futile and
expensive peace talks were held at regular intervals. The
Bosnian protagonists stayed in suites at the most expensive lakeside hotels and their wives went shopping at the
finest couturiers and jewellers, while their citizens killed

one another back home. Geneva is an overly-pristine city where even the plants in municipal flowerbeds are reputed to be staked upright, lest they wave untidily in the breeze. The city is also noted for its occasional violent thunderstorms and it was one of nature's pyrotechnic displays that inspired Mary Shelley to create Frankenstein and his monster. Another monster was in danger of being stitched together at the Geneva negotiations, a Bosnia held together with 'safe havens', enclaves and requiring the unceasing vigilance of international peacekeepers.

It always seemed odd that the Geneva gatherings were known as peace 'talks', since there were many occasions when the Bosnian Muslim leader, Alija Izetbegovic, the Croat Mate Boban, and the Serb Radovan Karadzic refused even to sit in the same room as one another, let alone hold a sensible conversation.

It was a strange life for the journalists, too. We would spend hours scuttling between the myriad rooms at the labyrinthine United Nations Palais des Nations, trying to glean any leaks emerging from the discussions under way behind closed doors. And there were leaks aplenty. Although the delegation's leaders often refused to talk to one another, their henchmen were only too keen to reveal what the other sides were saying, largely because they wanted to denounce their enemies' positions. It rapidly became clear that what all sides wanted was more land than was physically available on the map.

The UN building was like an over-large 1960s comprehensive school, with cork noticeboards in every room advertising the publication of the latest report on water-borne diseases in the Ivory Coast, or the effects of deforestation in the farthest reaches of Amazonia. There was next to nothing about the main reason the vast majority of the press was there, the Bosnian peace process.

There was also a canteen where journalists, minor diplomats and delegation spokesmen and women would meet for a beer or coffee. Soon after arriving for yet another round of peace talks, I was taken to one side in the cafeteria by John Mills, the newly appointed spokesman for David Owen. During a wide-ranging briefing, he made it clear that the Bosnian Muslims, not the Serbs, were refusing to accept a crucial aspect of the latest peace plan – one which had ostensibly been accepted by all the warring sides. 'They have basically been told to negotiate or perish,' said the spokesman. He shook my hand warmly as we parted.

The following morning, while I was walking across the main lobby at the UN building to buy newspapers, Mills came rushing towards me. 'That was an off-the-record briefing,' he bawled, as a group of journalists from around the world turned to stare. He was bearing a copy of *The Times* in which I had mentioned the 'negotiate or perish' dictum to the Muslims. The spokesman had not mentioned the confidential nature of our talk the previous day, as most experienced spokesmen would if they wanted information to remain secret, so I had felt able to use it.

The heated rebuttals and protests which followed *The Times'* disclosure of Muslim intransigence seemed yet more evidence that the international community wanted only the Serbs to be seen as difficult. Mills issued a statement to Reuters news agency, denying having issued the warning to the Muslims. *The Times* in turn protested to Lord Owen's office about the implication that I had invented the story.

During one of the most frenzied periods of the Geneva negotiations, in November 1993, the Muslim Deputy Prime Minister of Bosnia, Ejup Ganic, told the *Observer* newspaper that the Muslim side would never give in. 'We will destroy Croatia and return Serbia to the Middle Ages,' he was quoted as saying. The following month, the *Independent* said it had evidence that Bosnia's Muslims and Croats in Croatia were breaking the arms embargo which was then in force. Croatia had smuggled in at least sixteen Russian MI-17 helicopters, it said, while the Muslim-led Bosnian Army had managed to get hold of various pieces of new high-tech military hardware, including eight Hind helicopters.

And so the peace process continued; ceasefires were regularly announced, as were the deaths of countless thousands in Bosnia as the fighting carried on regardless. The rump Yugoslavia, comprising Serbia and Montenegro, was beginning to wilt under the weight of economic sanctions. In Kosovo throughout this time, an uneasy stand-off was prevailing between Serbs and ethnic Albanians. The threat of full-scale conflict between the two communities had boiled up and dissipated countless times in the past, but by the mid-1990s, pressure was building for the cataclysm to come. Macedonia was having its own problems; a session of Parliament in the capital, Skopje, was disrupted by a mass gathering of ethnic Albanians demanding federalisation of the republic. In Sarajevo, on 5 February 1994, an explosion cut down shoppers as they milled around the Markale market, with devastating consequences. With barely a second's hesitation, Bosnian Serb forces were blamed and an outraged world demanded vengeance.

## Chapter Six
# Massacre: Sarajevo 1994

Like a scene from *M\*A\*S\*H*, the sign pinned to sandbags
at Sarajevo airport said 'Champs Elysees'. It was one of
the first things you saw after obeying the UN peacekeepers' command to run as fast as you could from the
huge Ilyushin cargo plane, across the tarmac, to the relative safety of the low terminal building. We were ordered
to make a dash from the aircraft because Serb snipers
and artillery hidden in the hills around the airport were
apt to take pot shots at those arriving in the Bosnian
capital. Panting to catch my breath after sprinting with
the lead weight of an old-fashioned flak jacket in one
hand and a holdall bulging with emergency rations in the
other, I could not decide whether the Parisian street sign
was a symbol of wishful thinking or bitter irony.

It was November 1994, and I wanted to see how Bosnia
was faring nine months after the notorious Markale
market-place massacre in which sixty-eight people had
died and more than two hundred had been injured when
a single shell exploded in the small Sarajevo market. The
ghastly scenes had been filmed within minutes and a
horrified world left in no doubt that the Serbs were to
blame. The slaughter brought deeper American involvement in the Balkans, with the formation of the US-led
Contact Group and an American-negotiated alliance
between Bosnia's Muslims and Croats. The massacre also
ultimately paved the way for American air strikes on
Bosnian Serb positions in late summer, 1995. Furthermore, the killing brought about a deal whereby the Serbs

pulled back their heavy guns from the mountains surrounding Sarajevo and the Muslims reluctantly signed a ceasefire. The easing of the siege, and the relief for the people of Sarajevo, was a notable achievement.

However, to this day no one knows who fired the deadly mortar round on the Markale market. The only certainty is that an explosion rocked the tiny market-place soon after midday on that Saturday. Survivors and witnesses reported that they heard no characteristic whistle of an approaching missile, and this later led to some suggestions that a bomb had been placed under a market stall. A Western diplomat who was in Sarajevo at the time told me in 1999 that he was convinced the bombing was perpetrated by the Muslim-led Government. He had seen UN reports into the incident, he said, which unreservedly blamed the Muslims. As a diplomat, however, he could not go on record with this information. The Muslims were sure the Serbs would be blamed, and they hoped that outrage at the carnage would lead to air strikes against their foes and increase pressure for a lifting of the arms embargo which was in place against all the warring sides. Britain and France were vehemently opposed to lifting the embargo, although America had shown signs of wanting to arm the Muslims.

'On the morning of the explosion, some people were told it was not a good day to go to the market,' the Western diplomat said. 'There was also no shelling from the Serb positions that day, and the injuries were mainly from the waist down, as if a bomb had exploded *in situ*.' The diplomat said that another sign the Muslim-led Government had been responsible was that government media with cameras were on the scene 'within seconds', as if poised in advance to record the full horror of the carnage to gain as much world impact as possible.

Paul Beaver, spokesman for the respected specialist magazine, *Jane's Defence Weekly*, also has evidence that the UN was encouraged to suppress its investigations into the massacre. 'During two spells in Sarajevo, I interviewed

a number of technical experts about the market-place
bomb incident,' he told me. All the interviewees
demanded anonymity at the time but one of the British
Army ATOs (Ammunition Technical Officers) claimed
that reports to the UN Protection Force, Unprofor, were
suppressed because they incriminated the ABiH – the
army of Bosnia-Herzegovina.

'Nato soldiers attached to the UN force were
convinced that Serb artillery had not fired the fateful
round which killed and injured so many; they also exam-
ined the possibility that the ABiH had used one of its
own mortar positions. That too was discounted, according
to the officers and senior non-commissioned officers
interviewed.

'Instead, the position of explosion was, said the ATO
with considerable Northern Ireland experience, consis-
tent with an IED (Improvised Explosive Device) which
detonated at between one and two metres above ground
level. The ATO surmised that a command wire or time
fused device could have been planted on a market stall.'

Beaver added: 'The balance of probability points to
the ABiH and the motive is simply because the Sarajevo
Government wanted to bring the West into action against
the Serbs. The Western media was quick to blame the
VRS (Bosnian-Serb Army) and launched its air offensive. The case against the VRS has never been proven.'

The suggestion that the Muslims could have shelled
their own people began to be discussed by diplomats,
politicians and a small number of journalists after the
UN had conducted its investigation into the massacre
and concluded that no one could be sure where the shell
had come from. But most people, including nearly all
international news organisations, recoiled at the idea of
such self-inflicted mutilation. The vast majority of the
world's press and politicians accepted the instant suggestions that the Serbs were responsible; questions were not
encouraged and the general view was that, in any case,
the end justified the means; the siege of Sarajevo was

eased. By blaming the Serbs without proof, however, a precedent was set and the process of demonising them took deeper root.

I flew into Sarajevo, that November after the massacre, along with dozens of blue-helmeted UN troops from Scandinavia, after reporting to a cold hangar at Zagreb airport in the chilliest hour, just before dawn. Even before setting off, the flak jacket seemed more of a hindrance than a help. The protective vests should ideally be made to measure, but this one was used by anyone at *The Times* who felt the need and therefore seemed to fit no one well. The high neck, designed to shield the jugular, seemed tailored for a Baldrick while the lower extremities reached to my knees. It also weighed about twenty-five pounds and the troops travelling with me could not assist; they had their own even heavier burdens.

On board the huge aeroplane, the human cargo was relegated to ledges round the perimeter of the interior while massive crates of aid and equipment being taken to the Bosnian capital took centre stage, fixed down with chains and canvas straps. The only view on the world outside was from the cockpit way up front, while the rest of us travelled in semi-darkness in the windowless cargo bay. Because of the gloom, and the fact that we passengers sat sideways on to one another, it took me some time to realise that we had a VIP on board. Haris Silajdzic, Prime Minister of the Muslim-led Bosnian Government, was returning from negotiations abroad. Ever ready to talk to journalists, the handsome Silajdzic urged me to sit near him while he expounded his latest thoughts on the progress of the war. He, too, was forced to wedge himself into a ledge.

It was two and half years after the republic's Serbs, Muslims and Croats had launched into the most vicious conflict in Europe since the Second World War. Sarajevo had been besieged by Serb artillery for much of the time and thousands had died across the fledgling state. But the situation in the capital had eased greatly in the summer, thanks largely to the efforts of the UN commander, the Briton General Sir Michael Rose. After the Markale massacre, he had cajoled and bullied the Bosnian Serbs into pulling back their heavy artillery from the mountains they controlled, overlooking the capital, and brought about a drastic reduction in the retaliatory rounds fired by the Muslims. Rose was commander of the UN Protection Force in Bosnia for a year, from January 1994. During that time he resolutely opposed the use of a Nato air campaign against the Serbs. In his book, *Fighting For Peace*, he explained why he did not think it was possible to bomb the Serbs to the negotiating table in 1994 – the year before the eventual air strikes against them.

'The answer is simple. The two-week campaign against the Bosnian Serbs, in which 3,500 sorties were flown, nearly 100 cruise missiles fired and almost 400 different Serb targets engaged, did not alone end the war in Bosnia. The Nato air campaign in Bosnia in August and September 1995 formed part of a series of strategic actions taking place at the time. These included the use of artillery and mortar by the UN Rapid Reaction Force to neutralise the Bosnian Serb heavy weapons around Sarajevo, the Croat-Muslim federation ground offensive in the west of Bosnia, and most important of all, the emergence of a political settlement acceptable to all sides. The Nato air campaign was no more than a useful signal to the Serbs that the peacekeeping option had been suspended and that the West was now prepared to use a greater level of enforcement than before.' Rose significantly added: 'It also helped assuage US domestic opinion.'

Washington's need to keep Americans happy was probably also a key reason why the international community remained as quiet as possible about the results of the investigation which followed the market-place massacre. 'Unhelpfully, the US Administration aligned itself with the [Muslim-led] Bosnian Government and refused to consider the full demilitarisation of Sarajevo, although it

continued to insist on a withdrawal of [Serb] heavy
weapons from around the city,' Rose said in his book.

As I travelled to Sarajevo in the November following
the Markale massacre, Silajdzic was not happy; his
mission in life at this time was to persuade the international community to lift the arms embargo against the
Muslims. 'As Churchill said, "Give us the tools to do the
job,"' and he thumped a fist in his hand.

The Bosnian capital lies at the bottom of a bowl
created by surrounding mountains, and aircraft flying in
during the Bosnian war would make a last-minute steep
descent and swoop into the airport to minimise the risk
of being shot at had they taken a more conventional
approach. This strategy might have been exhilarating had
we been able to see out of the Ilyushin. Sitting in the
gloomy cargo hold, the sudden ear-popping drop was
disconcerting for the uninitiated. When we had finally
rolled to a halt, the rear of the giant plane was lowered to
form a ramp and we all began our dash towards the
terminal – the UN soldiers in well-disciplined order, me
in an ungainly lollop clutching the vile flak jacket,
handbag and holdall.

I had been invited to stay with a member of the
Muslim-dominated Bosnian Presidency, Mufid Memija,
and his family at their flat in the centre of the city. But
first I had to make the journey into town in a white
armoured personnel carrier driven by Egyptian peacekeepers. The road from the airport was one of the most
dangerous in Sarajevo, passing through areas exposed to
shells and snipers. The city was relatively calm now,
compared with the constant barrages which had shaken it
at the height of the siege. Nonetheless, long stretches of
road were eerily deserted, with the skeletons of apartment blocks standing as silent sentinels on both sides in
the cold, late autumn sunshine.

The flat where Mufid and his family lived was in an
elegant, stuccoed building near the Presidency building.
It could have been an apartment in a Regency house in

South Kensington, with plaster mouldings on walls and
ceilings, a huge, elegantly-tiled fireplace and spacious
rooms furnished with antiques. Polished tables and chests
of drawers were covered with immaculately clean and
ironed embroidered cloths, while fine lampstands had
been carefully placed around the lounge. The Memijas'
three-year-old son, Mido, played quietly on a Chinese rug
beneath imposing paintings which adorned the walls.
Mufid and his wife, Alma, were at pains to make me feel
at home. The generosity and kindness of the Muslim
family matched the warm spirit of Serbs I had met all
over the region. Ordinary people from all cultural backgrounds seemed to possess extraordinarily kind hearts; it
was hard to see how such magnanimous people could be
sucked into such vile wars.

The Memijas doted on their only child, perhaps to try
to ameliorate some of the misery of war. For although
their home was elegant, it was also cold. The couple dared
not let Mido go outside to play and he was known as the
Mushroom Boy because he was growing up in the dark.
He also had an ugly, puckered scar on his left leg, the
legacy of one of the almost constant power cuts, when he
had stumbled against a pan of boiling water in the blackness. Life for Alma was a constant grind of collecting
water from standpipes in the street, ironing at midnight
when the electricity occasionally materialised for a
couple of hours, and trying to find new ways to cook
beans, rice and flour. Mido's diet was supplemented by an
orange and vitamin drink provided by the UN and
known as '*humanitarija* juice'. The kitchen and bathroom
were littered with bottles of boiled water for drinking
and cleaning teeth, and buckets of unboiled water for
bathing, washing clothes and flushing the lavatory. The
supplies were collected in a rush during the two hours
every other day when standpipes were connected to the
mains.

Dusk fell soon after four in the afternoon, after which
candles and torches were the main sources of light. I soon

learned that you needed an octopus-like dexterity to cope with a candle, a bottle of water and a toothbrush. On my third day with the Memijas, I was treated to a bath, despite my protestations that the family should keep the water for themselves. Huge pans of water were put on to boil and thick towels were laid out. It was mid-afternoon and still light when I eased myself into the bath – as two loud explosions sounded nearby, shaking the building and sending me scuttling, naked, for cover near the bathroom door and away from the rattling windows. In my haste to spring back, I knocked over a bucket of water which had been so painstakingly brought up from the street.

Mido was often roused from sleep by shell-bursts and sniper fire. If his mother was out, he would find comfort in the arms of his grandmother, Saza, or Aunt Emina who spent hours huddled near the open oven door in the kitchen, trying to keep warm if the gas supplies were working. It was so cold in the flat most nights that I slept in my clothes on a mattress on the study floor, heaped high with blankets. Even so, the icy temperatures would numb my hands and feet and I would wake, shivering, several times a night. It was a relief to rise before dawn and stumble into the kitchen, where Saza and Emina were usually to be found drinking thick Turkish coffee and smoking endless cigarettes to calm shell-shaken nerves and to stifle appetites. Food was scarce and unappetising. Alma queued twice a month for the UN supplies which were keeping Sarajevans alive – flour, oil, cans of meat which she said 'even the cats won't eat'. She was also able to buy a little fresh meat and fruit and vegetables at inflated prices in the market. Mido was cosseted; he was given an egg scrambled with dried milk and salty cheese for breakfast, and reconstituted dried vegetables with fresh cabbage and onions for dinner. Every evening, the wide-eyed toddler would turn in circles on the Chinese rug. 'He has no park to play in, no friends, and he has all this energy,' said his grand-mother. 'He thinks all the world is old like us.'

Mufid and Alma were terrified that their son might fall prey to shells or bullets but there was a more silent killer on the loose in the Bosnian capital by the autumn of 1994. More people were being killed by gas leaks than by artillery and snipers, because families were cobbling together homespun connections to the city's mains. Britain's Overseas Development Administration donated a gas-detector van and sent a team to investigate the city's infrastructure. 'What we found was horrifying,' an administration spokesman told me, 'sixty thousand homes that were ticking time bombs, silently killing sleeping children with gas poisoning and with an explosive potential as deadly and unpredictable as any mortar.'

During the first winter of the war, desperate civilians cut down many of the trees lining Sarajevo's streets to use for fuel. In 1993, gas became the main source of energy but twenty thousand legally-connected homes were soon joined by sixty thousand households that were hooked up to the pipeline which ran from Siberia, via Belgrade. 'Often, the mains pipe is simply cut and a garden hose is clamped on and fed into the house's defunct central heating system,' the administration spokesman said.

It was to be another year before the Dayton peace agreement ended nearly three years of war in Bosnia, largely because all sides finally accepted that more fighting would not bring them substantially more than they already had. In Belgrade, Slobodan Milosevic played a leading role in the Dayton process after being persuaded to abandon the Bosnian Serb leader, Radovan Karadzic, in exchange for an easing of sanctions against the rump Yugoslavia.

The repercussions of the Bosnian conflict would linger, however; there is still no sign that the peace is deeply rooted enough to allow the departure of expensive international peacekeepers. Furthermore, the international perception of Serbs as warmongers riding roughshod over innocent victims in the region was revived by the West to galvanise public opinion when the Kosovo crisis erupted.

By the time the Kosovo conflict erupted in 1999, few Western politicians were going to point out – even if they knew – that the conflicts in Bosnia and Kosovo were hugely different in essence. There was no ethnic difference between Serbs, Croats or Muslims in Bosnia; the warring sides there were divided by culture and religion. In Kosovo, on the other hand, the Serbs and Albanians were of entirely different races. In Bosnia, mixed marriages were common, whereas they were almost unheard of in Kosovo.

# Chapter Seven

# Preparing for War

The ability of powerful nations to control the public's view of events is considerable, especially when the blinkers of patriotism are applied. Foreign policy the world over is rarely as black and white, or humanitarian and unselfish, as the propagandists would have us believe. Serbs often refer to the fact that Britain was only too pleased to have Communist Serbs on her side during the darkest days of the Second World War.

I met some people in England who failed to realise, even at the height of the Nato campaign, that Kosovo was actually part of Serbia and who believed that Milosevic and his forces had invaded the province. Such was the impression they had gained from reading tabloid newspapers and watching too much television. Propagandists rarely want the public to have too great an understanding of how the Kosovo cataclysm came to pass. It is necessary to look back more than a hundred years to see the shades of grey which give a truer picture than the black and white portrait drawn by Nato and the leading Western powers.

At about the same time as the American Indians were losing their battle for survival in the New World, ethnic Albanians on the far side of the world were trying to shake off an old invader of their own – the Ottoman Empire. The League of Prizren, created by Albanians to resist Ottoman rule, was formed in 1878 and three years later followed by the establishment of a provisional government. But it was another twenty years before the Ottomans were finally expelled from the region and

Kosovo became part of the new state of Albania. 'Why do you want a state when you don't even have an alphabet?' had been Bismarck's disdainful question to the Albanians while they were campaigning for their own country.

This state of affairs for the Albanians lasted just a year, however. In 1913, the Great Powers forced Albania to hand over the region to Serbia. The countries which imposed the handover included some of the very powers which were to attack Serbia in the closing year of the century – Britain, Germany, Italy, and France – as well as the Austro-Hungarian Empire and Russia.

The big turning point in the West's attitude towards Serbia came after 1989, when Yugoslavia began to fall apart at the seams. The edges were fraying as the two richest republics – Croatia and Slovenia – strained ever harder to break away. The timing could not have been better for them, or worse for Milosevic. Public opinion in Europe and America had been triumphant as the demise of Communism and the emergence of new capitalist-minded states were welcomed with open arms after the fall of the Berlin Wall. Few Western governments could resist the temptation to portray the collapse of Communism as a moral victory, one of right over wrong, white scoring over black, good against evil. It was a trait which was to spill over into the West's dealings with Yugoslavia; the insinuation being that Socialist Serbs were bad and everyone else was a hapless, innocent victim.

The opening shots of what were to be years of bloodshed in the Balkans began with a whimper on 25 June 1991, as Slovenia became the first to slip away from the Yugoslav Federation. A truce was signed less than two weeks later after forty-nine people were killed. Croatia's break was to be far bloodier.

Europe at that time was fixated with its own problems, especially the vexed question of the Maastricht Treaty, defining future relations between the member states.

Britain, ever the European renegade, wanted to opt out
of key clauses, much to the fury of France. Germany,
however, was more canny and tried to turn events to the
advantage of its old Second World War ally, Croatia.
Chancellor Helmut Kohl and his Foreign Minister, Hans
Dietrich Genscher, put heavy pressure on other
European states, and Britain in particular, to recognise
Yugoslav republics which wanted to go it alone. The
underlying German message to Whitehall was, 'You play
ball with us over recognition, and we will help you on
Maastricht.' John Major was Prime Minister at the time,
and he and other senior politicians have denied that
there was a link between recognition of Croatia and the
Maastricht negotiations. In her book, *Yugoslavia: An
Avoidable War*, the late Nora Beloff says, however:
'Though the then Foreign Secretary, Douglas Hurd, has
denied any linkage, virtually all the others who partici-
pated in the talks confirmed that a deal was done in
December 1991. The British told the Germans that in
return for German support on the desired "opt-out", the
Germans could count on British support for their
Yugoslav policy.'

While Western Europe became ever more entrenched
in its own problems, all-out war began to rage in Croatia.
Serbs made up nearly twelve per cent of the Republic's
population and many hated the idea of living under a
regime which they still associated with some of the worst
excesses of Nazism during the Second World War.
Throughout the summer and autumn in eastern Croatia,
Serb militias joined the Yugoslav Army in action against
Croatian forces. The Serb-dominated city of Vukovar fell
to the Serb-led federal army on 17 November, after an
eighty-six-day siege. Serbian forces also moved westward
in the autumn to blockade Croatian ports along the
Adriatic Sea.

By now, Tito's old Yugoslavia was in its death throes.

In December 1991, Macedonia and the republic of
Bosnia-Herzegovina formally announced they too would

seek independence. They were spurred on by the European Community, which announced on 17 December that it would recognise the independence of all Yugoslav republics which met certain criteria, such as stable borders, respect for minority rights and a free press. They had to hurry, though, because the deadline for declaring their desire to go it alone was set at just six days later, on 23 December. The date for recognition itself would be just after the Christmas and New Year break, on 15 January. In the end, even this time frame was not fast enough for Germany, which leapt ahead and recognised Slovenia and Croatia on 23 December. Macedonia – which turned out to be the most peaceable of the republics in the next eight years – was denied this right because Greece protested that the name 'Macedonia' contained 'territorial pretensions'. The Greek objection stemmed from historical tensions over the Greek region of the same name. In a typically Byzantine example of diplomatic legerdemain, the ex-Yugoslav Macedonia was eventually given the ugly tag of Fyrom. This may sound like a minor United Nations cultural mission to Ouagadougou, but is merely the acronym for Former Yugoslav Republic of Macedonia.

Meanwhile, in the rush to recognise Croatia, Germany overlooked one thing: had the republic met the conditions required to merit independence? The French arbitrator and lawyer Paul Badinter, who was in charge of a commission to decide on this crucial point, thought not. His commission declared on 15 January 1992, that only Slovenia and Macedonia had fulfilled all the requirements. Bosnia-Herzegovina, meanwhile, should hold a referendum to let the people decide whether they wanted to be recognised as an independent state. Despite this, Germany insisted that Croatia and Slovenia be recognised; Britain, Austria and Belgium led the way and fifty countries followed suit within days.

By then, Croatia's relatively short but brutal war was approaching a denouement. On New Year's Day 1992, the UN negotiator, Cyrus Vance, announced that both sides had accepted a plan to accept international peace-keepers. As one war reached its pinnacle, another was hard on its heels.

Later that January, the Bosnian Parliament announced that it would hold the proposed referendum on independence on 29 February and 1 March. Bosnia's Serbs boycotted the poll and barricades went up within hours of the vote, manned by armed Serb civilians on one side and armed Muslims on the other. Fighting erupted across the republic and, on 4 April, the first Sarajevo victim of the Bosnian conflict fell on Vrbanja bridge. The independence of Bosnia-Herzegovina was recognised three days later on 7 April, leaving the republic's Serbs feeling that the Yugoslav rug had been pulled from beneath them. They cast their eyes in search of arms and other support, and found themselves looking to Belgrade.

So began three years of bloody warfare where the road to hell was paved with a myriad peace conferences, ceasefire announcements, broken promises and lies. As the 1990s progressed, Serb leaders were increasingly compared – overtly and covertly – with German Nazis. It was perceived wisdom that there must have been at least tacit acceptance among the general population of atrocities committed against non-Serbs in Croatia, Bosnia-Herzegovina and finally Kosovo.

Ethnic cleansing has been a clever and evocative term, as used by the West, which has subtle undertones of Hitler's final solution. However, there is no similarity between the Third Reich and post-Tito Yugoslavia. The Holocaust was a concerted campaign to exterminate millions of Jews, gypsies and other races deemed inferior by German Nazis. The Nazis' victims, for their part, were largely innocents. The Nazis also, crucially, invaded other countries in pursuit of their aims. In Yugoslavia, the Serbs' main aim in all the wars of the past decade has been to terrorise non-Serbs into leaving certain areas. Many were killed in the terror and the policy was cruel, but it was not the same as systematic annihilation. Furthermore, the same methods were also used by Croats and Muslims, to a lesser degree it is true, but nonetheless to the full extent of their military capabilities. As already explained, the Muslim leadership in Bosnia is suspected by many Western experts of perpetrating the market-place massacre in Sarajevo in February 1994. Croats, for their part, were less than gentle in pulverising the Muslim quarter of the medieval Bosnian town of Mostar, or in expelling two hundred thousand Serbs from the Krajina region of Croatia in August 1995. Yet few in the West threw up their hands in horror at these and other non-Serb actions.

There was much talk in British newspapers during the Bosnian conflict of 'concentration camps' run by Serbs. Newspaper pictures of gaunt faces peering from behind barbed wire fences were eerily similar to the scenes discovered by the Allies at Nazi death camps in the closing weeks of the Second World War. However, the purpose of the Nazi camps was genocide – the mass murder of non-Aryan men, women and children. The main aim of Bosnian Serb prison camps was the deten-tion and interrogation of non-Serb males, often captured in battle. The regimes at the Serbian prison camps were undoubtedly brutal and many died but similar prison sites were also run by Muslims and Croats and no one ever tagged them 'concentration camps'.

Unlike the Nazis, the Serbs have shown no sign of wanting to trample across other countries' national borders. Despite claims by some Western diplomats and journalists that Serbs wanted a Greater Serbia, they at no time seriously wanted to extend their frontiers beyond the boundaries of post-Second World War Yugoslavia – territory which of course included Bosnia and Croatia.

The phrase *Velika Serbija* – Greater Serbia – was coined in the mid-nineteenth century by Serbian statesman, Ilija Garasanin, who used it in a paper designed to stimulate discussion about where Serbs should eventually settle in the Balkans. More than one hundred years later, the phrase *Velika Serbija* was picked up and portrayed by Croats, Muslims, Western politicians and some journalists as an indication of Serb hegemonism. Calls for Greater Serbia have also been made in modern times by some extreme Serbs, including the leader of the Serbian Radical Party, Vojislav Seselj, but expanding the territory of the Serbian homeland has never been a serious intention of the Belgrade leadership. On the contrary, the aim has been to preserve a viable Serbian state as the tectonic plates of political upheaval tore Yugoslavia apart.

Since the fall of Communism in the Soviet Union and the Eastern bloc, Europe and America have broadly seen Yugoslavia as a Socialist blot on the newly-capitalist landscape. Milosevic and those close to him knew this from the beginning but were determined to cling to power, not because they were particularly passionate Communists, but at least in part because of the privileges power has brought. Simultaneously, many of the highly entrepreneurial Yugoslavs envied the new money-making opportunities available to Poles, Hungarians and Czechs after Communism's demise. Opposition to the Milosevic regime has several times led to massive street demonstrations, especially in 1996 and 1997. But the West's decision to bomb Serbia over the Kosovo crisis cast the Serb nation as a whole into limbo and has forced the majority to unite against what they saw as a common foe. It is like a family feud. Internally there is widespread criticism of Slobodan Milosevic and his henchmen, but woe betide anyone from outside who tries to intervene.

Milosevic has repeatedly been described as a dictator by Prime Minister Tony Blair and others in the West even though he has been elected three times – twice as Serbian leader and once as Yugoslav President. Even though these polls were monitored by the Organisation for Security and Cooperation in Europe, they were widely criticised both inside and outside the country. Nonetheless, I believe it is inaccurate to describe the Belgrade regime as a dictatorship – that tag belongs to the likes of the former regimes of Idi Amin in Uganda or the Duvaliers in Haiti. By calling their leader a dictator, many Serbs feel that the West is calling into question their right to elect whom they choose.

One of the West's declared aims since the end of the bombing campaign has been the removal from power of Slobodan Milosevic. Apart from the fact that the world's powers were happy to deal with Milosevic when it suited them, notably during the Dayton talks to end the Bosnian conflict in 1995, most Serbs feel that the choice of who leads them is no one's business but their own. Far from undermining the Yugoslav leader, the Nato bombing coupled with crippling sanctions has increased Serbian hostility to the West to the advantage of Milosevic.

# Part II
# The Kosovo Conflict

## Chapter Eight
# Bomb 'em: March 1999

'We don't give a shit for the Information Ministry,' snarled the Yugoslav border guard as he looked with contempt at our British passports. 'Your bombs are killing our children.' It was March 1999, and the beginning of the Nato air campaign against Yugoslavia. Already it was clear that ordinary people in Europe and America saw Kosovo as a replay of Bosnia, and believed that the outcome could be similar with all sides accommodated in an eventual peace deal.

Dessa Trevisan, seventy-four-year-old veteran *Times* correspondent and a fireball of indignant outrage, decided to opt for the diplomatic approach. 'I must get across, or you will have to shoot me, you bloody bastards,' she spat back in Serbian. I hoped the diminutive, five-foot-nothing Dessa did not expect me to join her in this threatened act of desperation. After all, I was none too keen on bombs and explosions in the first place and, even if they eventually rolled out the red carpet in welcome, it was going to take a considerable amount of will power on my part to cross from the safety of Hungary into the new war zone of Serbia. To have to fight one's way across seemed the ultimate absurdity. The experience at the border was, however, a salutary lesson in how the West's demonisation of the Serbs had produced a bunker mentality which had driven them away from, rather than into, the arms of the international community.

Although Dessa was born in the Croatian capital, Zagreb, and grew up in Belgrade, she had been a British

citizen since 1950. We had arrived by minibus at the
Kelebija frontier post about half-way between Budapest
and Belgrade, never dreaming there would be the
slightest problem in crossing, beyond a possible delay.
Hundreds of journalists from Britain had vainly tried to
gain visas in the run-up to what had seemed an
inevitable Nato bombing campaign and we were among
the few who had managed to succeed. We had Dessa's
old friend and protégé, Vuk Draskovic, head of the
Serbian Renewal Movement and then Federal Deputy
Prime Minister, to thank for intervening with the
Information Ministry on our behalf.

'We don't give a shit for Vuk Draskovic, either,' the
border guard said as Dessa launched yet again into a
foot-stomping, walking-stick-waving tirade. It was all
very strange; I could understand why these surly and
perhaps understandably anti-British guards should
berate us for being citizens of a leading 'aggressor
nation', but why attack their own government?

The driver and passengers on the minibus which had
brought us from Budapest began to grow impatient,
especially when a chill wind started to blow unfettered
across the flatlands of Hungary and Northern Serbia.
We had been at the border for about half an hour when
Dessa and I were ordered to sit apart from the others in
a concrete-floored room with cold, metal benches.
Outside, we could see the minibus driver unloading our
bags, re-locking the back of the vehicle, climbing back in
his seat and starting his engine. The perversity of human
nature meant, however, that cowardice faded as the
minibus receded in the distance. Instead, because I now
felt at least temporarily safer, resentment grew at not
being allowed across the border.

A steady stream of Yugoslavs was meanwhile being
waved across the frontier, many of them returning from
shopping trips to nearby towns in Hungary, or to buy
petrol from the garage up the road. Fuel was strictly
rationed in Serbia and the black market rate in

Belgrade, of up to five Deutschmarks (£1.70) a litre, was way beyond most people's means. Others were taking advantage of the Tref duty-free shops which lined the road in no man's land. While waiting for hour after mind-numbing hour in the unfriendly concrete room, I learned that even a simple commodity such as tax-free shopping can have dark undertones in the Balkans. The Tref shops, I discovered, were owned by Marko Milosevic, twenty-six-year-old son of the Yugoslav President, and named after the Serbian word for the ace of clubs in a pack of playing cards. Tref was also the nickname of a close friend of Marko who had been murdered in a gangland fight.

Slender blonde-haired young women in lurid make-up and yellow micro-skirts disdainfully served cigarettes at less than the equivalent of three pounds sterling for two hundred, ten times cheaper than in Britain. Shelves in the stores were also stacked with finest whiskies, perfumes, and cosmetics from Paris, New York and Rome. The long-legged girls were doing a roaring trade and scooping up hard currency cash for the sports car-loving Marko. The Milosevic son and heir also runs a discotheque called Madonna in the Milosevics' home town of Pozarevac, a favourite night spot among the spoiled children of the wealthy.

Marco was the subject of some subterranean grumbling during the Nato campaign because, unlike other young men in Serbia, he has never undertaken National Service in the Yugoslav Army. The subject is a sensitive one and his mother, Mira Markovic, usually makes her wrath felt at any news organisations which refer to her son's innocence in martial matters. Stefan Niksic, the brave editor of an independent news magazine, *Nin*, ran a series of important and regime-challenging articles during and after the Alliance bombing. For instance, he carried an interview with a sacked army Chief of Staff, Momcilo Perisic, who set up his own opposition group after the bombing. One day, I asked Niksic if there was any subject he would not touch and he answered: 'Anything which concerns the personal lives of the Milosevic family.'

I was mulling over the paradoxes which make up the Milosevic family, while Dessa continued haranguing the guards. I had known the veteran correspondent for nearly a decade and she had always been loyal and generous in sharing her probably unparalleled knowledge of, and contacts in, the Balkans. Countless times, she had patiently explained Yugoslav history to me, arranged access to politicians others could only dream of interviewing, pointed out the importance of speeches which others ignored, or simply provided whisky and sympathy when life was getting me down.

I had been with her in Belgrade in the mid-1990s when she had been shot in the hand by a mystery assailant. She was also renowned for having removed a photograph of Milosevic from the walls of the government-run press club in the capital. For many years, she cheerfully and selflessly nursed her dementia-suffering mother at their home in Palmoticeva Street in the heart of old Belgrade, and now she was being refused entry to her homeland in its hour of need.

The steady stream of minibuses and cars making their way into Yugoslavia contained a large proportion of young men who said they were returning from well-paid jobs abroad to fight for their country. This was a time of huge uncertainty, with Nato threatening massive bombardment followed quickly by a ground invasion of Kosovo. Again, my over-fertile imagination was darting over doomsday scenarios which had Russia, Greece, Turkey, even Hungary drawn into an ever-escalating conflict and it was hard to look on the faces of these young men and not wonder how many of them would be alive this time next year.

The pace of events which had led to this first week of the war had been swift. After failed negotiations in

Rambouillet, when Milosevic had refused to pull back his forces from Kosovo, peace monitors from the Organisation for Security and Cooperation in Europe had been thrown out of the province, along with almost all other international observers and journalists. Serb police and troops had started forcing ethnic Albanians out of Kosovo into Albania, Macedonia and Montenegro after the slide towards conflict had become unstoppable.

Many of those travelling away from Yugoslavia appeared to be women with young children and the elderly, apparently seeking refuge from the newly-opened bombing campaign. It was hardly a stampede though, as the majority of those who wanted and were able to escape had done so already. Several seasoned war correspondents on *The Times* had applied for visas to travel to Belgrade, but all had failed. Instead, they set off to Albania and Macedonia to spend weeks interviewing the forlorn flood of refugees. The new Foreign Editor, Bronwen Maddox, had encouraged me to apply in view of my past links with the country, but neither of us nurtured much optimism. I spent about ten days in the run-up to the first missile attacks on 24 March, bombarding ministers and officials in Belgrade and London with visa requests. My old friend Dessa used her not inconsiderable charm and force of personality to press Vuk Draskovic, whom I also knew, to help me.

By the time the bombing started, I was on a promise but nothing would be certain until the document was stamped in my passport. Late in the evening of 24 March, I watched television in London with strangely detached awe as Belgrade firemen energetically and futilely hand-pumped water onto a raging inferno in the city centre. Four days later, Dessa and I received the call that our visas were ready. Twenty-four hours later, we were stranded at the border.

Dessa, who had been stunningly beautiful in her youth, now alternated between bouts of enraged tears and pure Balkan venom as time dragged on. 'Make sure

I don't do anything stupid,' she said at one point as we ambled outside for yet another cigarette. Back in the concrete room, where half a dozen customs police passed to and fro with expressions ranging from cold disinterest to outright hostility, Dessa launched herself anew at the large ample-bellied man who seemed to be in charge. She was like an enraged Tasmanian Devil on a bad day and, although I could not understand her Serbian expletives, it was clear that the uniformed man with a gun and truncheon at his belt was not amused. We were alone, and my mobile phone had faded and died in the few hundred yards between the Hungarian and Yugoslav border posts.

The official indicated by stern gestures that I should try to control Dessa's outburst. I put what was meant to be a comforting and stabilising hand on her shoulder, murmuring a reminder of her plea that I should prevent her from going overboard. 'Fuck off!' she hissed, throwing off my hand before returning to her tirade with renewed vigour.

Yet another lesson in Balkan psychology was about to be learned. Whereas all my instincts were to stay calm, firm, but very, very polite, it was Dessa's outbursts that won over the Yugoslavs' hearts. The officials slowly began to look upon her with pity, then awe, and finally and amazingly, with respect. By nightfall, we would all be drinking coffee, whisky and slivovic in a VIP room at the back as if we were honoured guests rather than *personae non gratae*.

For the first hour or so at the frontier, Dessa and I had been the only foreign citizens held in limbo, our passports held securely out of reach by officialdom making it impossible for us to go forward into Yugoslavia or retreat to Hungarian soil. Later, we were joined by three other hopeful journalists, including an Argentinian. These three men were also ordered to wait and the long day dragged on into dusk. The Argentinian had a mobile phone which worked and Dessa used it to telephone Vuk Draskovic's office in Belgrade.

While we had been travelling from London, a small but significant coup had taken place inside the Yugoslav Government. Vuk Draskovic was on the brink of dismissal as Deputy Prime Minister, and his friend, the Information Minister, was no longer in charge of issuing visas. That privilege now fell to the Yugoslav Army and the hardline Serbian Interior Ministry. Unless your name was on a list approved by the new visa gods in Belgrade, it was impossible to enter. The border guards at the frontier had no power whatsoever, so any further pleading or bullying would be futile. The diminutive Dessa proceeded to use the Argentinian's phone to make more tearful and enraged calls to the Yugoslav capital, all to no avail. Her misery was compounded when the man from Buenos Aires was allowed to pass at about 10 p.m.

It was then that the whisky, coffee and slivovic came out, our passports were returned, and we were free to spend the night in the nearby Hungarian town of Szeged. We were asked to return in the morning. Dessa perked up, but I thought I detected a gleam in the border guards' eyes which indicated that we would be stuck on the road to nowhere until we managed to get new papers.

What followed was five days of hell punctuated by a single shining moment of high comedy. For decades, Dessa had refused to take no for an answer from many of the crowned and Communist heads of Central and Eastern Europe when she ran into any obstacles to her job as *The Times* correspondent. She insisted on roaming up and down the Hungarian border to various frontier crossings, then back and forth to Budapest in what rapidly became clear to me was an impossible task.

The office in London began to demand my return while friends of Dessa – and my own conscience – forbade me to leave her. I became trapped between an immovable Yugoslav bureaucracy and the irresistible force called Dessa. Even at seventy-four, the veteran

journalist had the stamina of a Sumo wrestler. During
the five days of vain attempts to enter the war zone, she
barely slept and constantly prevented me from doing so
either as she insisted that I call Draskovic and other
high-ranking friends in Belgrade at two, three or four in
the morning.

Finally, after midnight on the fourth day, we tried to
penetrate a tiny border-crossing at Horgos in the hope
that Yugoslav red tape had failed to extend that far. The
Hungarians were bemused; why did an elderly lady with
a walking-stick and a woman in her mid-forties want to
travel to Yugoslavia? 'Tourism,' said Dessa. We must
have looked so absurd that it might almost have been
true and she repeated this claim at the Yugoslav passport control. Sadly, the ruse did not work, but an armed
and olive green-uniformed woman took pity on us.
Instead of greeting us with disdain, she directed us to
seats near a comforting radiator, made coffee and
offered us warming slugs of vinjak, Yugoslav brandy.

Eventually, though, sleep deprivation drove me to an
act of sheer desperation. One morning, I bundled a
wildly-protesting Dessa into a taxi outside the plush
Intercontinental Hotel in the Hungarian capital, having
decided that we would return to London. It was like
forcing a bad-tempered cat into a basket to take it to the
vet.

The uniformed hotel doorman and the taxi-driver he
had summoned looked on in amazement as I shouted
above the protestations emanating from the ostensibly
frail little old lady: 'Don't listen to her, drive to the
airport.'

'Ladies?' queried the driver.

'I am NOT going to the airport, I am going back to
the border,' insisted Dessa.

'AIRPORT!' I screamed at the driver, waving wads
of Deutschmarks at him from the back seat. 'Look I
have the money, I am the one who's paying, you must go
where I say.'

When we reached the airport, Dessa refused point-blank to check in her baggage, let alone proceed through passport control. At one point, I ended up dragging her and her luggage across the polished floor towards a concerned red-white-and-blue-clad figure behind the British Airways check-in desk. When Dessa clamped her mouth shut in grim defiance, she bore an uncanny resemblance to Mother Dolores.

Her tiny body suddenly went lurching off, half-sobbing, straight into the arms of a group of people I had never seen before in my life. I felt as if I was dangerously close to being arrested for abduction. The knot of people now embracing and cosseting Dessa turned out to be close family friends of hers. They not only provided the comfort and understanding which I was unable to give, but they performed the miracle of persuading her that the wisest course of action would be to return to London and apply for a new visa.

It seems to me that the frustration and misery of those few days at the end of March and the beginning of April highlighted one reason that Serbs have not endeared themselves to the Western press. Dessa and I were just two of hundreds – if not thousands – of journalists who were desperate to enter Yugoslavia to report the Nato campaign from within. Yugoslav government officials often complained that their views were ignored or misrepresented. At times, I felt this was true, but by making it difficult to visit the country in the first place, the Yugoslavs were in some ways their own worst enemies. Serbs travelling on the minibus which eventually abandoned Dessa and me at the border were also critical of their government; they were anxious that foreign journalists be allowed to witness the war on the ground.

Even after I finally managed to enter the country, the Belgrade regime made it extremely difficult for foreign journalists to travel around and witness the effects of the bombing. We were issued with 'war press cards' and

told we could go anywhere – provided we apply in
writing for permission to leave the capital. The forms,
complete with carbon copies, asked for information
such as the make, name and registration of the vehicle
to be used, the names, passport and war press card
numbers of the driver and passengers, estimated departure and arrival times. It was more like a flight plan than
a request to drive to another town and, in reality, the
vast majority of international correspondents were able
to venture out of Belgrade only when invited to join
government-run convoys. Road-blocks manned by
police ensured that any renegade journalists would not
get far. That said, I do not know of any print journalist
whose work was looked at before publication, let alone
censored. Television crews usually had to submit their
film for scrutiny but I did not hear of any who were
subsequently asked to change anything.

Ethnic Albanians continued to haemorrhage across
Kosovo's borders and they told a waiting world of mass
killings, terror and forced deportation. But no one really
knew what was happening on the inside. A couple of
one and two-day carefully-monitored press trips were
arranged by the Army Press Centre to show the effects
of Nato bombing on civilian targets, but very few journalists managed to spend any time or travel any
distance inside the province. Alastair Campbell, Tony
Blair's press secretary, caused outrage among correspondents later in the summer when he suggested that
journalists had not tried hard enough to cover the war
in Kosovo. That may seem a clever thing to say from the
safety and comfort of Downing Street, but his own
country's bombs were hardly an encouragement for
journalists to visit the province.

Contrary to what Mr Campbell implied, Kosovo was
the one place which every international journalist
wanted to visit. From the outset of the Nato campaign,
the region had become an information black hole. Two
notable exceptions who did manage to report from

inside Kosovo were Jacky Rowland of the BBC, who
spent two weeks there, and Paul Watson of the *Los
Angeles Times*. Watson managed through sheer cussed-
ness to stay in Kosovo throughout the Nato bombing.
When other correspondents were threatened and
ordered to leave, just days before the first missile strike,
Watson merely dug in his heels and stayed. The
Yugoslav authorities cajoled and harassed him for a
week or so, but in the end they just gave up and
accepted his presence at the Grand Hotel in Pristina.
Perhaps they initially thought that Alliance bombs
would persuade him to go. They were wrong.

While Watson was braving the first, heavy strikes on
Pristina, I was back in London bombarding the authorities in Belgrade by fax and telephone for a new visa,
preferably one which would admit me to the country.

I finally made it across the border just after midday
on 26 April after another agonising wait while the
border guards scrutinised my papers, telephoned
Belgrade to double-check that I should be allowed in
and finally gave me a grim smile as they waved me on. I
was taken by taxi from the frontier to the nearby town
of Subotica. Djovani, the driver, was not allowed to
cross into Hungary to collect me because all Serb men
between the ages of eighteen and sixty were on standby
for military service.

Djovani said it was too late to attempt the journey to
Belgrade that day, and insisted on taking me for coffee
and slivovic at his home in Subotica. The drive to the
capital would have taken about two hours by motorway
in peace time. But now that bridges had been bombed in
the en route city of Novi Sad, drivers were forced to
take circuitous back roads clogged with every sort of
transport from horse-drawn trailers to juggernauts.

Djovani was a small, balding, dapper man of about
forty who grinned a great deal and had seen better days,
when he was a wheeler-dealer in Trieste he said. Before
taking me to his home, he proudly showed me round his

home town with its tangle of red roofs and stuccoed
civic buildings. In one of the bitter ironies of modern
life, the local symbol of American culture – McDonald's
– was being used as a first aid training post. The war had
already stopped the supply of burgers, sesame-seed
buns, cola and processed cheese slices. Tables and chairs
were pushed to one side while young men and women
with vividly-applied cosmetic gashes lay on stretchers.
Their serious faces were in stark contrast to the grinning
McDonald's clown as bandages and tourniquets were
applied by Subotica's equivalent of the St John
Ambulance Brigade.

Djovani was married to a large, comfortable
Hungarian woman and had a toddler son. We sat for
hours in their plush newly-built house, drinking and
talking about their fears for the future. Soon after dusk
I had my first direct glimpse of Nato's war. Djovani's
lounge had large patio doors and they rattled
ominously, sending the taxi driver leaping to his feet and
out into his neat back garden. 'Come here and look,' he
called. The drone of several aircraft could be heard
overhead while, in the distance to the south, deep red
bursts of colour periodically illuminated the horizon.
'They are bombing Novi Sad again,' he said, shaking his
head as if trying to persuade himself that this was really
happening.

Early the next morning we set off for Belgrade. We
saw the pall of acrid black smoke from the bombed oil
refinery at Novi Sad from miles away, the fumes
belching an arc of choking fug over Serbia's second city.
Novi Sad's bridges were lying crippled at the bottom of
the Danube and we came across crowds of townsfolk
queuing for a makeshift ferry which was carrying people
to work on the far side of the river. The people were
surly and angry, in no mood to talk to a journalist from
the Western press. Rail passengers were also forced to
take the standing-room only ferry; trains from the south
halted on one side of the river where the travellers

disembarked, crossed by boat, then joined another train on the northern bank to continue their journeys.

Djovani was anxious for me to meet friends of his who owned a café in the city centre. It was here that I met Stefan Popov, a pilot for the national airline, JAT, and one of the most astonishingly brave or foolhardy people I have ever come across. As we sat in brilliant sunshine blotted by the ceaseless clouds of smoke from the refinery, Popov explained that he had just helped to fly JAT's entire fleet of Boeings through the war-zone skies of Serbia, and on to safety in Romania. He was not sure this had been a great idea, however, for he had the distinct impression that the Romanians had now impounded the sixteen aircraft.

The pilot then despatched his teenaged son to fetch me a copy of a book Popov had written about his aeronautical adventures. They included being shot down by a Serbian farmer during the Bosnian conflict. 'I used to fly aid to Sarajevo and I once decided to loop north over the Hungarian border on my way back,' he said. 'The farmer thought I was invading and he shot at my twin-engined aircraft. He hit the engine and the oil pressure fell away. I had to make an emergency landing in a field.' The farmer and his neighbours ran towards his makeshift landing strip, but were not to be persuaded by Popov's explanation that he was one of them. At gunpoint, they locked him in a barn for the night while local police verified his identity.

The afternoon was drawing on and we had to get going. No one in their right mind travelled after dark during the Nato bombing campaign and Djovani had to make his way back to Subotica after dropping me in Belgrade. As we crossed Pancevo bridge on the outskirts of the capital, more than a hundred people with anti-war posters formed a chain alongside the iron girders which formed part of its massive structure. Their message was, 'If you want to bomb this bridge, you will have to bomb us, too'.

It had taken me nearly four weeks to reach Belgrade
– but now I was ready to start reporting the war.

# Chapter Nine

# Belgrade by Night: May 1999

The little old lady looked as if she had three eyes. On closer inspection, it was the effect of the shrapnel which had drilled into her forehead and killed her. One of her shoes had been torn off and the radishes she had just bought at the market lay like splashes of blood near her outstretched hand.

Next to her in the pretty cobbled street sprawled a man of similar venerable years. An ominous deep red stain formed a halo on the ground surrounding his head. Round the corner, in the adjoining street, two slim female legs extended from a blanket-covered mound.

At first, the dead had seemed almost camouflaged among the rubble, splintered trees and broken glass but once you began to notice them, the bodies were everywhere, some covered in tablecloths and blankets, others simply lying exposed where they had fallen. The little streets at the back of the market looked as if an army of Al Capones had hit town and opened fire with sub-machine-guns. There was barely a square inch of wall, tree, car or human being which had not been raked by shrapnel. Houses which had been pretty hours before, with picket fences and window-boxes bursting with blooms, were now riddled with scars from the strafing. Widows in black leant on their garden gates, whimpering into handkerchiefs, as they surveyed their dead neighbours lying amid the broken glass, gashed trees, smouldering cars, and crumpled bicycles. Plastic bags lay strewn near many of the dead, spilling parcels of fruit, eggs and vegetables, fresh from the market but now never to be eaten.

It was Friday, 7 May 1999 in the southern city of Nis, and Nato had made a mistake. Instead of hitting a military building near the airport about three miles away, the bombers had dropped their lethal load in a tangle of back streets close to the city centre. At least thirty-three people were killed and scores more suffered catastrophic injuries; hands, feet and arms shredded or blown away altogether, abdomens and chests ripped open by shards of flying metal.

This had been no 'ordinary' shelling, if such a thing exists. The area had been hit by cluster bombs, devices designed to cause a deadly spray of hot metal fragments when they explode. The Yugoslav Government had accused the Alliance of using these weapons in other attacks which had cut down civilians, but the suggestion had been mostly laughed to scorn in the West. Now the evidence was plain to see. Dozens of bright yellow canisters containing shrapnel had failed to explode and lay among the detritus. Some were propped up against the sides of pavements. It made you wonder who had dared to touch, let alone move, these ghastly instruments of war.

Within minutes of the attack, the Yugoslav Government had rounded up any journalists in Belgrade able to leave for Nis immediately, to show the world what had happened. We had formed a convoy and driven at breakneck speed for nearly two hundred miles along a motorway which would soon be impassable because of another bombing raid. Now Renzo Cianfanelli and I were picking our way cautiously among the unexploded bombs and the dead. One weeping survivor told us that the slender legs protruding from a blanket belonged to a young woman who was eight months pregnant. An elderly woman was carried, complete with the kitchen chair on which she was sitting, from her home and into the street by two strapping young men. She wanted to be with her friends rather than grieve alone. A middle-aged man grabbed our arms and ushered us into the courtyard by the side of his house. Lying in a shed by the side of his kitchen was yet another unexploded yellow canister.

Renzo had brought Irena, his statuesque, raven-haired interpreter, and after interviewing survivors, we set off for the hospital. The glass shelter where the car-park attendant usually sat was in ruins, for the bombs had even struck here. The attendant was dead and an ambulance crew, scrambling to rush to deal with the injured, had had a narrow escape from an exploding bomb when rushing to their vehicle after the air raid siren had wailed. Inside the hospital, a woman with a blood-soaked dressing on her leg was screaming in agony in a ward filled with shrapnel-maimed casualties. The scars of this and other Nato raids on Nis were likely to remain for years.

Nis is a huge industrial city in south-west Serbia, ruled by political foes of Slobodan Milosevic. The Mayor, Zoran Zivkovic, is a leading member of the Democratic Party and he rules the city in coalition with members of Serbia's other main opposition group, the Serbian Renewal Movement.

In the Alice-in-Wonderland world of Balkan politics, the Mayor and the local leader of the Serbian Renewal Movement, Bratislav Stamenkovic, went before a priest in one of the city's Serbian Orthodox churches a couple of years ago to swear an oath of allegiance to one another. They were motivated to do this because the national leaders of their respective parties loathe one another and they wanted to reassure the Nis electorate that their own local alliance was more solid.

Vuk Draskovic, priest-like head of the Serbian Renewal Movement, and Zoran Djindjic, golden-boy leader of the Democratic Party, used to be allies themselves, once. They led massive street protests against the Milosevic regime in 1996 under the banner of *Zajedno* – or Together. However, the movement failed to draw support among the masses and the protests ended in

bitter squabbles between the two party chiefs. Many
observers suspect that America had a hand in splitting up
the *Zajedno* allies, because the West felt at the time it
needed Milosevic to help implement the new Dayton
peace agreement for Bosnia. Draskovic and Djindjic
travelled to Washington together as allies – but returned
in separate planes and were never friends again.

I have asked both what happened during that visit, but
neither will do more than hint that something happened
in the US which divided them. The Nato bombing
campaign only enlarged the gulf between them. Djindjic
was scathing when Draskovic accepted the post of
Deputy Yugoslav Prime Minister in February 1999, just
before the war started, accusing him of complicity with
the Milosevic regime. Draskovic accused Djindjic of
cowardice for leaving Serbia for the far safer shores of
Montenegro during the bombing.

These internecine squabbles were the despair of
many ordinary Serbs who wanted to see a united opposition and that is why the Nis coalition partners
probably felt they had to swear on the Bible to win the
confidence of the city electorate. After Nato's cluster
bomb attack on Nis, ordinary Serbs united in condemnation of the Western powers. It was to be a similar
story all over Serbia; the more Nato pounded the
country, the more people stood together in defiance
against the outside world. It was the political leaders
who remained divided.

Nato, meanwhile, was forced by to concede that it had
used cluster bombs in Nis. Many had thought that these
weapons were banned under the terms of the Geneva
Convention but someone in Brussels claimed that their
use was allowed 'in open countryside against ground
troops'. The fact that dozens of civilians had been mown
down on market day in a city centre was deemed a regret-
table mistake. It was an error which was not to deter the
use of cluster bombs time and again afterwards. Mary
Robinson, former Irish President and head of the United

Nations Human Rights Commission, visited Nis a couple of weeks after the cluster bombing and spoke out strongly against the Nato action there. Her words were reported in the West, but many news organisations subsequently seemed to regard her condemnation as slightly barmy.

I had been in Serbia for ten days when the Nis cluster bombing occurred. I had seen and heard the effects of many explosions in and around Belgrade by then, but this was the first time I had seen so many civilian dead. Until then, I had felt I was watching the war through the wrong end of a pair of binoculars. It all seemed strangely detached.

This is probably partly because I and most other foreign journalists were staying at the luxury Hyatt Hotel in New Belgrade. The hotel, with its polished marble floors, potted palms, tinkling fountains and discreet army of staff, was calculated to cocoon guests from the rough-and-tumble of real life. Hundreds of journalists, television cameramen and sound technicians from every corner of the world were ensconced there, most of them dressed in jeans, crumpled multi-pocketed jackets and walking boots. It must have been one of the rare occasions when the hotel staff were more sartorially pristine than their guests. It was hard to know what the hotel workers made of us, though they always seemed overwhelmingly friendly and eager to please. In May, at the height of the bombing, the hotel heard it had won the Hyatt of the year award. Nonetheless, it must have been hard for some of the staff to smile at reporters from countries which were bombing them and turning any journeys home at night into perilous ordeals.

The main dining room was closed for the duration of the war and a buffet-style restaurant became the main focus of Hyatt life. One Spanish journalist would regularly exasperate the waiters but amuse the rest of us by leaping to answer the restaurant telephone in a singsong voice: 'Third World War, can I help you?' Everything in

Serbia had to be paid for in cash since foreign bank accounts had been frozen as part of the international sanctions against the country. The price of even a coffee and a sandwich at the Hyatt could have fed a Serbian family for a week, while the cost of a round of drinks in the Duke Ellington bar would have made the Hyde Park Hilton seem underpriced. Even cash-stuffed foreign correspondents could not have lasted more than a few days in this way, so the hotel enabled our newspapers and television stations to pay into a Hyatt account abroad which somehow bypassed the sanctions.

One of the strangest sensations I had at the Hyatt was to swim in its palatial pool in the basement health club and gaze outside, past exotic palms and towel-bedecked loungers, to a scene of utter devastation. Across the street was the bombed-out wreckage of the ruling Socialist Party headquarters. As I ploughed back and forth in the pool, I could see the torn remains of blinds and curtains blowing from every shattered window in the towering high-rise building which had twice been hit by Tomahawk cruise missiles in April. Nato had had to come back for a second strike because the first time they missed the vital television mast on the roof. Now the mangled wires looked like a vast, crumpled, dead spider sprawled on top of the building.

Upstairs, in the vast Hyatt lobby, there was one regular visitor who always arrived in a style to which the five-star hotel had been accustomed in happier times. Zeljko Raznatovic, better known as Arkan the indicted war criminal, would parade with an entourage of bulging-jacketed, shaven-headed bodyguards and his micro-skirted wife. Arkan led a paramilitary group, the Tigers, in Croatia and Bosnia, and was suspected of having deployed these men in Kosovo. We all assumed that his frequent trips to the Hyatt tea-room were his way of trying to show that he could have had no involvement in Kosovo because here he was, having a highly civilised drink in Belgrade. Arkan sipping coffee, wearing a dark suit and a smug smile, always looked out of place, like some famous footballer on his wedding day. It was always hard not to imagine his large frame ordering fatigue-clad men into combat.

After the Nis cluster bombing, Renzo, Irena and I arrived back in Belgrade just before 11 p.m. We had filed reports to our newspapers while driving back and were just about to draw breath over a beer in the Hyatt when a thunderous explosion shook the hotel. The lights dimmed and waiters scurried round the restaurant urging us all to move away from the plate glass windows. A second boom announced another explosion a minute or so later. Jeans-clad television crews scrambled for their cameras and sound equipment then ran eagerly outside, while I stepped more cautiously into the night.

'It must be the bridge,' many journalists surmised as we moved outside. The Gazela bridge spans the Sava River and carries one of the main roads linking Old and New Belgrade. It was regarded as a prime Nato target and any driver brave enough to venture out at night, when most of the bombing took place, would race across the bridge at breakneck speed and with bated breath, for fear of being caught in the expected raid. In the end, the bridge was spared, reportedly because the French Government intervened on its behalf.

So what had been hit? At that moment a taxi squealed to a halt in front of the hotel, disgorging a breathless Irish reporter who had been returning from dinner at a restaurant near the river. 'They've got the Chinese Embassy,' she said. The embassy, a few blocks away from the Hyatt in New Belgrade, burned furiously for hours after the missile slammed into it. Three journalists working for the Xinhua official Chinese news agency had perished, along with Nato's hopes of avoiding any more damaging mistakes.

Only an attack on the Russian Embassy could have been more embarrassing. By dawn, after the dead had been lowered from an upper floor of the smouldering ruin, millions of Chinese were baying for Nato's blood. Western embassies in the Chinese capital were besieged and Jamie Shea, the Alliance spokesman, was trying to explain the seemingly inexplicable. A Yugoslav military building had been the intended target, he said. A mistake had been made in entering the compass co-ordinates in the computer equipment which guided the 'smart' missile.

Conspiracy theories abounded for weeks, with reports about a traitor from the West deliberately sabotaging the computer co-ordinates. In October, the *Observer* said it had information which indicated that the embassy was deliberately bombed by Nato because the mission was believed to be sending signals to the Yugoslav Army.

One of those who perished in the embassy blast was forty-seven-year-old Xinhua correspondent, Shao Yunhuan, a graduate of the Beijing Foreign Language School who spoke fluent Serbian. Her husband, Cao Rongfei, was First Secretary at the embassy and he was seriously wounded. Ten days before falling prey to the cruise missile, Shao wrote in the Chinese international affairs journal, *Cankao Xiaoxi*, about her own experiences watching other people die.

'It was 2:00 in the morning, April 23rd. My colleagues and I were watching the news on the Serbian TV. As usual and as expected, we again heard the explosion of bombs. However, this time it was extremely loud. We felt the whole building shaking. Suddenly, the TV screen went blank.

'When NATO attacked the TV station, there were about a hundred people working inside. It is said that up to now there are at least ten dead and seventeen injured, and we still don't know how many people are trapped inside the ruins. Next afternoon, over a hundred journalists from different countries led by several Germans gathered at the Hyatt Hotel to protest at Nato's bombing of the TV station and donated money to those families who had lost their loved ones. A German journalist spoke with a trembling voice, saying "Several days ago, a Serbian journalist friend asked me if my workplace was safe. I told him that I was safe. Now I am here, but this Serbian journalist has himself died."

'In the afternoon, we went to the Republic plaza where anti-bombing concerts were often held. We witnessed no music and singing today. It was very quiet. There were flowers and candles. According to updated information, since the 24th of March, Nato has flown about 7,000 sorties, dropped about 6,000 tons of bombs, and fired over 2,000 missiles … Not long ago, I read a news item in *Witness*. It reports that a mother of three had a nervous breakdown because she could no longer stand the bombing and fear. She killed her three children and then committed suicide. This reminds me of a philosopher's words: I would choose death in a situation worse than death.'

The night that Nato bombed the Chinese Embassy, the Hotel Yugoslavia was also bombed. The building was a favourite haunt of Arkan and one casualty there was a boutique in the building owned by his wife.

While up in my room writing a report on the embassy bombing for a late edition of *The Times*, the lights, television and air conditioning stopped working. Looking out of my window across the city, it was clear that we were in the grip of a major power failure for, apart from one or two car headlights, there was not a pinprick of light anywhere. Exactly a week before, Nato had started using a new weapon which exploded above ground and showered power stations with graphite dust, throwing the electricity generators into chaos.

The graphite bombs downed electrical supplies to the vast majority of Serbia that night and the new weapon was judged such a success by Nato that it was subsequently regularly deployed. It is not known what effect the power failures had on Slobodan Milosevic's military machine because the regime was highly secretive about the army. Casualty figures were never released, for instance. The electricity cuts caused huge misery to the civilian population, however.

Soon after midnight on 1 May, Dr Branka Nikolic was about to perform the trickiest part of an emergency caesarean at the Narodna Front Hospital in Belgrade when the lights went out. The patient was an ethnic Albanian woman, one of the community in whose name the bombing was being carried out, and her child was in danger of dying before being born. Calling for candles, the young, overworked doctor prayed she would not inadvertently cause death or injury to mother or baby as she continued to operate in the half-light. 'It was a very serious situation, they could have died,' she said. Medical staff in the premature baby unit were meanwhile struggling to keep alive the tiny scraps of humanity whose incubators had ceased to function.

Misery was also felt by ordinary Serbs at home. Next morning, families who had carefully collected, cooked and frozen stockpiles of food in anticipation of the war were wringing their hands in despair as the supplies defrosted. In the Hyatt, we were relatively immune to the power cuts because the hotel had an emergency generator. A shortage of fuel to power the generator meant, however, that it was used sparingly. Someone aptly described the hotel as a 'large American fridge' because it was a vast, air-conditioned unit where none of the windows opened. After graphite bomb attacks, the generator would just about cope with powering lights in corridors and most bathrooms, as well as a low level of air conditioning. At these times, no hot food or drinks were available and woe betide anyone who had failed to charge mobile phones or computers while the power was working.

Most people in Belgrade tried to carry on living as normally as possible, but the war began to take its toll as the weeks passed. Food prices rose and cigarettes became almost unobtainable outside the black market. This was a huge problem in a nation of chain-smokers, especially at a time when nerves most needed steadying. A packet of cigarettes, which cost the equivalent of fifty pence in peacetime, was at least twice as expensive when bought from the small army of dealers who began to congregate in underpasses and near markets all over town, and had to be paid for in precious Deutschmarks.

Few people took cover in air raid shelters after the first two weeks of the bombing. These were usually basements beneath apartment blocks, or underground cafés and sports clubs and, after a while, most people just trusted to fate and stayed in their beds. The elderly tended to avoid the shelters from the beginning, because they remembered carpet bombing from the Second World War and they dreaded being buried in rubble. Serbs also began to regard hiding in a basement as a sign of weakness. By mid-May, the air raid shelters had become so obsolete that a young Serbian woman and I had great difficulty in even locating one when I wanted to write about life underground.

Nada lived in London, but had decided to spend much of the war with her parents in Belgrade. The mournful wail of the air raid siren cut through the afternoon bustle, the cue for Nada and I to begin asking at shops and kiosks for directions to a shelter. We were treated as if we were harmless idiots. 'Why do you need a shelter? There is no need to be afraid, you will be all right,' said one young man as he put a calming hand on Nada's shoulder. 'Have you heard something? Will there be an attack?' said a woman selling pizza. Most just shrugged and looked at us strangely but no one seemed to know where we could take cover. In the end, we were directed to a basement youth club.

The young man in charge spent about ten minutes trying to persuade Nada she really had no need to worry and that no one used the shelter. Nada, in turn, was having increasing difficulty keeping a straight face. A bold and confident young woman by nature, she was finding it hard to look fearful. The young man eventually seemed to decide that we were beyond reason, so he changed tack and gave us a detailed description of how safe the basement was: 'The room is nine metres under ground level and is protected by three metres of concrete,' he intoned. When we finally descended, we found three old men playing cards. They were there because they had nowhere else to go, not because they were afraid.

Although Serbs carried on with life as normally as possible during the day, they did stay home at night. During daylight, the pavement cafés were as busy as ever but after dusk, Belgrade became a ghost town. Almost all restaurants, bars, theatres and night clubs were closed and the city was as dark as Bucharest had been in the gloomiest years of the Ceausescu era. Some after-dark activities, such as theatres and discos, began to operate in the afternoons to compensate.

In Republic Square, anti-war rock concerts were held every day, giving the city centre an almost Woodstock feel. The pedestrian shopping street, Knez Mihailova, filled with dozens of stalls selling anti-war postcards, jokes, T-shirts and badges. The main symbol of anti-war sentiment was a target – the message being 'Come on, then, bomb us!' The postcards were nothing if not forthright: 'Columbus, fuck your curiosity!' said one anti-American favourite; 'exPLANE me why?' went another with a picture of a Nato Tornado aircraft. Top of the popularity stakes was a reference to the Stealth bomber which was shot down in April, to the deep consternation of Nato: 'Sorry, we didn't know it was meant to be invisible,' were the words on one postcard.

The Yugoslav authorities were naturally keen to help journalists cover the effects of the bombing on civilians. We were all encouraged to interview the Environment Minister to hear about pollution after the bombing of a huge chemical plant at Pancevo, or the Health Minister after a Belgrade hospital was attacked. But the one subject on which most journalists were fixated was Kosovo – and hardly anyone seemed to be getting there. Everyone had made his or her application to visit the province and everyone was told, day after day, to be patient and come back the next morning. Meanwhile, all the outside world knew of life in the province was provided by accounts given by the tide of ethnic Albanians which continued to pour across into Albania, Macedonia and Montenegro.

The Yugoslav Army ran the main press centre in a building a couple of hundred yards from Republic Square. The scene there was usually one of utter chaos, with hordes of bearded, sweating journalists shouting in every language from Swedish to Swahili at overworked, overstressed civilian officials trying to cope with an over-whelming demand for war press cards and permission to make reporting trips outside the capital. The concept of queuing was abandoned as a sea of hands waving pieces of paper was thrust at two women and a pleasant-faced man who tried to cope with the deluge of requests on computers which regularly failed because of electricity cuts.

Most days, there was barely room to move in the stifling, smoke-filled rooms as television crews and news-paper correspondents jostled to connect with their interpreters and fixers. There was a large press confer-ence hall deep within the bowels of the building, past a lobby filled with gruesome black and white photographs of bomb victims. Here, army spokesmen bedecked with enough medals to build a battleship would speak for an hour or more and disclose next to nothing.

It was after yet another day of futilely pleading for permission to travel to Kosovo, that I bumped into a group of Greek journalists in the Duke Ellington base-ment bar at the Hyatt. They smiled complacently at my frustration: 'You reeely want to go to Kosovo?' one asked. 'There is a way.'

And so they told me about Daniel Schiffer, a Franco-

Italian who they said had taken an Italian television crew
to the front line in Kosovo a week earlier. It cost a great
deal of money, they did not know exactly how much, but
they would contact an Israeli friend who had Schiffer's
mobile telephone number.

Forty-eight hours later, I sat in the lounge bar upstairs
waiting for the man who described himself as a humanist
and philosopher. 'I 'ave long, wavy black 'air and I wear
a dark suit,' he had said by telephone when we had
arranged to meet. In the curmudgeonly way of journalists
who want to keep a possible scoop to themselves, I was
slightly dismayed to see Elaine Lafferty, a journalist from
the *Irish Times*, sitting alone and within easy earshot at
the next table. The lounge bar was usually the last place
frequented by the press.

In walked a studiedly French-looking man with collar-
length locks, an expensive overcoat slung over his
shoulders, head cocked on one side and a smile on his
face. He had obviously been extremely handsome in
leaner, earlier years, and possibly still saw himself as a
latter-day Adonis. He was flanked by two enormous men
in dark glasses – one smiling, one not.

'Delightful to meet you,' said the man who was
evidently Schiffer as he bent over to kiss the back of a
hand which I had extended with the aim of it being
shaken. The two apparent bodyguard hulks swept past
me and sat down with Elaine Lafferty.

Schiffer explained all. He regularly made ''umanitarian visits' to Kosovo, but he was very particular about
whom he took along for the ride. He was disgusted by the
Nato bombing and he wanted 'responsible' Western journalists to see for themselves. Then, like a salesman trying
to pitchfork a punter into a sale, he stressed that he had
many other journalists queuing up for the privilege. A
fast decision was crucial. 'You can go anywhere you like,
I can take you to the front line, yes, yes; we can meet with
the Mayor of Pristina, you can talk with as many
Albanians as you want.' It would all be above board, he

said, and undertaken with the knowledge and consent of
the Army Press Centre.

How much would it all cost? Schiffer looked morti-
fied. 'I do not take any money, I do this for 'umanitarian
reasons,' he said. I must have looked agog with happiness,
for he was quick to add, 'Something for the driver and
interpreter, though.' He refused to discuss the subject
further, insisting that he never accepted payment and
always left one of his large companions to negotiate the
'something'.

It was becoming clear that Schiffer also wanted to take
Elaine Lafferty on the same trip but had failed to
mention this doubling-up either to her or to me. We were
all then enjoined to sit around the same table, with the
exception of Schiffer who looked pained at the prospect
of discussing money.

I now had a chance to examine more closely the two
enormous men with Schiffer. Nenad Golubovic seemed
to speak no English, drank lemonade, did not smoke and
had the finely-honed muscles of a man who takes his
exercise deadly seriously. Nebojsa Radojevic smoked,
drank whisky and his bulk owed more to eating out than
to working out. He spoke English with a curiously old-
fashioned accent, like an upper crust character in a
British 1940s film. He smiled as he explained that, for us,
he would make a 'special price' to cover the cost of 'security, army passes, petrol, car hire, translation services,
food and accommodation' – 4,000 Deutschmarks each.
This was an enormous sum, equivalent to about £1,300, or
over a year's pay for most Serbs.

Nonetheless, this was a rare chance to visit Kosovo and
*The Times* did not demur at the cost. Although it was plain
from the beginning that Elaine Lafferty and I would have
to try to put some distance between ourselves and Schiffer
to speak to any ethnic Albanians, we would be able to
travel without an army escort. We would also be able to see
the Kosovo countryside for ourselves and we could take
advantage of Schiffer's Serb contacts in the province.

I checked with the Army Press Centre and was told
that travelling with Schiffer was fine by them. It was not
fine, though, with some of the Western journalists. Not
wanting to disappear with three strangers who had
already taken my money, without letting someone
neutral know when we were due back, I made the
mistake of telling an American woman who worked as
an Italian radio reporter and with whom I had shared
many a Hyatt supper. 'No way would I go with him; my
station just would never allow it,' she said, looking as if
she had climbed to the Everest equivalent of moral high
ground.

Next day, Nebojsa came to my room, sat at my desk
and carefully counted out the bundles of Deutschmarks I
had managed to scrape together. We were to leave that
evening and spend one night in Cacak, about sixty miles
south of Belgrade, before heading into Kosovo the
following morning. My mouth was dry and my heart
pounding with trepidation as I willed my feet forward,
out of the relative safety of the Hyatt and into the
unknown. I made a last call to my father, knowing the
mobile would cease to function within half an hour of
leaving Belgrade.

Of course, the chances were that we would return
safely and that Lafferty and I would have seen what
everyone else was desperate to see. I could not help
thinking, as we set off into the dusk, about the truly brave
British and other Allied men and women who had para-
chuted into enemy territory during the Second World
War to carry out vital underground missions. I also
wondered where Jamie Shea, the Nato spokesman, was at
that moment.

Soon after nightfall, Nebojsa pointed out an unusually
bright light in the starlit sky. 'There is our friend,' he said,
'it is a Nato spy satellite.' There was predictably little
traffic on the road to Cacak and we reached the town
about an hour and a half after leaving Belgrade. Nenad
pressed the accelerator to the floor as we approached a

long, wide bridge leading into the town – a classic Nato target. There were barely any street lights, but the moon was high and bright enough for us to see the massive, mangled wreckage of the vacuum cleaner factory which had been pulverised by Alliance missiles in April.

After checking into the clean and thankfully well-lit hotel where we were to spend the night, Schiffer professed a desire to eat at his favourite Italian restaurant, while Nenad disappeared to stay with his wife and two children who lived in Cacak. The hotel seemed to be an annexe to a Skoda car dealership, or the proprietor had an extremely weird taste in décor. Starched white tablecloths in the cavernously huge dining room were prominently adorned with the Skoda emblem. Elaine Lafferty and I were asked whether we would like to share a room, an idea which was swiftly abandoned in the face of the glares we shot back at this suggestion. It was not that we failed to get along; it just seemed a cheek in view of the vast sum we had paid for the trip. Schiffer, meanwhile, insisted on showing us the suite of rooms which seemed to be permanently held in readiness for him, complete with jacuzzi, fully-stocked bar and kitchen, and two bedrooms.

The Franco-Italian again professed a yearning for pizza at his favourite Cacak restaurant, entailing yet another foray into the night and another breath-holding dash across a bridge. It was a futile venture because the pizzeria was in the grip of a power cut and could not even offer a cup of coffee. Back in the hotel, Nebojsa, Schiffer, Elaine and I ate together in the enormous dining room where dozens of tables with their Skoda tablecloths and Skoda paper napkins were laid in forlorn readiness for guests who never appeared.

Afterwards, up in my room, I turned on the television. The only available channel was broadcasting black and white pictures of monasteries in Kosovo and images of medieval battles, to the accompaniment of stirring patriotic music. A small bowl of yellow roses was placed near the window; the following morning I picked one out and placed it in my buttonhole. It seemed a rare thing of beauty amid the ugliness of war.

# Chapter Ten

# Into the Unknown: May 1999

We crossed into Kosovo just after midday on 20 May 1999. The small knot of Yugoslav troops in a sandbagged lookout position seemed more like Dad's Army than the first line of defence as they waved us through.

It had been VIP treatment all the way from Belgrade, with police and army checkpoints clearing a path for us. Foreign journalists were usually stopped, questioned and sometimes searched if they managed to get army permission to venture out of Belgrade. Schiffer, on the other hand, was treated with almost presidential deference. This was to be useful in providing Elaine Lafferty and me with easy access to senior Serb officials in Kosovo. Instead of having to track down and make appointments to see mayors, police chiefs, or hospital directors, Schiffer presented us as his entourage wherever he went.

What was to prove more difficult was finding ethnic Albanians and speaking to them out of earshot of Serb officialdom. Elaine, Schiffer and I had been crammed in the back seat of the Toyota Carina during the drive from Belgrade, with Nenad in front at the wheel and Nebojsa sitting comfortably alongside him. Nenad, with the split-second reactions of a rally driver, pushed the Toyota to the limit but always seemed in complete control.

Nato bomb damage had become steadily heavier as we drew near Kosovo. Huge iron rail bridges strung between mountain gorges looked as if they had been attacked by giant tin-openers, mines and quarries stood empty, and the narrow road was shrapnel-pitted and strewn with rocks and debris as it wound through a string of villages built along

the River Ibar, near Raska, just north of the Kosovo
border. The damage to bridges made life difficult, but not
impossible. Human adaptability is amazing. Banks of earth
and gravel had been built to form makeshift new river
crossings, sometimes just a few yards from once-pretty
stone bridges now with gaping black holes ripped in them.
Houses near the bombed bridges invariably bore witness to
the power of the explosions, with roof tiles scattered like
playing cards and windows blasted away. Death notices
pasted to telegraph poles seemed to indicate that several
civilians had perished in these attacks. High mountains
surrounded us on all sides and we had long ago lost telephone contact with the outside world as we crossed into
Kosovo, a land seen at this time as the heart of darkness by
the rest of the world. We saw very little of the Yugoslav
Army, apart from a couple of ramshackle lorries and dusty
buses full of troops heading away from Kosovo. The main
evidence of a military presence was the imprint which tank
tracks had stamped on the narrow country roads. The landscape seemed deserted. High overhead, the deep azure sky
was criss-crossed with vapour trails of Nato jets.

The first town we reached in Kosovo was the coal
mining centre of Kosovska Mitrovica. Here, the Mayor,
Nikola Radovic, rushed to meet us as if we were long-lost
relatives. The townspeople felt totally cut off and isolated
from the outside world, he said, with no telephone links
with Pristina, let alone Belgrade. We were taken to a
crowded building which was being used as a makeshift
town hall and local radio station. Everyone had abandoned the local government and other official buildings
for fear of them being bombed.

Across the road, in the market-place, a queue of ethnic
Albanians and gypsies was waiting to receive unemployment and other social benefit payments. Hardly anyone
was able to work, the Mayor said, because the massive
Trepca mine on which the town depended had been
closed since the fifth day of the bombing campaign.
Nearly forty thousand of the town's eighty thousand

population relied in some way on the mine for a living, said Zdravko Trajkovic, Socialist Party President of the Mitrovica region, as he guided us to a heavily-bombed area of the town.

The six-storey police station had been targeted one Sunday afternoon a couple of weeks earlier, he said. We all picked our way across a scene of devastation. Mattresses, phone wires, police uniforms, books, tin mugs and shoes poked from the mountain of rubble. Apartment blocks near the flattened police station were uninhabitable, with windows, roofs and some internal walls blown out. A large school had also been caught in the shockwave and was now unusable. Six hundred Serb children and nine hundred ethnic Albanians aged from eight to fifteen had lost their classrooms in the bombing, said the Mayor. I was surprised that children from both communities had attended the same school but it transpired that the institution had not been quite the oasis of ethnic harmony it first appeared: Serbs had been taught there in the mornings, Albanians in the afternoons. It was impossible to tell whether this had been with the mutual agreement of both communities, or whether it was another example of the parallel lives often lived by ethnic Albanians. What was clear, though, was that children had been segregated from an early age.

There had been about twenty-seven thousand ethnic Albanians in Kosovska Mitrovica before the bombing campaign had started, the Mayor said. Most had left in April, but in the past week five thousand had returned, he added. 'Can we speak to them?' I asked. 'They will be frightened to say anything because there are some KLA among them,' he answered. It was impossible to tell if this was true and, in the end, the only ethnic Albanians we were able to talk to in the town were the elderly queuing for their pensions. Even here, we were trailed by a Serbian radio reporter with a tape recorder.

The Mayor and the regional president fêted us with a lunch of bread, meat, salad, wine, beer and slivovic before sending us on our way to Pristina in a flurry of dewy-eyed embraces.

It was a time of intense battles on the ground between the KLA and Yugoslav forces near the western towns of Djakovica and Pec. The Albanian fighters had been vanquished as an organised army from almost every other part of the province in a series of bloody skirmishes in March and April but the small roaming bands of KLA snipers still managed to terrorise Serbs in the countryside and the main body of the Albanian-led guerrilla movement was to make sweeping inroads through the province in the following three weeks, culminating in its triumphant return alongside Nato in June.

In mid-May, towns in Kosovo were teeming with displaced people while the countryside was largely deserted. There were large numbers of ethnic Albanians in Kosovska Mitrovica, Pristina and Prizren, although many seemed under pressure to leave, both from the Serbs and from the KLA, who wanted every Albanian to join the exodus which was mesmerising the world. Thousands of ethnic Albanians had fled to these towns to escape the battles in the countryside or because they had been hounded out of shops and small businesses they had run in other parts of Kosovo. In at least some cases, these shopkeepers seem to have been put under pressure to leave by someone other than Serb forces. Official Serb notices had been pasted to many shops with Albanian names over the door, telling the owners that they should not abandon their businesses.

The countryside, meanwhile, was eerily bereft of human life. Civilians – Serb, ethnic Albanian, gypsies and Montenegrins – were terrified of venturing past these ghostly settlements, which were seen as ideal hiding places for marauding KLA snipers. Ethnic Albanian villages were easily distinguishable from the rest, because their homes and gardens were unusually surrounded by solid walls 'like a harem to keep their families in', said

Nebojsa. Most ethnic Albanian villages that we saw were also marked by one or two burnt-out or still smouldering homes.

The image that was being projected in the West at this time was that all ethnic Albanians were being subjected to mass deportation, rape and killing. Certainly these evils were perpetrated, but I began to build up a more subtle picture, based on seeing these villages at first hand, speaking to some ethnic Albanians who stayed behind, and later talking to disaffected soldiers and militia men who took part in the Kosovo battles. Widespread brutal killings were carried out in periodic raids by Serb police and shadowy paramilitary forces in 1998. Another fierce purge of ethnic Albanians began in early 1999 and only intensified as the threat of air strikes became certainty. Paul Watson of the *Los Angeles Times*, the only Western reporter in Kosovo throughout the Nato bombing campaign, says that the main campaign to sweep away the KLA once and for all, no matter what the consequences for innocent ethnic Albanians, began in the second week of March and ended on 20 April. This was when the main refugee exodus took place.

'There was a dramatic change on April 20, when people stopped being driven out,' he told me later in the Grand Hotel. 'But those who hated the Albanians used the chaos of the air strikes to over-react.' Watson also believed that there was more than one reason for the refugee crisis. 'Many left because they were driven out, but an equal number left to escape the Nato bombardment and some left because of the fighting between the KLA and the Yugoslav Army.'

By mid-May, the KLA's seven command control centres had all been destroyed and the remnants of the rebel army were mostly dug in around Djakovica. The fighting on the ground at this time was between regular Yugoslav Army troops and KLA guerrillas. Since the KLA lived in villages and not barracks, women, children and the elderly were caught up in the fighting. It is not clear how many on either side perished in these battles, or how many died because of the Nato bombardment. About five thousand Yugoslav Army troops are believed to have died in Kosovo during the Alliance campaign, but many of these are likely to have fallen in battle with the KLA.

When the Yugoslav Army finally pulled out of the province in June, Nato commanders were horrified to discover that weeks of bombardment had barely dented the Serb military machine and that they could account for a mere thirteen tanks damaged or destroyed while thousands more rolled undamaged out of Kosovo. The Serbs proved to be masters of disguise and fakery. Many of the tanks and artillery pieces which Nato commanders in Brussels had triumphantly proclaimed to have been destroyed were wire and paper replicas or cunningly arranged lumps of wood and old tyres. Allied jets would pummel these worthless fakes for hours, while Yugoslav troops sat smirking from their tanks and armoured personnel carriers, under camouflage cover and safely out of harm's reach.

Nonetheless, by the time of our arrival in Kosovo, casualties were beginning to mount. There were rumours of several hundred Yugoslav Army troops dying in one massive Nato bombardment of ground forces near Djakovica in mid-May. Wounded soldiers were also beginning to return home with stories of devastating KLA ambushes. The Government in Belgrade wanted to keep news of deaths and injuries away from the capital, so most of those conscripted to fight in Kosovo came from provincial towns in southern and central Serbia.

It is no surprise then that it is in this region that Slobodan Milosevic faced the first serious wartime challenge to his rule. On 18 May, more than four thousand stone-throwing women led street protests in the towns of Krusevac and Alexandrovac, calling for an end to the Kosovo fighting and the return of their menfolk. 'We want sons, not coffins,' they chanted. The mayors of both towns were attacked and reserve troops, emboldened by the women's action, declared they would disobey orders to return to the front line.

The following evening, in a little-reported statement, a Foreign Ministry spokesman in Belgrade declared that President Milosevic was 'prepared to cut a deal' to end the Kosovo crisis. There is no way of knowing if the street protests helped prompt the statement, but Mr Milosevic is bound to have been disturbed by the demonstrations, which occurred in the traditional heartland of his ruling Socialist Party.

In Kosovo, we in the Schiffer party set out on the final leg of our journey to Pristina. As we pulled away from the last suburbs of Kosovska Mitrovica, we passed a graveyard on a slope overlooking the town. Scores of new graves had been dug and many bore photographs of young men of typical military service age. In practice, any man aged between eighteen and sixty-five was eligible for call-up and none was allowed to leave the country during the Kosovo crisis. Many young men from the south, where most of the conscripts were netted, travelled to Belgrade, hoping to evade call-up by living in semi-hiding with friends.

By mid-May, young women across Serbia lived in a state of perpetual tension for fear that their boyfriends, husbands or brothers would be marched away to war. Those whose menfolk had already been conscripted were terrified they would never see their loved ones again. What no one knew was that, after the war, many recruits would be forced to stage protests and build barricades before they could wring their army pay from the cash-strapped Government.

The Kosovo landscape became flatter and deathly quiet as we approached Pristina. Not even a dog or chicken seemed to remain in the string of ethnic Albanian villages which straddled the long, straight road heading south-east to the capital. In most of the villages smoke billowed from one or two blackened houses, in mute but vivid testament to recent violence; however the majority of homes seemed undamaged.

We also saw dozens of mosques which were similarly unmolested. This was in stark contrast to the widespread burning and destruction later inflicted on Serbian Orthodox churches by ethnic Albanians who returned with Nato. Several Orthodox cemeteries were also vandalised, including one in Prizren containing the grave of Goran Zdravkovic's mother. The young doctor's mother died of cancer when he was a teenager and Goran has vowed to return one day to wreak vengeance on those who defiled her grave. 'When I go back, it will be for me, not for my country; it will be very different,' he once told me in a menacingly low voice.

When Pristina finally appeared on the horizon, in the distance we could see grey-white clouds of dust being thrown up by a Nato bombardment of the airport. I felt deeply uneasy when our route took us round the perimeter fence of one of the largest power stations I have ever seen. The huge cement cooling-towers on the outskirts of the city must have looked extremely inviting to bombing crews in the wide blue expanse above us. The site was so enormous that it took about ten minutes to circumnavigate, even at Nenad's high-speed manoeuvring rate.

Shortly after, Elaine Lafferty and I emerged, cramp-legged from sitting three abreast in the car for several hours, onto the forecourt of the Grand Hotel in Pristina. The city paradoxically seemed more relaxed than I had seen it in the past. The last time I had visited the Kosovo capital had been in 1993, when Serb militias were in evidence on every street corner and a self-imposed curfew kept most people off the streets after dark. Arkan, leader of the paramilitary Tigers, had owned a share in the Grand Hotel and the scent of latent terror had been overpowering.

Back in 1993, two large, stubble-chinned and morose

men had emerged from the shadowy recesses of the vast
and grim lobby as I had checked into the hotel. When a
stony-faced female receptionist had moved to hand me
the ridiculously large brass key fob, I had found myself
flanked by the men, one of whom then grabbed the key
as I was about to take it. In sheer desperation, I had
snatched it back, 'accidentally' jabbing the man hard as I
spun round and fled, hotfoot, to my room. I had stayed
there, locked in, until my driver from Belgrade returned
from a foray to find a restaurant where we might eat that
evening.

Now, despite the perils of day and night bombardment
from the skies, Pristina looked more at ease. This could be
because the estimated seventy thousand ethnic
Albanians in town were seen as posing no threat. The
KLA had been wiped out in the capital and many of the
Albanians had arrived from other parts of Kosovo to
escape Serb forces or the heavy Nato bombing near Pec
and Djakovica.

The Grand Hotel still looked the same as in years
gone by, a grim monolith of flat, socialistic design with
gloomy lobby and frayed red carpet. The same low, wide,
black plastic seats were placed in squares around the hall
and the lifts still did not work properly. The sheets and
blankets in the hotel were clean; the corridors, floors and
lifts filthy. Old orange peel, cigarette packets, torn and
greasy paper bags were piled up in corners or over-
flowed from long unemptied ashtrays. The dim lights –
when there was not a power cut – were a blessing since
the half-light prevented you seeing the grime in too
much detail.

The two big differences between 1993 and 1999 were
that the men and women manning the reception desk
now beamed broad and genuine smiles of welcome, and
the bar was bereft of alcohol. Beer, wine and spirits had
been banned throughout the city as part of a law and
order campaign. It was a rule which was broken from the
top. Wine and beer were produced for our table at dinner

that evening and, next morning, we were all given hefty slugs of slivovic in the Mayor's office.

Only a handful of journalists were staying in the hotel, including a Serb working for Reuters news agency, Paul Watson of the *Los Angeles Times*, two Greek photographers and Jacky Rowland of the BBC. A media centre had been set up on the first floor, where a single telephone line to the outside world allowed us to hook up computers, send faxes or simply dictate reports to our offices. Since there were so few of us, there were also mercifully few squabbles over access to this line. Some people also had access to satellite telephones, fantastically expensive but effective pieces of equipment.

We had arrived during a relatively tranquil period in Pristina. For the first two weeks of the Nato bombing, in late March and early April, the Grand Hotel had been rocked nightly during heavy bombardment of the city centre. Now, Nato's targets were mostly on the outskirts, such as a Jugopetrol fuel storage depot. However, even explosions on the edge of town were often strong enough to shake yet more glass out of the windows in the dining room downstairs.

After a quick Coke and a sandwich, we set out from the gloom of the lobby into the blinding sunshine to take a walk round the city centre. The main police station, the post office and several rows of private homes looked as if a giant fist had smashed down on them from the heavens. Nato bombs had torn through the buildings, leaving their tell-tale scorchmarks and the usual debris of former human occupiers mixed in the rubble. The houses had paradoxically belonged to ethnic Albanians and the locals were quick to tell us that they had heard horrendous screams coming from the burning ruins of one home hit in the raid, where seven members of one family had perished.

Separatist ethnic Albanian books and pamphlets lay scorched and half-buried among the pulverised bricks and mortar of another flattened home. I pulled one of the books from the debris; it contained a photograph of a mock funeral which ethnic Albanians had held in Pristina in the early 1990s to mark 'the death of Yugoslavia'. Other photographs showed close-up views of children with livid scars and mutilations, presumably from injuries purported to have been caused by Serbs.

Our meanderings through the devastation were punctuated by the occasional thump of explosions in the distance. So far, Elaine Lafferty and I had been constantly accompanied by Schiffer, Nenad and Nebojsa. As we retraced our steps to the main square between the bomb-ravaged police station and post office, we saw that several hundred ethnic Albanians had gathered there. Entire families, mostly with a few bags, cases and other belongings, were sitting or standing listlessly in the heat. Elaine and I were desperate to talk to them, but away from our Serbian chaperones. Whispering together, we hurriedly decided to split up; I would try to keep the Schiffer contingent busy on one side of the square while Elaine talked to Albanians on the opposite side. Then we would reverse roles.

At this moment, several buses with the destination 'Macedonia' written on the front pulled into the square. The ethnic Albanians were instantly roused from their lethargy and began swarming round the vehicles as surly-looking drivers looked disdainfully down on their prospective passengers. Schiffer and Nebojsa were at my side the instant I began to try to find an English-speaking Albanian. 'Would you like to talk to them? I will translate,' said a smiling Nebojsa. 'Look, there is no heavy police presence here,' said Schiffer, 'no one is harassing them.' It was true that the number of police was no greater than you might see on any London street, but I knew there were more ways than one to press unwanted people to leave.

Nebojsa began addressing one young family in Serbian. 'Why are they going?' I asked, playing the game. The family mumbled something incoherent which

Nebojsa translated as: 'They are leaving to escape the
Nato bombing.'

I spotted Elaine in earnest conversation with a couple
queuing to board one of the buses. Schiffer also saw her,
tried to beckon her to his side, and eventually moved off
to join her. I meanwhile thanked Nebojsa, made as if to
follow Schiffer, but dodged behind another bus.

'Anyone speak English?' I asked quietly but urgently
as I moved up and down the line of people waiting to
climb on the bus. 'Are you with Serbian television?'
came a young man's voice. I was quickly able to reassure
him and his brother that I was a British journalist, which
to them equalled friend of Nato and the ethnic
Albanian community. 'Why are you leaving?' 'Because
we are being forced to go,' they said. 'The police have
told us we must go on these buses.' They turned their
backs on me as they saw a worried-looking Nebojsa
approaching.

Back in the hotel, Elaine took me to one side. She had
been talking to an English-speaking man who also said he
was being forced to leave. When Schiffer had approached,
he insisted on questioning the man anew for Elaine's
benefit. This time, however, when Schiffer claimed the
man had insisted he was leaving to escape the Nato
bombardment, the ethnic Albanian had shot back with:
'No – I am leaving because of the police.' As Elaine said,
it was a brave thing to do. The problem for all journalists
trying to cover this secretive and plot-filled region was
that it was well nigh impossible to tell who was telling the
truth. The general impression we gained that afternoon
was that ethnic Albanians were under pressure to leave
the country.

Paul Watson, of course, had been in Pristina
throughout. This, in part, is how he described what he
had seen to readers of the *Los Angeles Times*:

'Once Nato added its air war on top of Kosovo's civil
war, the Serbs retaliated against the closest, and most

defenseless, target: the same ethnic Albanians Nato had come to save.

'At first, there was no panicked exodus from Pristina's ethnic Albanian neighborhoods, even though Serbian death squads wasted no time trying to provoke one.

'Five Serbian policemen put out the message that no one was safe, seizing the leading ethnic Albanian human rights lawyer, Bajram Kelmendi, 62, and his two sons, ages 16 and 31, and shooting all three.

'After failing to blow up the Kelmendis' house with a bomb placed under the front step, the police led the lawyer and his sons from their home shortly before 1 a.m. March 25, just a few hours after the bombing had started. Then they murdered them and dumped their bodies at the roadside in Kosovo Polje, a suburb of Pristina.

'An accomplished lawyer herself, Bajram Kelmendi's widow, Hekibe, knew that there was no case without solid evidence, so as she spoke in a sitting room full of about 20 mourning women two days later, she gave damning testimony: She had seen the murderers' faces and would know them for certain if she lived to see them again. They had already taunted her by driving by the house in the car they stole from her son.

'On the night of the abductions, as she lay face down on the floor with a police rifle aimed at her head, Hekibe heard one of the Serbs ask on his radio if he should bring her along too.

' "Leave her behind," the voice crackled back over a walkie-talkie. "We don't need her."

'Several days later, the campaign of terror took another sinister twist in what was probably my most painful moment in the war. From my fourth-floor hotel room, I heard a man's voice shouting from the street below. I looked down on thousands of people being force-marched by Yugoslav troops through the city to the railway station, where they were packed into rail cars and deported to Macedonia.

'I ran down eight flights of stairs and out the lobby

door. I stood in shock as a long column of ethnic Albanians about 15 people across – maybe 7,000 in all – moved silently past.

'The first person I spoke to, a man walking with his wife and two children, said in broken English that police had ordered them all to leave.

'I was watching a crime, and there was nothing I could do to stop it.

'Unlike foreign journalists based in Belgrade, none of us in Pristina were under direct military or police control, and we did not need permission to leave the city.

'There was one restriction: We could not go into what the military and police called "operational areas," which could be identified by the long columns of refugees streaming out.

'I was able to reach all of Kosovo's main cities and towns at least once, some of them several times, and I saw a much more complicated picture than the one relayed by refugees fleeing across the border. There often seemed to be a direct link between KLA or Nato attacks and Serbian revenge against innocent ethnic Albanians.

'In towns like Djakovica in southwestern Kosovo, empty streets would fill with people over time, and then empty once again as Nato bombing intensified and Serbian rage boiled over.

'The war was almost over before the Yugoslav army got around to setting up a media control office in Pristina, but even then it was easy to get through road-blocks without an escort. Still, it wasn't until Serbian forces began to withdraw in the face of Nato's advance that I was able to see close up what Nato and the UN war crimes tribunal in The Hague said was a mass grave.

'But by the time I reached the remote village of Izbica in the destroyed Drenica region on June 16, the bodies had been dug up and taken away.'

Our first impressions of the causes and effects of the refugee crisis therefore seemed to differ from the official

Nato line which was that all the ethnic Albanians who flooded into Macedonia, Albania and Montenegro had been forced to leave at Serb gunpoint. Although this seems to have been the main reason at the beginning of the air strikes, at least some seem to have left later because they were fleeing Nato's bombs, and some were pressed to go by the KLA. More evidence of this emerged after the bombing ended, when I was able to piece together a clearer picture of what had happened in Kosovo while the world was locked out. Meanwhile, we were to see more of the death and mayhem caused by the air strikes.

The day after our arrival in Pristina, Elaine Lafferty and I were taken to see Pristina's Deputy Mayor, Zivorad Igic, who treated us to two hours and six hundred years of Kosovo history. The Mayor himself, Dusan Simic, was away, being treated in the same Belgrade hospital as John Simpson of the BBC. Both had suffered leg injuries, Simic playing football and Simpson when he tripped and fell outside his hotel. A large man in military fatigues sat in on our talks with the Deputy Mayor, describing himself as a journalist.

We returned to the Grand Hotel to discover that one of Yugoslavia's largest prisons had been bombed that morning, and that many of those inside were ethnic Albanian prisoners. The jail, at Istok in central Kosovo, was like a scene from hell, said other journalists who had driven out to see for themselves while we were ensconced in the mayoral parlour. Nato said it had been aiming at an electrical plant nearby; Serb officials said the Alliance was trying to spring hundreds of KLA members from the prison.

A hole had been blasted in the perimeter wall and there were two giant craters nearby, but there had been no chance for any prisoners to escape, said the returning journalists. Many – Serbs and Albanians – had been wounded in the explosions and had been seen screaming for help as prison guards merely lined up outside to make sure no one managed to flee the blitzed compound. The journalists, including Jacky Rowland, had a narrow escape themselves when Nato came back to drop more missiles. No one had tried to help the one thousand trapped and wounded prisoners inside, according to the journalists.

At noon the next day, Saturday 22 May, I was standing next to the hospital bed of a young man with bandages over his eyes who was clutching in agony at the rough blankets covering him. His ceaseless writhing and low moans brought concerned looks from doctors and nurses, but they did not have enough pain-killers to make him more comfortable, they said.

We were in the town of Gnjilane in southern Kosovo and the young man was one of more than sixty wounded when two cruise missiles slammed into the Binacka Morava industrial estate where they worked. Five people had been killed, including two canteen ladies. Gavrilo Nicic, a forty-five-year-old building worker, lay covered in burns, cuts and bruises in the bed next to the pain-racked young man. 'I have never had a day's illness, let alone been in hospital before,' he said. 'It is very shameful of England to take part in this bombing because England has a tradition of fairness in the world.'

The Gnjilane bombing was barely to rate a mention abroad; it was a legitimate target, after all. Any industrial site was regarded as fair game and among the most heavily-damaged facilities on the bombed estate was a bus service garage. I tried to remind myself that the buses now reduced to blackened shells could have been used to deport ethnic Albanians or to transport troops. It nonetheless seemed hard to accept that it was civilian workers, women as well as men, ethnic Albanians as well as Serbs, who had borne the brunt of the air strike.

The hospital director and his senior medical staff invited us for a chat in a smoke-filled office. Over plum brandy, they poured out their misery and anger at having to deal with the casualties of war.

The 480-bed Gnjilane hospital had one hundred doctors and two hundred nurses before the war, half of them ethnic Albanian. 'The Albanian doctors disappeared the day before the bombing started,' the hospital director said, 'along with seventy Albanian patients undergoing dialysis treatment.' The implication was that the KLA had forewarned the Albanians about Nato's imminent action and that these doctors and patients had fled across the border to Macedonia. A more sinister view would be that they had tried to escape the Serbian backlash they knew would accompany the bombing.

A woman doctor cut in: 'This is a very hard time for us. Two Albanian children have just lost legs because they started to play with an unexploded cluster bomb, we have ambulance crews injured when they go out to help bomb victims.'

The industrial estate bombing had caused typical injuries, another doctor said: 'Severe head wounds, lost hands, lost legs, blast wounds, crushed legs, damage to eyes, ears, everything.'

A United Nations team was spending three days in Kosovo at this time and we had seen their convoy of pristine white four-wheel-drive vehicles set off each morning on their mission to ascertain the need for humanitarian aid. The UN group had already visited Gnjilane and I asked whether the hospital had been offered any help. 'I would love to see the UN team, but we have not had any contact,' the hospital director answered. 'They passed by but they didn't stop.'

# Chapter Eleven

# Two Wrongs: March–May 1999

'I want you to understand how one ordinary Serbian soldier serving in Kosovo felt during this war,' said Radovan. The softly-spoken twenty-eight-year-old health worker from a small town in central Serbia was conscripted into the Yugoslav Army a week before Nato dropped its first bombs on the night of 24 March 1999. Radovan, whose real name cannot be used, went on to describe life behind Serb lines in Kosovo.

'As you probably know, most of us were not professional soldiers but ordinary people who had to leave our families and jobs and go away to war.'

Radovan was one of many demobilised soldiers I spoke to in the June and July, soon after Nato rolled into Kosovo, as I tried to discover what had really happened in the province during the air strikes. I met them during a series of visits to towns in southern Serbia such as Vranje, Kursumlija, Leskovac, Prokuplje and Nis which were teeming at that time with Serbs – civilians as well as newly-demobbed soldiers – who had been forced to flee Kosovo when Nato entered the province accompanied by a KLA bent on revenge.

Back on 24 March, the first day of the war, Radovan was still in his home town but had been put into uniform, assigned to barracks and had been separated from his family. He remembered the first bomb which he personally saw. 'There was a big flash in the sky and after a few seconds I heard the detonation and I thought, "Oh my God, this is really happening." I don't belong to any nationalistic organisations but I thought that the West was making a big mistake by starting the war. I couldn't help asking myself over and over, why us? Why didn't anyone punish Turkey when they attacked the Kurds or when they invaded Cyprus? I wondered why the Americans, who have killed millions of people such as American Indians and Vietnamese, and who have big problems at home with racial discrimination and high levels of crime, have the right to come in my country and act the peacemaker.'

Within days, Radovan was sent down to Kosovo where, as an educated man, he was put in charge of a squad of thirty people. His description of life on the front line suggested that most killing of ethnic Albanian civilians was carried out by special forces and not by regular troops. 'All of us were reservists, we had done our National Service in the past but now were being called up to fight in this time of national emergency. We were very afraid at first but, as time passed, so our fear lessened. We passed through most of Kosovo including many villages from Klina to Djakovica. We faced two big dangers, one from Nato in the air and one from the woods where Albanian terrorists were lurking. All the time, Nato attacked us very hard, but especially towards the end. During the last fifteen days bombs were falling close to us every day, the explosions were three to four hundred metres away. More than fifty bombs were dropped near us during this time.'

Radovan told his story in June, before Nato admitted that the bombing campaign had inflicted relatively little damage on the Yugoslav Army's military machine. 'We were very lucky because no one from my squad was hurt. We also lost very little military equipment, despite what Nato thought. And that was the same throughout the Yugoslav Army because, in spite of the heavy bombardment, little damage was caused to our hardware. We had one big amusement. We made fake tanks out of cardboard and Nato aimed at these and bombed them all the time. We were very happy that we deluded them,' he said.

The soldiers were settled in empty houses, Radovan claimed, and they were given food three times a day. 'We were able to get cigarettes too, but we smoked more than usual so there was sometimes a shortage of tobacco. As luck had it, our families were also able to send us parcels of food and cigarettes.' While life on the front line turned out to be bearable for Radovan and his men, they all worried deeply about their families back home, fearing that wives, children and mothers may be suffering under Nato's bombardment.

'One day one of my men heard that his village had been bombed and he fell into hysterics. It was very sad and frightening to see him like that. As in any war, many people were involved and they behaved in many different ways. There were good and bad people from both our side and the Albanian side. Nato was the only side which was completely bad.' Did Radovan witness, or take part in, atrocities against civilians? Although there was no way of verifying his account, his description of his relations with non-Serbs in Kosovo was echoed by other ex-soldiers who served in different areas.

'I was trying to maintain discipline among my people. We were based in a village where Albanian Catholics were living and our relationship with them was very good. We didn't disturb them, we didn't drive them out from their houses and we paid for everything we took [meat and vegetables]. But I was a witness to the fact that it was not like that everywhere. There were places where Serbs and Albanians were in intense conflict. In the village where we were based, people could live and work normally but the villagers were frightened when we arrived. Then they were afraid again when we left because they didn't know what to expect from Nato or from the terrorists. They were just ordinary people, like us.'

All the troops said that morale had been bolstered enormously by the shooting down of the American Stealth bomber over central Serbia at the beginning of the conflict. 'We didn't have modern anti-aircraft weapons but our forces managed to shoot down the Stealth bomber. It was good to know that a little country like ours could defeat this invisible aircraft. But we also knew that Nato had thousands of planes and we could not beat all of them. Anyway, we were told that our army brought down about seventy aeroplanes and thirty pilot-less aircraft. Personally I didn't believe this, or that bombing the Chinese Embassy would stop the war. It was just one more thing to blame Nato for.

'We were very happy when we heard that the war was going to stop and that we would soon go home. At the same time, we were unhappy because this war caused many victims from both sides, with many refugees from both sides, many homes destroyed, many people left without jobs because so many factories and workplaces were bombed. When we were travelling home, we were afraid of what we would find. Would we come back to our jobs, like before? We knew nothing could be the same again.'

I also gleaned important information from Nikola Barovic, a prominent Belgrade lawyer and human rights activist who has in the past defended many ethnic Albanians and others who have fallen foul of the Yugoslav state. He believes that the mass exodus of Kosovo's ethnic Albanians may have been kick-started by a malicious rumour as much as at the barrel of a gun.

Speaking in Belgrade in August, he described the opening days of the conflict, when special forces are believed to have embarked on the fiercest phase of their campaign to terrorise and hound non-Serbs out of Kosovo. 'I was watching on television as countless thousands were walking through Pristina at the beginning of the war and I assumed that Serbs were behind them with guns,' said Barovic, whose late father was also one of Yugoslavia's leading human rights lawyers. In July, after Nato had entered the province, the barrister visited Kosovo and Montenegro and met ethnic Albanian lawyers he had known for years, to discover how they had fared in the Kosovo cataclysm.

'I was told that the Serb secret police had spread a rumour at the beginning of the campaign that the Turkish Ambassador and the Turkish Consul would be waiting at the bus and railway stations in Pristina, ready to take ethnic Albanians to safety in Turkey,' he said. It was a cunning trick which had been carefully prepared, he added. The Serbs had reportedly rehearsed how best to spread misinformation by disseminating a previous rumour to the effect that the Croatian President, Franjo Tudjman, was on his deathbed. Tudjman was indeed suffering cancer in March, and he died of the disease in December. But in March, he was not critically ill. Nonetheless, the report gained such credence that some British national newspapers updated their obituaries of the Croatian leader. Denials from the Croatian capital, Zagreb, had merely fuelled the rumour. 'The Tudjman story was treated as a school exercise in how to spread rumours in Kosovo,' says Barovic.

This is not to deny that many ethnic Albanians were killed or terrorised into leaving Kosovo by gun-toting members of Serb special police and paramilitary militias. However, the situation was more complicated than that portrayed by Nato. The impression propagated in the West was that Serb forces had embarked on a series of massacres of ethnic Albanians in 1998, simply because the Albanians were campaigning for independence from a rotten regime in Belgrade. The West had intervened on humanitarian grounds, and launched the air strikes when Serb forces failed to stop attacking the Albanian community and pull back from Kosovo. Then, as the bombing started, the Serbs had begun systematically to exterminate large numbers of ethnic Albanians and to herd the rest out of the country. This simplistic view was aided by blanket world television coverage of the ethnic Albanian refugees as they swarmed out of Kosovo. Weeping men, women and children told the same story again and again of men being separated, taken away and killed while the rest were ordered out on pain of death if they disobeyed.

What Western viewers were not told was the Serb side of the story; that the KLA had become so strong in 1998, that parts of Kosovo became no-go areas for Serbs, and that some Serb families were living as virtual hostages in some Albanian-dominated villages. The Serb forces – army, police and shadowy paramilitaries – were put under great pressure both by Kosovo Serbs and by the Belgrade regime to act. In the spring and summer of 1998, they decided enough was enough and embarked on a fierce campaign to sweep the KLA from the province. Many perished in these battles, both Serbs and Albanians.

When the Nato bombing campaign started, the Serbs intensified their drive, fuelled by unprecedented venom because they now blamed the Albanians for bringing down the might of Nato missiles on their heads. Atrocities were doubtless committed and many Albanians were killed, but the Serbs I spoke to insisted that most of those who perished had been real or suspected KLA fighters. If true, this is a crucially different situation from the image of wholesale slaughter aimed at exterminating a race. It is also important to remember that many of the demobilised soldiers I spoke to had been conscripts, ordinary civilians called up to fight in a time of war and who were often as critical of the Belgrade regime as they were of the West. They all told similar stories of swoops on ethnic Albanian villages, aimed at destroying the KLA. They also said they had heard of atrocities committed by secretive paramilitaries who had not distinguished between armed guerrillas and civilians, including women and children, when they went into battle.

The men's accounts also tallied with information provided by Barovic after he visited Montenegro in July and met ethnic Albanian lawyers he had known in Kosovo before the war. The lawyers told him they were forced to leave their homes by men in uniform. Many

were beaten up as they were put onto buses or bundled
into cars to leave Kosovo. However, says Barovic, they
did not directly witness any systematic campaign of
killing. This is not to say that Albanians were not killed or
to minimise the brutality of some Serb forces, merely to
put it into context.

Barovic blames the Kosovo crisis on the Serbian
Government for 'failing to keep order for the past ten
years'. However, he also accuses the Nato-led Kfor
peacekeeping force of failing to protect Kosovo's Serbs
and other non-Albanians after taking control of the
province in mid-June. 'The Yugoslav Government of
course always said it was against torturing and killing and
in favour of the equality of minorities. It blamed "uncontrolled groups" for such things. Now Nato says the same
thing when Serbs are killed, beaten up and their homes
burned – that it is "uncontrolled groups".

'The Geneva Convention is very clear,' says Barovic.
'Whoever controls territory is responsible for security. It
is no excuse to say you do not have enough resources to
protect the civilians.' The lawyer has been scathing about
the Yugoslavian Government in the past, especially over
its human rights record. He has defended many ethnic
Albanians from Kosovo and has denounced the police
when his clients have been beaten up. He was himself
assaulted in 1997, after throwing a glass of water over the
ultra-nationalist leader of the Serbian Radical Party,
Vojislav Seselj. Seselj counts the extreme right-wingers
Jean-Marie Le Pen of France and Vladimir Zhirinovsky
of Russia among his close personal friends and is Deputy
Prime Minister of Serbia. Barovic says he lost his temper
during a television debate when Seselj began disparaging
the lawyer's late father. 'I am not an aggressive man, but
I am sorry to say I was provoked beyond endurance and
I threw a glass of water over him.' While Barovic was
drinking coffee after the programme, Seselj's bodyguard
walked up, punched him in the face and broke his nose.
Seselj and the bodyguard were accused of assault, but the

case was dropped when Seselj claimed parliamentary immunity.

'I have defended Croats, ethnic Albanians, everyone who needed defending; someone who has become a member of a minority group; someone challenging authority,' says Barovic. The barrister was also scathing about what he called the 'war pornography' of much television coverage of the Albanian refugees. 'They described killing as if they enjoyed describing it,' he says. His words reminded me of how strange it had felt to watch the refugee scenes from the Macedonian and Albanian borders on satellite television from Belgrade, while running the gauntlet of Nato bombs in the Serbian capital.

I remember one report in which refugees from a village spoke of seeing one hundred of their male relatives being taken away. There was little doubt, according to the reporter's account, that the men had been singled out to face summary execution. Next day, however, one hundred men from that village were filmed arriving at the border in a bus. Would some small doubt now be cast on the many refugee reports that all men separated out were being murdered? No. Instead the reporter announced the men's arrival with the words: 'They are the walking dead.'

The picture that emerged from my interviews with the ex-conscripts in June and July was that the Drenica area of western and central Kosovo had become all but sealed off to Serbs in 1996 and 1997, as the KLA built roadblocks and held cars and buses to ransom. 'They were like highway robbers, taking money and jewellery from everyone on board, Serbs and Albanians,' said one.

Vengeance from Serb forces when it came had been swift and vicious. 'By the end of 1997, Drenica was seen as a small Albanian state inside Kosovo,' said one of the newly-demobilised troops. 'And everyone was asking why the army did not react.' Each town's police force then formed special units who were better trained than the regular police and who wore masks when they went into action. In February 1998, these special units gathered for a decisive battle against the Drenica KLA, and circled the entire area, according to one former soldier who had served in several joint operations with the police. They were reinforced by other special militias sent from Belgrade. One of these special units was especially feared, and went under the name of Frankie's Boys, named after their shadowy commander.

Scores of fighters on both sides were killed in the battles for Drenica, which were denounced as war crimes by the West. Ethnic Albanians began holding large demonstrations calling for Nato air strikes. Police and the regular Yugoslav Army meanwhile set out to demolish road-blocks which had been set up by the KLA in central, southern and western Kosovo, and to rescue Serb families living alone in ethnic Albanian-dominated villages 'because they were under constant attack. We were like the American cavalry to these families; we were just trying to save them,' said another ex-soldier.

In the summer of 1998, most wealthy and powerful ethnic Albanians had left to live abroad as the campaign to provoke air strikes gained momentum. The police, using steel-plated armoured cars, continued their drive to push the KLA back from the Drenica region. 'We would form a half-circle with the cars round a village and use them as cover as we moved in,' said a former policeman. 'Usually the women and children came streaming out, but we never touched them. The Albanians did not usually have as much ammunition as we did, say thirty or forty bullets each while we had three hundred each. When they ran out of ammunition they would try to flee, but we had traps set up to catch them'. When the Albanian gunmen had no hope of winning a battle with the police and army, they would throw down their weapons and attempt to flee, the former policeman said. If they were caught, paraffin-soaked rags were used to swab the suspects' hands, necks and shoulders, to ascertain whether they had been in recent contact with traces of explosives, a key giveaway if they had been firing weapons. Those whose swabs were positive were usually taken away and shot, the ex-policeman said, unless they were aged fourteen or less, when they were taken prisoner.

'During these battles a lot of houses were destroyed and a lot of Albanians were killed. Serbs who were rescued from the villages usually left forever, while the Albanian women and children who ran away from the fighting eventually just returned. Of course Albanian women and children were sometimes killed in the fighting – when there is shooting all around, everyone is at risk. I cannot imagine myself shooting at a woman or child on purpose. We were brought up in the spirit of the old soldier ethic.'

By the summer of 1998, the Albanians began to put up walls, using blocks of concrete, and barriers of lorries, across roads round Pec, Djakovica and Prizren, according to many ex-soldiers. Then, in July 1998, Frankie's Boys and Ministry of Interior troops were brought in for two big sweeps against the KLA, one near Prizren and one near Pec, in a drive to open up these roads.

Frankie's Boys were seen as the SAS of these special units, being extra-fit, highly disciplined, wearing masks, and often equipped with SA-80 guns. 'It is one of the best guns for anti-terrorist operations,' said one former soldier, 'it has very good sights, is very light and easy to carry.' The SA-80s are believed to have been taken from Dutch peacekeeping troops at Gorazde during the Bosnian war, according to defence experts in the West. Frankie's Boys were regarded with awe by the regular Serbian soldiers: 'We would be shooting and shooting and using, say, five hundred bullets in fifteen minutes while in that time Frankie's Boys would use ten bullets and not utter two words,' said a vet from central Kosovo who served in the Yugoslav Army in that summer of 1998. 'They had high-tech radios with better channels than we had and they only talked to one another. They had nicknames such as Frog, Snake or Maverick and if we were in a joint action, they always sat apart from us at mealtimes.'

The psychological toll on some of the conscripts began to tell by late summer, 1998. 'I was allowed back into civilian life,' said one, 'I couldn't bear it psychologically any more. I was watching my friends dying around me, killed by the KLA, and I felt I could have been killed five or six times every day.' Then came the nightmares: 'The first came after I was asked to carry a policeman whose leg had been smashed by a dumdum bullet. They just threw him on my back like a sack while we were under fire. When we were out of the range of fire, I cut his trousers back. He was lying on his back, screaming in pain, and I saw that his leg was hanging on by just one piece of skin. I cut it off and applied a tourniquet. I was with him when we drove him to hospital and he screamed all the way, for sixty kilometres. In my nightmare, I dream of his screams, and see his bones bleeding.

'The other nightmare was caused after a battle in a village where we could see all the women and children escaping. From one window in a house, a man kept shooting at us. Eventually, one policeman managed to get beneath the window and he threw in a grenade. After the battle for the village, I went in that house with my commander and we saw the man who had been shooting at us; he had been thrown to the back of the room and was dead. Sitting next to the window was a woman, staring at me. She was dead, but in her lap was an ammunition clip which she had been feeding to the man. After that, I often dreamt of her, looking at me with those eyes.'

Another former conscript, who had been an army doctor, described his 'hardest fight for a man's life'. A young policeman had been shot in the chin and throat and was lying on exposed ground between Albanians shooting from a village and the police firing back from behind the cover of their armour-plated cars.

'I started to dodge from car to car to get as near as possible, but a sniper saw me and started aiming at me. I was doing all I could to stay alive, but my colleagues became so fascinated watching me that they forgot to carry on shooting to give me cover.' The army doctor eventually made a dash towards the badly injured soldier, a young boy from Kraljevo whose throat was so swollen that he was suffocating. 'He was begging me with his eyes to help. When I first reached him, I was so out of breath that I could not speak either. I was carrying ten kilograms of medical equipment and we were both panting and trying to talk.' The doctor carried out an emergency tracheotomy to let him breathe.

By the end of summer, 1998, Serb forces felt they had swept the KLA from many areas, including Prizren and Orahovac. In October that year, when peace monitors from the Organisation for Peace and Cooperation in Europe arrived in the province, Kosovo was quieter than it had been for years, the demobilised soldiers said. It was to be the calm before the storm. Fresh fighting broke out as a new round of KLA guerrilla raids on police and soldiers were met by revenge attacks by Serb forces, each side blaming the other for rekindling the violence.

'From then, everything went wrong and we knew the bombing would happen,' said another former policeman. 'In Kosovo, almost all of us had satellite television and we could see how the world was reporting what was happening in Kosovo. They said we were massacring people when in reality we were involved in two-way battles. It was unbearable to watch the reports. No one talked about the deaths of Serbs. Everyone talked about Albanians killed at Racak, but no one mentioned 250 Serbs kidnapped from Orahovac. It was such a low, disgusting media game.' It was clear from talking to Serbs who had served in the Yugoslav forces in the run-up to the Nato campaign, that they viewed the killing of ethnic Albanian fighters taken prisoner as acceptable; they could not understand why people in the West would regard this as criminal. To them, a massacre would involve the murder of innocent men, women and children. 'Everyone saw us as monsters with knives in our mouths. But we have our own code of ethics, so we know how to fight and what the limits are. I personally cannot imagine what a massacre is like.'

The demobilised soldiers and police also described how they had survived the Nato campaign. The Alliance knew by the end of the bombing campaign that it had been tricked into attacking mock tanks and artillery, but the scale of the duplicity may have been far greater than thought.

Microwave ovens were regularly used to disrupt Nato radar signals. One former conscript described how he dreaded being ordered to use the kitchen equipment. 'We used microwave ovens powered by a battery pack,' he said. 'When you turn it on and open the door, the microwaves would confuse Nato radar and draw their fire away from our military equipment. The trouble was, the oven then became a target. You had to dash across into the middle of a field, turn it on, then run like hell and take cover because they were nearly always bombed immediately afterwards. But it meant that our *matériel* was saved.' A spokesman for *Jane's Defence Weekly* later told me that microwaves emitted by telecommunications towers could also lure missiles off course. Although Serbia had hundreds of these towers, there were many thousands in Hungary and Bulgaria and the concentration of microwaves in those countries is believed to have led to some HARM missiles diverting from their targets in Serbia and landing instead in these neighbouring countries.

The Serbs also used black plastic to masquerade as rivers, after covering and camouflaging real rivers and bridges nearby. They also made fake plastic runways alongside real, camouflaged airstrips. 'Two bits of wood covered with camouflage nets would look like aircraft,'

said a demobilised soldier who had been based near
Prizren. 'We made fake tanks and Howitzers from wood
and tyres, then put boxes of smouldering sawdust
beneath them to attract heat-seeking missiles. We could
make two or three hundred of these in a night. When we
withdrew at the end of the war, the Germans who arrived
in Prizren were amazed.' To protect real tanks from the
attentions of heat-seeking missiles, they were covered
with polystyrene foam and constantly doused with water
to cool them down, the ex-soldiers said.

As I heard these accounts, I thought back to the days
and nights I had watched and heard Nato bombing the
airport on the outskirts of Pristina. I was amazed at the
end of the bombing campaign that Russian troops – who
had raced to the airport ahead of Nato – and then the
Alliance, had been able to use a runway which had apparently been blitzed time after time for weeks.

When the Nato bombardment began on 24 March,
army barracks across Kosovo were among the first
targets. They were mostly empty, though, for the troops
had been moved to other accommodation before the first
Alliance missile had been fired. I had also scoured the
Kosovo landscape for signs of Yugoslav Army troops, but
had barely seen any. Their capacity for melting into the
countryside was remarkable. Sometimes while driving
through the province, I would look back at what had
appeared to be an empty village, to catch the merest
glimpse of camouflage uniforms moving among the trees
and undergrowth.

Time after time while I was in Kosovo, the Serbs' fear
of the KLA was brought home to me. Once, while on our
way from Pristina to Gnjilane to see the effects of the
industrial estate bombing, Nenad suddenly seemed even
more alive with tension than usual. He and Nebojsa
pulled automatic pistols from their jackets and we heard
the click of the ammunition clips being slotted in place. A
sheen of sweat had formed on Nenad's brow; he had seen

a deserted road-block of tyres on a bend in the road ahead. While my instincts would have been to squeeze the brake, Nenad slammed his foot hard on the accelerator and we burst through the barrier. All Serbs were terrified of KLA ambushes on these ghostly roads.

To me, the dangers from snipers on the ground and bombers in the sky began to seem about equal. The power of the bombs rained down by Nato was brought home to me yet again while we were in Gnjilane. Vladimir Kuzmanovic was just showing me where he had found his friend's dismembered foot, amid a mound of rubble strewn with clumps of singed insulation wadding on the industrial estate, when the air raid sounded anew.

'I saw them coming, you know. Two Tomahawks, travelling quite slowly …' Kuzmanovic was as keen to stay and finish his account of the bombing as I was anxious to move away. The local Serb official who had brought us to the site was becoming panicky. The bombers could come back at any time; after all, 130 missiles had been dropped around the town since the war began. Kuzmanovic persisted: 'When I saw them coming, I shouted to the others, "Just lie down." I lay down and I was fine, just one piece of wall hit the back of my leg.' Despite the building worker's apparent immunity to cruise missiles, the rest of us were becoming desperate to leave. The nerve-jangling wail of the air raid sirens filled the air as we finally took our leave of Gnjilane and set off back to Pristina.

Schiffer was returning to Belgrade the next day and I needed to return to try to extend my visa. Elaine Lafferty announced that she would stay in Kosovo until Schiffer returned a few days later. This would leave me more room in the back of the car on the journey to Belgrade; it would also leave me alone with three men I barely knew, including the tight-lipped and enormous Nenad.

He seemed extremely angry because I had arranged to pay a Greek photographer staying at the Grand Hotel to develop and wire some photographs back to London. 'You English are so stupid,' he had hissed, banging his giant fist down on the dusty dressing-table as we waited for the photographer to return to his room. Nenad had wanted to develop and send the photographs himself. He seemed quite menacing, cooped up in the tiny room lit only by the beam of a pencil torch, as the hotel was in the grip of yet another power cut.

When we had first met in Belgrade, Nenad and Nebojsa had rushed to carry bags and open doors for Elaine Lafferty and myself. Chivalry was as dead as the electricity the morning I set off to return from Pristina. No one moved a muscle as I fumbled up and down six flights of stairs in the dark to retrieve my luggage. It was plain that I had deeply upset the entire Schiffer party by engaging the Greek to help with the photographs. A cool atmosphere prevailed in the car until we had crossed the border and were back in Serbia proper. Nebojsa then sat back and closed his eyes to listen to the Serbian folk-rock tape he had inserted in the cassette-player. The words went: 'The more you bomb us, the more united we will be. We now know what it means to be Serbian.'

It seems I misjudged him. Nenad was no numbskull driver with more brawn than brains. When we reached his home town of Cacak once more, Schiffer decided to stop off at a photographic studio to have a professional portrait taken of himself, flanked by Nenad and Nebojsa. The Franco-Italian humanist-philosopher already appeared on several rolls of film taken by Nenad in Kosovo, but these were to be more statesman-like images.

While waiting for the pictures to be developed, Nenad invited us to his home. We were led up the path to a new detached house in a leafy suburb of the town, where his wife, Mira, and two teenage children were waiting to greet us with coffee and wonderfully warming vinjak. Nenad obviously did very well in his multifaceted import-export business; the kitchen would have been well-equipped by Surrey standards and the lofty, parquet-floored living room was equipped with new television, video and plush blinds. But it was what I saw in a corner of the room which made me feel slightly ashamed about my earlier qualms about Nenad.

A religious icon was hung over a table laid out with an intricately covered Bible, candlesticks, a metal crucifix and incense burner. This shrine was obviously held in high esteem by the family, and Nenad crossed himself as he sat down. There was something in the way Nenad cradled the Bible in his massive hands which made it seem inconceivable that he could be mindlessly violent. I would remember this scene when Nenad was stroking Elsa's face a week later, after the road-tunnel bombing which killed Nebojsa.

Nenad's wife was extremely slender with high cheekbones and shoulder-length permed black hair. She was to prove extremely brave over the coming weeks in supporting her husband when he decided to undertake almost suicidally dangerous visits to Kosovo after Nato and the KLA had taken over the province. At a time when all Serbs in Kosovo faced being kidnapped, beaten, and shot by ethnic Albanians, Nenad delivered humanitarian aid to those fellow countrymen unable or unwilling to flee north to safety.

# Chapter Twelve

# Missed Again: May 1999

The police chief's idea of happy hour was between eight and nine o'clock in the morning. It was the third week of May 1999 and Radisa – affectionately known among the Western press as Radishes – grinned delightedly as he poured three hefty measures of whisky; one for me, one for Julian Manion of the BBC, and one for himself. Accustomed as I am to public houses, even I winced inwardly at the prospect of undiluted Scotch for breakfast.

I had been in Yugoslavia for almost a month and if I wanted to go to Kosovo again I needed to extend my visa, which was due to expire in a few days. This was a complicated business involving visits to Information Ministry officials, the Army Press Centre and the police station, the latter being reputedly the trickiest obstacle to overcome. Tales were rampant among some of the international journalists about correspondents who had been given twenty-four hours to leave the country after failing to satisfy the police.

I was given to understand that the offer of a bottle of whisky to the authorities would in no way be construed as attempted bribery. But now, as I waited on a bench in the corridor, outside door 16a on the third floor of the police station, I knew I could not bring myself to hand over the brown paper bag containing the bottle. To do that sort of thing in England you risk being accused of perverting the course of justice. So I handed the task over to Marija, my interpreter, who clearly saw nothing even vaguely amiss in offering gifts to police chiefs you have never met before.

When we finally gained access to the inner sanctum, Marija gave an almost imperceptible shrug as she handed over the parcel which the policeman absent-mindedly shoved in a cupboard before grabbing an already opened bottle to fill our glasses. Radisa had a gap-toothed grin which made him look like a cross between Terry-Thomas and Sid James. Could this amiable-looking chap really be the man who had struck terror into the hearts of some war-hardened hacks?

Sitting, sipping the fiery, cheap whisky at an hour when I had not yet had even a cup of tea, I realised I was being closely watched. Any signs of reluctance to drink with gusto when the sun was barely above the horizon, let alone over the yard-arm, would perhaps be regarded as suspect. After all, Serbs often pointed out that it was non-drinking, non-smoking, politically-correct Americans who were among the worst anti-Serb warmongers on earth.

Foreign journalists were not allowed to go to the police station alone; we had to take an interpreter with us. This was even though some senior police spoke English and some foreign correspondents spoke excellent Serbian. Taking an interpreter was all part of the system. The idea seemed to be that the translators should intercede if journalists failed to appreciate the subtle and sometimes not so subtle hints about how we should approach our task.

When war broke out, an army of students and postgraduates had swarmed around the Press Centre vying for positions as interpreters. For them, it was rich pickings: between 100 and 150 Deutschmarks a day, which was as much as many Serbs earned in a month. Marija, who was twenty-six years old, was recommended to me by a young woman who was acting as interpreter for a Swedish journalist. She turned up for her interview with me half an hour late and made it plain that her father was not at all enamoured of the idea of his daughter working for someone from an 'aggressor country'.

Marija turned out to be a reasonable interpreter, a lousy timekeeper and a loyal friend. She also had a fierce pride, typical of the people of Cacak, the central town where she had been born. Sitting in the police chief's office, she looked as if she would choke when the policeman told her to empty the ashtrays. When angry or upset, Marija would cock her head on one side and twirl a strand of her shoulder-length hair round her index finger. She was vigorously twisting one of her tresses now, as Radisa kept shooting asides to her in Serbian, the gist of which seemed to be that she should know her place. In the end, Radisa drank his whisky, looked through files with my photograph clipped to the front, grinned once more and told me not to worry. I duly received the visa extension.

Once or twice after that, I saw Radisa in the lobby of the Hyatt. But next time I went to the police station he had been moved to a new post and we all had to get accustomed to a new police chief. The system of registering, renewing and extending visas was beyond many people's comprehension, involving queuing at various counters for the privilege of paying various taxes and fees. The authorities also ensured that all foreign journalists lined up at least once a week at a window set aside especially for us, just inside the entrance to the police station. Teetering on top of five steps, in precisely the right place to block the entrance and annoy everyone passing in or out, it was probably the most uncomfortable spot in the building that anyone could think to place the foreigners. After queuing here to deposit the latest paperwork, you would reach the window and greet the stony-faced woman on the other side. She had a special talent for choosing that precise moment to bring down the shutter and demand that you return a couple of hours later.

These were irritating but relatively minor inconveniences and it had to be remembered that many of the foreign press corps were from countries raining down missiles on Serbia. In view of this, there was surprisingly little hostility shown towards us. The real obstacles to reporting were the inability to travel outside Belgrade without permission, and the danger of being bombed. The Serbs – both officials and ordinary people in the street – seemed to want the West to understand their viewpoint and showed an almost childlike appreciation for those of us who were 'sharing' the bombing.

By the time I returned from my first wartime visit to Kosovo on 22 May, the air strikes had been under way for two months and civilian as well as military casualties were beginning to mount. Before trying to return to the southern province, I wanted to try to take stock of the war so far, and to see whether misery among the civilian population was putting any real pressure on Slobodan Milosevic.

On the Tuesday night before Elaine Lafferty and I had set out for Kosovo, three patients had been killed when Nato scored a direct hit on the Dragisa Misovic hospital in the Dedinje suburb of Belgrade. The deaths were only the latest in a series of Nato blunders which were starting to prompt questions abroad. Civilians were being killed every day and in all parts of Serbia, from Subotica near the Hungarian border in the north, to Kosovo villages, close to the frontier with Macedonia in the south. Few of the Nato-inflicted fatalities were regarded as newsworthy in the West, especially while the world's television cameras were focused firmly on the columns of refugees crowding out of Kosovo. The Alliance was forced to admit some mistakes, however, even though Nato ultimately blamed Slobodan Milosevic for these, saying he had started the war in the first place.

On 5 April, at least five civilians perished and thirty were badly injured when three cruise missiles, ostensibly aimed at a barracks in the southern mining town of Aleksinac, fell a third of a mile short of their target and hit a row of houses instead. Air Commodore David Wilby of Nato said: 'It is possible that one of our weapons fell short of the target. Despite our meticulous and careful pre-attack planning, the law of statistics will, at some stage, go against us and we will be exposed to technical defect.' The results of the 'technical defect' can be seen in photographs taken by the local coroner, of a man decapitated as he tried to flee his demolished home and an elderly woman who died as she slept in her bed.

On 12 April, ten passengers were killed and sixteen injured when the train they were travelling in was incinerated by an air-launched missile as it crossed a bridge which Nato wanted to destroy. The train, en route from Belgrade to Salonika in Greece, was hit near Leskovac in southern Serbia. Nato said that the pilot of the aircraft which launched the missile had been so busy flying his aircraft and aiming at the target that he failed to notice the train approaching.

On 14 April, up to seventy ethnic Albanian refugees in two convoys were killed by Nato bombs as they fled villages in western Kosovo. The Alliance said the pilots thought they had been attacking Yugoslav Army units.

On 27 April, Nato again missed its target when attacking a military barracks in Surdulica in southern Serbia. As in Aleksinac, ordinary homes were hit and at least sixteen civilians were killed. The Alliance said that it had struck the barracks, but did not rule out civilian deaths. General Giuseppe Marani said: 'After more than four thousand attack sorties, one bomb went astray. We put all our effort in avoiding collateral damage. Things like this can happen and in fact they happened.'

On 28 April, a stray Nato bomb hit the Bulgarian capital, Sofia. No one was injured when the missile hit a private house. Bulgaria's President, Petar Stoyanov, said no one had 'expected such developments'.

On 1 May, at least twenty-three people died when a Nato missile aimed at the Luzane bridge north of Pristina hit a passenger bus. In Brussels, Colonel Konrad Freytag said: 'Unfortunately, after the weapon's release, a bus crossed on the bridge but was not seen by the pilot whose attention was focused on his aim point during weapon trajectory.'

On 7 May, the cluster bomb attack which killed and injured dozens in Nis brought the following Nato response. Major General Walter Jertz said: 'I can tell you that we did not target – repeat we did not target – civilian hospitals and we do not target any civilian targets whatsoever.'

That night, the Chinese Embassy was hit. Washington blamed an out-of-date map and said it had intended to bomb the Yugoslav Federal Directorate of Supply and Procurement, two hundred yards away. Conspiracy theories later abounded, including reports that a spy had deliberately fed the wrong information into the missile-guidance computer.

On 13 May, up to two hundred ethnic Albanian civilians were killed in one of the worst single incidents of the war, when Nato bombed their refugee convoy at the village of Korisa in south-west Kosovo. About six hundred refugees, mostly women, children and elderly men, had taken shelter for the night at Korisa after Nato bombs near the Albanian border forced them to abandon an attempt to leave the country.

Nato initially said it had merely bombed 'legitimate miltary targets' at Korisa. Then Western journalists in Pristina managed to reach the village and described scenes of burning tractors and trailers and scores of charred and mutilated bodies. Nato subsequently said that it deeply regretted any accidental civilian casualties and that military equipment had been seen in the area. Britain said that it blamed the regime of Slobodan Milosevic for the deaths as it was his forces which had provoked the conflict through the ethnic cleansing of Kosovo. 'How dare they now produce crocodile tears for people killed in the conflict for which they themselves are responsible,' said Foreign Secretary Robin Cook. The Prime Minister, Tony Blair, said: 'Of course we regret these things deeply when they happen. But that should not make us flinch from placing responsibility for this conflict squarely on the shoulders of the person, Milosevic, who has begun this conflict.'

On 30 May, at least eleven civilians were killed and another forty were injured when Nato bombers launched a daylight raid on a bridge in Varvarin, south-central Serbia. Witnesses said four cars fell into the River Velika Morava. Rescuers who went to aid the injured were hit in a second attack. Nato spokesman Jamie Shea said the alliance had bombed a 'legitimate designated military target'. He added: 'There is always a cost to defeat an evil. It never comes free, unfortunately. But the cost of failure to defeat a great evil is far higher.'

On 30 May, Yugoslavia reported that at least twenty people lost their lives when Nato bombed a sanatorium and neighbouring old people's home in Surdulica, where civilian homes had been hit in the earlier blunder on 27 April. Nato spokesman, Colonel Konrad Freytag, said that warplanes had struck an ammunition storage depot and a military barracks. This was also the day on which two German pilots took off from a base in Albania and bombed a mountain road tunnel near Prizren – a small earthquake in the Nato scheme of things with just one driver-interpreter dead.

On 31 May, Alliance missiles hit an apartment block in Novi Pazar, south-west Serbia, killing at least eleven people and injuring a further twenty-three. Nato admitted that a bomb had gone astray during an attack on an army barracks in the town. Jamie Shea said that five of six missiles hit their target but one overshot.

By the end of May, there had also been dismay at Nato headquarters when it emerged that jettisoned bombs had fallen near a tourist beach in Venice. An Italian fishing boat was destroyed when it had the misfortune to catch one of the Alliance bombs in its nets.

Nato went on the defensive: it had carried out 31,000 campaign flights, half of these being combat missions,

Jamie Shea said. 'When we started this operation, we were conducting around thirty sorties a day. Now we are conducting up to 350 attacks every night. There has not been a ten-fold increase where bombs have gone astray. If anything, the proportion [of mistakes] is getting better. Better because Nato planners take every conceivable precaution to strike accurately.'

Two of the more 'accurate' strikes had occurred in late April, but here again it was the innocent who largely suffered. On 21 April, Nato bombed the Milosevics' private residence in the select Dedinje district of Belgrade. The President was not at home, but the nearby house of the lawyer Nikola Barovic suffered severe cracks in the main load-bearing walls. Two days later, on 23 April, St George's Day and Shakespeare's birthday, a massive missile attack smashed open the building which housed RTS State Television in the centre of the city. At least ten people died, most of them make-up girls, tea boys and technicians.

The parents of these youngsters later asked bitterly why all the bosses had left at least an hour before the blast, and why the children of some senior party members had been warned to stay away that night. Many people subsequently believed that the Government had been told in advance of the planned attack but failed to alert junior employees.

The ferocity of the blast shocked many people in Belgrade, especially since the building was in the heart of the old town and close to many ordinary houses and apartments. The owner of the private Radovic jazz club in the precincts of St Mark's Church, at the back of the television centre, found a human hip among the rubble which rained down from the bombed building onto his premises. One of the saddest aspects of the blast was that it knocked state television off the air for only a short time, before a makeshift studio was rigged up elsewhere.

In the first two weeks of the bombing, a sense of national outrage had seen most of the population defiant and angry. Two months on, however, they were becoming war-weary. Five hundred thousand people had been thrown out of work because their factories and other workplaces had been bombed, according to trade unions in Serbia. The wages of those still in work were being eroded, and the cost of many essentials began to rise. The price of foods with a long shelf-life doubled in May, as freezers became unreliable because of the power cuts. Water shortages also began to make themselves felt, because the electricity failures caused by graphite bombs were hitting the pumping system. The Yugoslav Red Cross reported that more than a million people had been made homeless by the air strikes by mid-May, either because their houses and apartments had been destroyed, or because they had fled heavily-bombed areas. The worst affected towns were Pristina, Novi Sad, Cacak, Nis and Valjevo.

As is often the case, the young seemed to adapt faster to the realities of war than the old. A couple of weeks after the television station blast, I was invited to dinner by Serbia's answer to Liz Taylor. As one of Yugoslavia's most famous actresses, Svetlana Bojkovic had written to Glenda Jackson, the British Transport Minister, asking her fellow thespian to appeal for an end to the air strikes. I first met Miss Bojkovic in her dressing room at the Atelije Theatre in central Belgrade. Plays were being performed, free, at 5 p.m. to enable audiences to return home before nightfall, and a queue for that afternoon's play had already begun to form when I arrived, three hours in advance. Miss Bojkovic and her director husband, Musa, were sipping slivovic in the theatre bar as we began to discuss the approach to Glenda Jackson. 'We have both played your Queen Elizabeth the First and I am appealing to her artistic nature,' said the actress. It must have been the politician in Glenda Jackson who read the letter, however, for she did not reply.

It was a clear, balmy night when Svetlana Bojkovic asked me to dinner, and the french windows in her

*One Woman's War*

antiques-furnished flat opened onto a balcony festooned with grapevines. Katerina, her beautiful twenty-six-year-old actress daughter by a previous marriage, emerged from her bedroom where she said she had spent much of the day asleep. The table was aglow with fine cutlery and polished glasses and Frank Sinatra was singing to us in perfectly-pitched tones from the CD player as we sat down to sample the delights of goose liver pâté, toast, cheese and salad. It could have been a gathering of beautiful people anywhere in Europe but this was Belgrade in late spring 1999 and Nato was about to drop in. From somewhere close by came the boom of a loud explosion, followed by a more distant and muffled thump, then a third bang, this time closer.

Rada, a forty-something journalist working for a Belgrade evening newspaper, spun round in alarm – the loudest explosion seemed to come from the direction of her home. 'It could be the bridge,' said Svetlana Bojkovic. I leapt for my mobile phone and telephoned a contact at the Information Ministry, who had already ascertained that the target had been a Jugopetrol storage tank just across the river. Rada's worried expression lifted and Katerina sighed: 'Could we discuss something other than the war?' Right on cue, Sinatra crooned the benefits of being young at heart.

The difference between the generations was exemplified that evening. Svetlana and her husband, in common with most people over thirty-five, were anxious about the future and bewildered about the bombing. They may have been privately critical of the Milosevic regime, but to the outside world they presented a united front. They wanted repeatedly to pick over the events which had led to the air strikes. Katerina was typical of the young; the last thing she wanted to do was fret over what could not be changed. Most young people also wanted to leave the country and work abroad, seeing no future in a country treated as a pariah state for much of their lives and with no improvement in sight.

When Katerina failed to turn the talk away from war, she determined at least to inject some humour. 'What do you call a cross between Bill Clinton and a sheep?' She paused before bleating, 'Tony B-L-A-A-A-I-R.' The rest of the meal passed without more interruptions from Nato. Nonetheless, many phone calls were needed before a taxi driver could be found who was brave, hungry or foolhardy enough to make the dash across the bridge to take me back to the Hyatt on the far side of the river.

Petrol prices were beginning to reach phenomenal heights on the black market – up to five Deutschmarks a litre. Even public transport suffered fuel shortages and it was hard to chastise the unpunctual Marija when buses and trams often failed to run at all. Even when they did appear, the vehicles were in such dire need of repairs that it seemed miraculous that they could bear the weight of passengers at rush hours. Sometimes, I expected hundreds of pairs of legs at any moment to break through the rusty chassis and propel the bus like Fred Flintstone and his car. Another common result of the bombing was a plethora of road accidents, caused because traffic lights often abruptly ceased working in the regular power failures. Time after time at major intersections in Belgrade, you would see wretched-looking drivers staring nonplussed at bent bumpers and smashed glass while queues of traffic built up behind them.

The hot and sunny May weather helped to soften some of the misery of the physical and economic tribulations of living under Nato bombardment. Pavement cafés and restaurants were still teeming with customers and, to a casual observer, life might almost have looked pleasant. However, most people had only enough money for a single coffee or beer, which they would linger over for hours. In any case, the frequent power cuts meant that many restaurants could offer only cold food. Stores selling clothes and other non-essentials for daily life also tended to open for just an hour or so a day, if at all.

By mid-May, we were becoming accustomed to

wartime hardships and few people were stirred, let alone shaken, when the air raid sirens sounded. This was real life, and a bomb-free existence was just a hazy memory. Behind the scenes, though, politicians and diplomats were struggling to find a peace agreement. From the beginning, Nato and the Western governments had great difficulty placating Russia and China, which were deeply uneasy about the air strikes. On 6 May, one day before the Chinese Embassy blast, foreign ministers of Russia and the seven most developed countries in the world met in Bonn and agreed on a peace plan. The so-called G8 Principles included the withdrawal of Yugoslav forces from Kosovo, the deployment of international peacekeepers, the return of refugees, and an interim administration in Kosovo. The proposals turned out to hold the key to peace, for they formed the basis of the eventual ceasefire. Russia's special envoy to the Balkans, Viktor Chernomyrdin, was to play a pivotal role in this new peace process.

The Chinese Embassy bombing could therefore hardly have come at a worse moment; five days after the explosion, Russia threatened to pull out of the negotiations. President Boris Yeltsin said his appeals for peace had been ignored in the West and that 'Russia cannot settle for the role of mailman carrying messages between countries involved in the conflict'. Igor Ivanov, the Russian Foreign Minister, was equally angry after he held talks with the American Deputy Secretary of State, Strobe Talbott. Describing the Nato leadership as hawkish, Ivanov said he had been alarmed to learn that the Alliance intended to continue and expand the air strikes against Yugoslavia. 'Russia cannot sit idly by and watch Nato bomb Yugoslav towns and villages,' Ivanov said. It was to take much fence-mending, especially by the Finnish President, Martti Ahtisaari, before the diplomatic search for peace gained momentum again.

Many more civilians as well as soldiers were to die before Slobodan Milosevic formally accepted the G8 Principles. In the end, the Yugoslav leader agreed to the peace terms on 28 May – one day after he and four of his closest military and political advisers were indicted as war criminals. It took a further twelve days for details of the Yugoslav withdrawal from Kosovo to be agreed and the bombing to stop.

The UN's international war crimes tribunal in The Hague charged Milosevic; Serbian President, Milan Milutinovic; Deputy Yugoslav Prime Minister, Nikola Sainovic; Chief of Staff of the Yugoslav Army, General Dragoljub Ojdanic; and Serbian Interior Minister, Vlajko Stojilkovic, with crimes against humanity allegedly committed in Kosovo after 1 January 1999. Arrest warrants were issued and the tribunal's chief prosecutor, Louise Arbour, ordered the freezing of the foreign assets of the five men. The indictments won the whole-hearted support of Britain, France and Germany, but Italy was lukewarm while China and Greece expressed reservations, arguing that they might obstruct the long-term peace process in the Balkans.

The *Spectator*, required reading for much of the British establishment, went further in its criticism by running a blistering attack by journalist and human rights historian, Kirsten Sellars, on the ethos of war crimes tribunals. 'The human rights ideal was itself born of political convenience, as a smokescreen behind which the great powers could pursue their own interests, oblivious to the needs of those they purported to help,' she wrote in the 28 August edition of the magazine. 'America, the crucible of human rights and chief architect of the UN's 1948 Declaration on Human Rights refused to accept the Genocide Convention until 1986, on the grounds that it encroached on American sovereignty. British governments have been equally cautious. Although the Attlee government signed the European Convention on Human Rights, it did so only after securing the condition that UK citizens were banned from taking cases to the human rights courts in Strasbourg. The ban was lifted in 1964.' Ms Sellars went on to say that 'only losers ever stand trial

for war crimes … when Churchill was told that 12 top
Nazis had been sentenced to the gallows after the
Nuremberg trials in 1946, he mused to General Hastings
Ismay, "It shows that if you enter a war it is supremely
important to win it – if we had lost, we would have been
in a pretty pickle." '

Ms Sellars concluded by pointing out that the Hague
tribunal which indicted Milosevic was forced in 1998 to
drop charges lodged three years earlier against a Serb
accused of raping prisoners at the Serb-run Omarska
camp in Bosnia. The accused, one Gruban, was, it transpired, a fictional character from a novel by Miodrag
Bulatovic called *Hero on a Donkey*.

'A local journalist fed the story to a sensation-hungry
American reporter in a Bosnian café who in turn passed
the information to The Hague,' Ms Sellars wrote. 'It was
"confirmed" by the conveniently anonymous Witness F.
It would be funny if it weren't so tragic.'

The week that Milosevic was indicted, I had problems
of my own concerning money abroad. Schiffer and
Nebojsa had indicated that they would take me on a
second visit to Kosovo, this time with two cars and in the
company of Renzo Cianfanelli and three Portuguese
journalists. *The Times* was keen that I should go, even
though the price this time was 1,000 Deutschmarks
higher, at 5,000 Deutschmarks. This was because we
would be staying longer, said Nebojsa. There was only
one snag; the thick wad of around 9,000 Deutschmarks
which I had brought with me to this cash-only society a
month earlier had by now dwindled to a pathetic bundle
of about five 100-Deutschmark notes. The elastic band
which had once held the bankroll together had long ago
fallen loose and lay discarded at the bottom of my safety-
deposit box in the Hyatt strong-room. Functioning in a
world without plastic or even the ability to have money
sent from abroad required a huge amount of planning.
My visa, in common with almost every other journalist's,

was single-entry. If I crossed the border even for an hour or so to collect money from Hungary or elsewhere, I would not be allowed back without going through the weeks-long application procedure all over again. Even then, there would be no guarantee.

I tried to borrow the money I needed from Reuters news agency and the BBC. They too were running low on funds and keenly awaiting the arrival of back-up colleagues who would replenish their coffers. Some journalists had opened bank accounts in Belgrade on the understanding that, given a few weeks' notice, money could be sent in from abroad. Most abandoned that route when it became known that several thousand pounds had gone mysteriously missing en route from the bank of a British daily newspaper, via Moscow and Bulgaria, to Belgrade.

*The Times* then pondered sending the Foreign Desk secretary laden with Deutschmarks to meet me in no man's land at the Serbian-Hungarian border. But at the last minute, I heard in Belgrade that an Israeli radio journalist was to arrive from Tel Aviv via Budapest the following day. The cash handover took place after a highly complicated manoeuvre, in which a freelance journalist in Budapest collected the money from a bank there and drove, with minutes to spare, to meet the Israeli as he was transferring from Budapest airport to the minibus that was to take him on to Belgrade.

While getting hold of cash may have been a hassle for foreign correspondents, it was well nigh impossible for many Serbs – especially the innocent. Those whose names were linked with tales of corruption and evil-doing on the killing fields of the Balkans had probably made other, more underground arrangements to launder and collect ill-gotten gains long before the Kosovo conflict. My experiences of trying to transfer money legally from abroad were a salutary lesson in how far the tentacles of war can strangle day-to-day life for ordinary people.

The day before I left for Kosovo once more, Sergio de Mello, head of a UN mission aimed at ascertaining the humanitarian cost of the war in Yugoslavia, described the situation as 'disastrous'. Speaking after twelve days touring the country, he said he had witnessed incredible amounts of stress among the ordinary population as a result of the presence of an invisible enemy which could attack at any time. Key problems caused by the bombing included unemployment, destruction of basic services, transport, health, electricity and water supply systems, he said.

On Friday, 28 May, a few hours after handing over the 5,000 Deutschmarks to Nebojsa, again in the confidentiality of my room, eight of us set out for Cacak en route to Kosovo. It was a time of intensifying Nato attacks.

That night, three cruise missiles hit two power plants in the Bezanijska Kosa and Ledstani suburbs of Belgrade, blacking out almost the entire city. An industrial estate on the edge of the southern city of Nis was hit by twenty-one missiles; two people were killed when ten missiles were aimed at various targets round the central town of Aleksinac. Several bombs exploded around the state television transmitter on Mount Crni Vrh, a few miles from Pirot. And more than 170 cruise missiles and conventional bombs were dropped on targets across Kosovo.

# Chapter Thirteen

# Kosovo's Last Days: May 1999

A stray horse ambled up and down Kosovska Mitrovica's near-deserted main street, occasionally breaking into a canter as if testing the extent of new-found freedom. It was my second visit to Kosovo during the Nato campaign and the only signs of human life were the knots of militiamen leaning on Kalashnikovs and one or two elderly people carrying empty shopping bags past abandoned stores and kiosks. An atmosphere of testosterone-driven aggression hung heavy in the air. Three soldiers lolled against the door of the 'Non-Stop Café', which was shuttered and barred.

What had happened here? It was only eight days since I had last been in Kosovo yet it seemed to have changed beyond all recognition. Where the streets and squares of Kosovska Mitrovica had been bustling with people, they were now barren. The Schiffer party had made its usual courtesy call on the Mayor and other regional officials, and now Cianfanelli and the Portuguese journalists were being given their first view of the bombed police station and damaged school. Since I had seen these just a few days earlier, I set off to try to see the town alone. Nebojsa soon caught up with me, but no one could disguise the fact that the place was almost a ghost town.

After being guided back to the Schiffer group at the bombed-out police station, I asked Zdravko Trajkovic, the regional Socialist Party president, where everyone had gone, including the elderly ethnic Albanians we had seen a week earlier, queuing for their pensions.

Trajkovic spoke more vehemently and more angrily

than during my previous visit. 'One day last week, eighteen bombs were dropped here in just over an hour. Now
people have left to live in the woods in the surrounding
area. They are afraid to be inside their houses, so they
sleep outside,' he said. 'Five thousand cluster bombs
have been dropped in the Mitrovica area, also enriched
uranium from Tomahawk cruise missiles. The Albanians
are agricultural workers but they cannot now farm
because of the cluster bombs. The future looks bad for
everyone, all nationalities. No one wins from a war.'

All he said may have been true, but this still did not
account for the increased militia presence on the street
and the accompanying tense atmosphere. Trajkovic went
on to say that the authorities had to be on the alert; the
KLA could come back at any time. Several Serbs had
been kidnapped or ambushed in the previous seven days,
he said, including mourners from the funeral of a bomb
victim.

It soon became apparent that the KLA had made
huge inroads into Kosovo. During the week that I had
been away, the guerrilla army – working mostly in small
groups – had pushed their way back almost to the
outskirts of Pristina. Rural roads in most of the province
west of the capital were now regarded by ordinary Serbs
as sniper-held territory and few ventured to use them.
Eight days earlier, the KLA snipers could terrorise Serbs
in perhaps a quarter of the province; now they held sway
over more than half. Many people believed that Nato
was working with the rebels. 'A favourite tactic is for the
KLA to ambush a group of police or soldiers, pull back
immediately and leave Nato to finish them off,' said one
soldier.

We continued our journey towards Pristina, diverting
from the previous week's route in order to visit
Lazarevo and its towering concrete memorial to the
1389 Battle of Kosovo Polje – the field of blackbirds.
Lazarevo is barely large enough to qualify as a village,
but it was here that King Lazar led his Serb forces to a

defeat enshrined in Serbian consciousness as a symbol of the nationality's bravery and fortitude.

There was no sign of any blackbirds as we climbed the gentle slope to the base of the monument, looking out over a plain towards Pristina about three miles away. The only airborne creatures that afternoon were butterflies and fighter pilots flying so high overhead that we could see their aircraft's vapour trails but could hear no engine noise. Bursts of grey-white dust were being thrown up by explosions in the middle distance.

I began to think about the pilots. Many Serbs regarded them as cowards, because they usually flew at such a high altitude that they faced little danger of being shot down. Questions were being asked in the West about whether this strategy was the reason for some of the Nato blunders; that they bombed from such a great height that they could not see what they were hitting. They were also seen as isolated from the reality of the devastation caused on the ground by the high-tech environment of the cockpit. It would be like playing a computer game, many Serbs said. Weeks later, when I met Nikola Barovic, the human rights lawyer from Belgrade who has defended many ethnic Albanians and other minorities in the past, he had his own thoughts on this. 'Nato soldiers have been conditioned to think of all Serbs as guilty,' he said after visiting Kosovo in the weeks after the Alliance-led force arrived in the province.

But that Saturday in Lazarevo, the Yugoslav forces still had two weeks left to hold sway over the province. I turned to examine the 1389 battle memorial, inscribed with the words of King Lazar's curse – an eve-of-battle pledge that any Serb who failed to fight 'would have no male or female child, or reap anything from the land, not wine or bread'. A red plastic flower had been tucked incongruously into the Serbian coat of arms on a plinth next to the memorial, which was erected on the six hundredth anniversary of the battle in 1989. This was also the year in which Milosevic stripped Kosovo of its autonomy.

A restaurant for Serb pilgrims to the site had been damaged in a bomb attack. Renzo Cianfanelli began stepping over the rickety threshold of the battered wooden building, when Nebojsa warned him to stop. 'That sign,' he said, pointing to chalk letters – *pazi minerano* – scrawled on the doorpost, 'it means "danger of mines".' I beat a hasty retreat from the immediate area while the unfazed Cianfanelli continued to peer inside.

Once back in Pristina, we discovered that Elaine Lafferty had left for Skopje in Macedonia. But Jacky Rowland and Paul Watson were still in town and they explained that the apparent advances made by the KLA were being matched by a surge in Nato air strikes. Pristina was nonetheless still teeming with people, in contrast to the scenes in Kosovska Mitrovica. There seemed to be even more displaced ethnic Albanians in the capital than there had been the previous week, and I wondered if any of them were from the now almost-silent mining town. I made a solo foray out into the square from where Elaine Lafferty and I had seen the buses leave for Macedonia. I could find no one from Kosovska Mitrovica but one English-speaking family of ethnic Albanians paused briefly to speak. They said they had left their home near Gnjilane ten days earlier because they felt threatened by the Nato bombing. They did not want to leave Kosovo altogether even though police in Pristina were pressing them to take one of the regular buses to Macedonia.

Back near the hotel, I met two elderly sisters who ran a sandwich bar from a kiosk. The women had already suffered one huge upheaval, when they were among the two hundred thousand Serbs forcibly ejected from the Krajina region of Croatia in August 1995. They were afraid of the Nato bombing, they said, but were even more worried by the uncertainty surrounding their future. I was to remember the sisters and their soft, gentle voices, many times in the coming weeks. I was to wonder what had become of them after Nato had entered Kosovo with the KLA hard on their heels.

In Brussels, Nato planners were discussing how to isolate Yugoslav forces near the Albanian-Kosovo border. Fierce battles between the Yugoslav Army and the KLA were underway near Kosovska Mitrovica and throughout western Kosovo. More KLA groups had crossed from Albania into the mountains near Prizren and were pushing back Serb forces from positions on Mount Patrik, between Djakovica and Prizren. These KLA groups were fresh from training camps in Albania, where they had been well-armed. The night before we, in the Schiffer group, set out for Prizren, some Nato officials were probably planning the following day's actions. Only one road into Prizren now remained relatively safe from KLA snipers – the mountain route from Brezovica. If this were bombed and blocked, it would leave the important border town of Prizren isolated. The Alliance had begun exploding bright flares over Prizren and the surrounding area which turned night into day as they slowly floated to earth, allowing reconnaissance photographs to be taken to plan the following day's air strikes.

That evening, Nebojsa was about to eat his last meal on earth at the Grand Hotel in Pristina when an ear-splitting explosion sounded nearby, shaking the ground and rattling the already cracked and polythene-covered plate glass windows in the vast dining room. Someone, somewhere had provided us with beer, wine and whisky in defiance of the alcohol ban and our glasses were full when the bomb exploded. Carlos Julio, Elsa and I dived instinctively beneath the table and I found myself clutching a still-full glass as we crouched under cover.

We emerged feeling slightly shamefaced to find Nebojsa and Nenad shaking with laughter, mopping tears of amusement from their eyes. 'If the bomb had been powerful enough to break the windows, we would all have been dead anyway,' said Nebojsa. 'It is destiny, so there is no use hiding under the table.' A couple of minutes later, another thunderous explosion brought more peals of laughter from Nenad and Nebojsa and more leaping for cover by the rest of us. We all decided to move further from the windows and deeper into the interior of the dining room while we ate. Elsa and I had little appetite, but Nebojsa tucked into a hearty meal, totally unperturbed by the intermittent blasts outside.

He was too busy to eat breakfast before we set out for Prizren early the following morning.

Snow still capped the summits of the highest peaks as we climbed into the mountains towards the ski resort of Brezovica. Radovan Urosevic, director of the media centre in Pristina, told me that he once managed and part-owned the resort which we would pass through on our way to Prizren.

Nenad and Nebojsa made frequent telephone calls to contacts they had in the Yugoslav Army and police, apparently to discover the safest routes. There had always been rumours that Serb forces knew in advance about at least some Nato targets. This view had taken deeper hold after the bombing in April of the state television studios in Belgrade, when all the bosses and most of the sons and daughters of senior party members had been strangely absent from the building when the deadly missile struck. During my visits to Kosovo, Nenad and Nebojsa always seemed supremely confident that they were receiving up-to-date and accurate information about which roads were safest from KLA snipers on a given day, and where Nato bombers were likely to concentrate their attacks. I assumed this was because the Yugoslav Army and police were efficient at tapping into Nato communications. Others suggested that it some-times suited the Alliance to leak where some air strikes would take place.

That Sunday, 30 May, as we made our way towards

Prizren, I only hoped that Schiffer's two aides were equipped with the latest information, especially since the Alliance was evidently stepping up the number of air raids. Elsa, her cameraman and Carlos Julio were being driven by Nebojsa in the Volkswagen Golf, while Cianfanelli, Schiffer and I shared the Toyota, with the skilful Nenad at the wheel.

A few miles east of Brezovica, we passed the burnt-out ruins of a large hotel and restaurant. 'The owner is an Albanian, a super, super man,' said Schiffer. 'He has gone to Albania.' Graffiti on buildings and bridges seemed to indicate local support for Vojislav Seselj, the ultra-nationalist leader of the Serbian Radical Party whose bodyguard had punched the human rights lawyer Nikola Barovic in Belgrade.

The road began to twist between alpine meadows ablaze with spring flowers which seemed to make a mockery of the war. There was a far heavier Serbian police and army presence on this road running south and west from Pristina to Prizren than I had seen elsewhere in the province. Once or twice, Nenad stopped to talk to fatigue-clad men resting on their rifles, smoking and drinking coffee beneath roadside trees. 'They have bombed the bridge into Prizren,' said one policeman at the village of Strpce, near Brezovica. 'You can still get there, but you will have to walk into the centre.' We pressed on. Then, at Srecka, about eight miles from our intended destination, we were told by another policeman that a tunnel on the road ahead had been bombed and he thought we might not be able to get through.

Nenad wondered whether we should begin to make other plans but Schiffer was determined. He had made appointments with the Mayor and other officials and he wanted to keep them. A few minutes later, at just after nine in the morning, we entered a road tunnel to find that the way ahead was completely blocked by rubble from a recent bombing.

The last time I saw Nebojsa alive, he had folded his arms comfortably across his chest and watched as we clambered over the rubble to begin our descent on foot into Prizren. He was to stay and look after the cars. His destiny was all but sealed.

# Chapter Fourteen

# No Place Like Home: Serbia, June–July 1999

The man calling my name looked familiar as he walked hesitantly towards me. He had something of the look of Lonnie Donegan about him, yet I could not remember where I had seen him before. It was a hot and glaringly sunny day in Belgrade and I was just rising from a table outside the Moskva Hotel after having a coffee there with Branka, a senior journalist from state television in Pristina.

It was early July, nearly three weeks after Nato-led troops had entered Kosovo and the Balkan world had been turned upside down. Kosovo was undergoing yet another haemorrhage of humanity as Serbs, gypsies and even some ethnic Albanians – those accused of conspiring with Serbs – began to flee rampaging gangs of KLA supporters who were looting, killing and burning homes in the province. These atrocities often occurred in front of peacekeepers who said they did not have enough resources to cope.

While Serbs streamed out, ethnic Albanians poured in, both those who had fled in March and April, and others who were arriving from Albania for the first time. Those from Albania proper included KLA hardliners who had helped co-ordinate the guerrilla war against Serbs in Kosovo for years. The atrocities committed against civilian Serbs in the presence of Nato gained some coverage in the international media, but nowhere near as much attention was paid to Serb suffering as had been

given to ethnic Albanian misery during the Kosovo
conflict. This was partly because newspapers and television were fast becoming bored by the Balkans; by August
the vast majority of the thousands of journalists who had
covered the crisis since March had left the region and
moved on to other stories.

By late June, Kosovo was effectively a separate country;
there was no longer any Serbian language radio, television
or newspapers, no Yugoslav border controls between
Kosovo and Macedonia or Albania, and the dinar had
effectively been replaced by the Deutschmark. Yugoslav
troops who had fought for the territory felt angry and
betrayed at being ordered to abandon the province. Insult
was added to injured pride when many of those who had
been called up were told they would have to wait for their
army pay, usually the equivalent of around £150 sterling.

From the end of June, demonstrations broke out
across the country as disillusioned Serbs began to
demand Milosevic's resignation. The West piled on the
pressure by declaring that no reconstruction aid would be
forthcoming while Milosevic was still in power. This
remained Western policy until November when America,
under pressure from Europe, decided that the holding of
free and fair elections in Serbia would be enough to ease
sanctions and allow economic help to rebuild the war-
ravaged economy.

Late June and July were probably the most dangerous
weeks for the Yugoslav President. Even Seselj, the ultra-
nationalist leader of the Serbian Radical Party and
Deputy Prime Minister of Serbia, looked as if he might be
about to abandon ship. During the air strikes, Seselj had
vowed to resign from the coalition government with
Milosevic's Socialists if Nato troops set foot in Kosovo. In
June, he announced his resignation, but was told he would
not be allowed to quit until the State of War had been
lifted. Some then suggested that his resignation
announcement had been a mere public relations exercise
and that he was conveniently forced to stay on. Probably

only he knows for sure. Whatever the truth behind Seselj's move, Milosevic required all his powers of manipulation to ride out the weeks immediately following Nato's arrival in Kosovo.

The Yugoslav leader had two key cards in his hand, and he played them with masterly skill. One was his knowledge of the Serbian people, especially the masses of farmers and industrial workers from the Socialist Party heartland of southern and central Serbia. Milosevic hoped that the more the West demanded his overthrow, the more the population would resent being told what to do by those who had until recently been bombing them. Secondly, Milosevic knew that the two main political opposition groups had been deeply divided for over two years, and he tried to ensure that this rift only grew wider.

The Yugoslav leader could feel relatively sure that his closest advisers would not abandon him – thanks in part to the Western powers. In May, while the Nato bombing campaign was still underway, the European Union had invoked a travel ban and other curbs against three hundred politicians, military, police and business figures closest to the regime. By June, many had nowhere to go, even if they wanted to desert.

People in the capital have always been seen as an intellectual élite and psychologically different from those in the provincial towns and countryside. In Belgrade, Serbs were relieved that the bombing had stopped, but they were also weary and worried about the future. Few in the capital were ready in late June to risk more unrest and possible bloodshed by provoking the authorities with protests and demonstrations.

It was in Belgrade that Nebojsa had been buried, during the first week of June. I had been in London then, mostly writing for *The Times* and trying to acquire a new visa to enable me to return to Serbia. There had been a glitch because some Western journalists complained to the Army Press Centre about those of us who had travelled with Schiffer, saying we had breached the rules by not travelling

with an official convoy. Whether this was because of
professional envy that we had managed to reach Kosovo
outside the confines of a brief Yugoslav Army-chaperoned
visit, or whether they genuinely objected on moral grounds
was impossible to say. However, the complainants did not
bother to check their facts. Elaine Lafferty and I had
declared our intentions to go with the Franco-Italian
before our first trip; I had also openly discussed plans for
my second visit with the police when extending my visa. In
the end, I was able to prove this and now here I was, newly
re-ensconced in a Belgrade free of bombs.

Branka, the Pristina television reporter, and her sister-in-
law, Sladja, came to see me because they were having
enormous difficulty transferring money from their bank
account in Pristina to Belgrade where they were camping in
a relative's flat. Branka had fled Kosovo after being beaten
up by an armed youth who was among a mob which
stormed the television studio where she worked. She was
told she would be killed if she did not leave Kosovo for
good. 'I asked what I had done wrong, I am just a professional journalist. He said, "Listen to my order; leave Kosovo
in two hours or the whole world will hear that a Serb journalist has been cut in pieces by an Albanian."' Branka said
her studio manager had told Kfor about the threats, and the
Nato-led peacekeepers said they would try to protect the
television workers. But in the end, the peacekeepers merely
emptied the building of both Serbs and the armed
Albanians, she said. 'All my colleagues have fled and all our
apartments have been robbed. Kfor said it would protect us
but there were just not enough of them to do that.'

Most of the interpreters used by Kfor were Albanian,
she added, and they failed accurately to translate what
Serbs were saying when they asked the peacekeepers for
help. 'One Serb was telling them that a neighbour had
been murdered, but the Albanian described the attack as
a "provocation",' she said.

Marija, my interpreter, looked increasingly upset as
the two women told their story. She was typical of many

younger generation Serbs who were horrified by the problems faced by the refugees. Older people tended to be far less sympathetic and some were positively hostile. It was only four years since two hundred thousand Serbs had been forced by US-advised Croatian troops to leave the Krajina area of Croatia, where many of their families had lived for hundreds of years. Those Serbs, too, had received scant sympathy from the Belgrade regime and many had been resettled in Kosovo in 1996.

The Serbs fleeing Kosovo after Nato's arrival were even more unwelcome. People feared there were not enough resources to go round in the war-stricken economy. Moreover, many believed the Government's false assurances that all was well in Kosovo; all Serbs who had left should return and those who did not were merely parasites.

I was shaking Branka's hand to say goodbye when the Lonnie Donegan look-alike called my name. 'You remember me? I am Zoran, reception desk manager at the Grand Hotel in Pristina,' he said in near-perfect English. It was rapidly becoming clear that the pavement café outside the Hotel Moskva was a favourite meeting place for the few Kosovo Serbs who had managed to reach Belgrade. Most of those fleeing the violence in the south were being held back at towns near the Kosovo border by a mixture of police road-blocks and the imposition of regulations which prevented them working or living legally in the capital.

'I would not disturb you, but I am desperate,' said Zoran. 'I just wanted to say that if you have any work for a driver and translator, I have a good car.' His tale was typically tragic; he and his wife, together with their five-year-old son, had barely escaped with their lives, he said. They had been told to leave or be killed and had endured a terrifying drive from Pristina to Kursumlija, a small town just outside Kosovo in Serbia proper. Zoran's wife and child were now living more than two hundred miles away with Zoran's father-in-law in the countryside, while he was staying with his brother about twenty-five miles from Belgrade. But his brother had problems of his own because his wages as an electricity worker had been cut, so Zoran did not feel he could stay there for long. Salaries were being slashed across the country in a government attempt to control the war-ravaged economy.

I was pleased that Zoran had spotted me among the crowds of Belgrade, for I needed a driver to take me to the protests that were being held in towns all over Serbia. Zoran told me he had trained as a lawyer and his excellent grasp of English meant I could dispense with Marija's services on out-of-town trips. This arrangement would also enable me to write and file reports to *The Times* while being driven from town to town, something I would not have been able to do had I hired a car and driven myself.

All the opposition protest rallies were being held in the evenings, great for the local population anxious to avoid the heat of the day but less than perfect timing for journalists trying to meet first edition London deadlines. The only way to send these reports was by dictation from my mobile phone, a device which often stubbornly refused to pick up a signal from the protest venues. Zoran could whisk me to the nearest hilltop or wherever the precious signal could be received, while I used this time to write.

First, though, I wanted to investigate the plight of the Serb and other refugees from Kosovo and we decided that Zoran should drive me to Kursumlija and other towns near the Kosovo border where those who had fled were believed to be staying. We spent the first night in Nis, the industrial city in the south which I had last visited on the day of the cluster bombing which had killed more than thirty civilians in early May. The drive then had taken about three hours; now it took twice as long. The Nato bombing had intensified later in May and now all traffic had to divert regularly from the motorway to bypass holed bridges and missile-smashed tarmac. Road travel throughout Serbia had become a gruelling experience, with horse-drawn carts, pantechnicons, little exhaust-puffing Yugos and BMWs all competing for space on the shell-pocked roads. It could take well over an hour to travel ten miles along a near-dirt-track diversion round a bombed stretch of motorway. A series of heavy summer storms intensified the misery by causing breakdowns in ill-maintained cars and, more alarmingly, disguising the many pot-holes. The deluges filled the craters with rainwater and lent road surfaces a false appearance of sublime smoothness.

The suspension on Zoran's 'good car', meanwhile, would have made my childhood go-cart seem Bentleyesque in comparison. The ageing and leaky Golf was as sensitive to slight irregularities, such as a stray piece of gravel, as the princess was to the pea. When it hit one of the ubiquitous pot-holes, it was like hitting the Grand Canyon. The result was that Zoran constantly peered tensely ahead and constantly swerved violently right and left in an attempt to avoid real or imagined craters. He knew his car was hardly fit for these long journeys, and he knew that I knew it; but we never spoke openly about this because he was so obviously deeply embarrassed and probably fearful that I would cease to use it. We had struck a deal whereby I would pay him three times the cost of the black-market petrol needed for a given excursion. It was obviously money he desperately needed. He was far from alone.

The morning after arriving in Nis, I found Zoran and a middle-aged woman sitting at a table in the country club where I had spent the night. The woman was in tears; her name was Svetlana Dimic and she had been a cleaner at the Grand Hotel in Pristina. She had left Pristina at her husband's insistence because the city had become so dangerous for Serbs after the KLA's arrival with Kfor. 'We didn't have enough money for bread and, after Kfor's arrival, our district was cut off. I couldn't go out, let alone go to work. There was violence on every street corner.'

But now she was preparing to take a bus back because she wanted to attend the funeral of a cousin who had been murdered. 'He was slaughtered, the KLA cut his throat,' she whispered between quiet sobs. 'He was kidnapped one day and my husband discovered what had happened to him by chance. His name was on a list of those killed which had been posted on a door in Pristina.' The former hotel cleaner said she would probably have returned soon, anyway, because she felt isolated in Nis. 'I feel like an alien here in Nis,' she said. 'I have been staying with an aunt in a one-bedroom flat. There are six of us and, though I am frightened to go back, I do not want to stay here either.'

We watched as the tired, plump woman climbed aboard the dusty bus that would take her back to Kosovo.

Zoran became quiet and tense on the drive south from Nis to the border town of Kursumlija, which gets its name from the Turkish word for 'bullet'. His wife and son were in a village nearby, he said. He would dearly like to visit them but was in an agony of indecision because he did not want to upset his son. 'If he sees me, he will not want to let me go again so it is probably best that I do not visit him at all,' he said. 'I cannot be with them here because I must look for work and there is nothing here. There are too many refugees, all looking for work which does not exist.'

The Government in Belgrade was doing its best to try to press the Kosovo Serbs to return because their presence in Serbia proper was an embarrassing reminder that Slobodan Milosevic had lost the province so often described as 'the cradle of Serbian civilisation.' If the Serbs could not be persuaded to risk their lives and go back, then life would be made difficult for them. All employers in Serbia proper were forbidden to take on workers from Kosovo and parents were told that their children – who made up about half the refugees – would not be allowed to enrol in schools outside the province. Doctors, nurses and teachers from Kosovo were told they would be sacked if they did not return, and all refugees were told they could not apply for residency permits. This piece of paper was needed to enable people to claim social security payments, and to buy petrol coupons.

We reached Kursumlija in mid-morning, after passing police at a road-block a couple of miles out of town who were trying to prevent refugees travelling north, towards Nis and Belgrade. On the outskirts, soldiers lolled around a stationary tank which carried a sign proclaiming 'It isn't our fault'. It seemed that at least half the people in the town were refugees, many of them camping in a school and sports hall. Others sat nursing children and cups of coffee in dozens of little cafés round the main square. But the bright sunshine could not cast even a false light on the plight of the Kosovo Serbs.

One of them, Zeljko, told me about his brother who was languishing in jail. He and his family had fled Kosovo after their apartment was taken over by gun-wielding ethnic Albanians. When the authorities had insisted that the family return to Kosovo, Zeljko's brother, a teacher, had agreed to go back to investigate, but insisted that his wife and two children stay in Kursumlija until he was sure it was safe for them to go back. A few days later, after barely escaping alive, his brother had fled the province for a second time. When he went to the sports hall to seek out his family and tell them that there was no way they could return to Kosovo, they were nowhere to be found. Another refugee broke the news that his wife and children had boarded a bus to Kosovo the previous day; a local policeman had told them that he had sent a message assuring them all was well in Kosovo and that they should join him in Pristina as soon as possible.

His brother had gone berserk. He went searching for the policeman and, after finding him, began lashing out at him. The policeman hit back, but the distraught teacher then pulled a gun and shot the officer in the stomach. Now the family was trying to raise enough money to pay for a lawyer to defend him when his case came to trial, said Zeljko.

Everywhere Zoran and I went in Kursumlija, stories of human tragedies were waiting to be told. Yet even as I listened, I knew that the reaction of many in the West would be that these were Serbs, and that they must share at least some of the guilt for past atrocities committed against Kosovo's ethnic Albanians.

Unlike the Albanians who had fled Kosovo in March and April and fallen into the arms of a waiting and compassionate international community, these Serbs were now finding little or no protection from the peace-keepers in Kosovo and were being shunned by their own government and people.

'Milosevic and his government lied to us for years, saying they would protect us,' said one of the Kursumlija refugees. 'I am revolted by my government,' said another, 'it is an awful experience to be a foreigner in your own country.' All spoke of beatings, houses and flats burned, neighbours murdered and friends kidnapped in Kosovo. It was plain that they believed it would be suicidally dangerous to return.

At one café, a dark-haired young woman in her twen-ties was nursing a toddler and a three-month-old baby. In Kosovo, she had been a kindergarten teacher and her husband an electrical engineer. Their toddler suffered kidney disease, she told me, and needed dialysis treat-ment but was being prevented from travelling to Belgrade to receive it there. 'At the moment we have enough medicine, but we do not have enough food, just a few cans of beans and some tomatoes. I do not know how I am going to get the dialysis for my daughter.'

Zoran and I eventually moved on from Kursumlija. The former lawyer had made an important decision; he would like to visit his father-in-law's farm because he had managed to make a telephone call and believed his wife would be there. There would be no risk of upsetting his son, because the boy was being cared for in another village that day. We arrived late in the afternoon at the whitewashed farm in the village of Resinac. The main house and the outbuildings seemed deserted, but for a young and yelping puppy tied to a fence and a few chickens scratching around in the yard. Fruit trees surrounded the farm, which was approached via a leafy track well away from other houses. It seemed an oasis of calm and tranquillity in a world gone mad.

Zoran disappeared towards some sheds behind an orchard to try to discover the whereabouts of his family while I played with the sharp-toothed puppy. It was some time before voices announced the arrival of Zoran, his wife and mother and father-in-law. With typical rural hospitality, I was invited inside to drink coffee and home-made apricot brandy.

I was just revelling in the scenes of pastoral charm when I asked about a large black and white photograph on the living room wall. A handsome young man in his prime was flanked by two small boys. The style of clothes and the age of the frame indicated that the picture had been taken long ago, in happier times. The seemingly endless cycle of Balkan violence was about to reassert its presence on that sunny afternoon.

Zoran's father-in-law was one of the small boys in the photograph, the other being his twin brother, and they were standing at the feet of their father, a member of the Partisans. Days after the picture was taken in 1941, German Nazis had descended on the village, killed his father, mother and twin brother and burned down their home. Zoran's father-in-law survived only because he was playing in the hills with friends. He had returned, aged five, to find a scene of slaughter and devastation. Now, nearly sixty years later, he was giving shelter to another five-year-old – his grandson – who had been hounded out of his home.

Strictly speaking, those who fled Kosovo were not refugees but internally displaced, although to all intents and purposes they had fled to another country. Their numbers steadily increased throughout the summer until, by September, about two hundred thousand were estimated to have left Kosovo, according to the UN High Commissioner for Refugees – well over ninety per cent of the non-ethnic Albanian population.

Serbia has a population of eleven million and could not easily absorb this number; soon there were signs of the refugees in most towns. They were sleeping in parks in Belgrade and Nis, some camped out in lorries and tractors, about two hundred were put up at a rundown boarding house on Mount Avala just outside Belgrade.

In August, the respected American group, Human Rights Watch, said: 'Already swamped with hundreds of thousands of refugees from Croatia and Bosnia, and in the midst of an economic crisis and the aftermath of the Nato bombing campaign, the Yugoslav Government is ill-equipped to feed, clothe and house an additional group of displaced persons.

'There are reports that displaced Serbs from Kosovo have been prevented from entering the city of Belgrade and some Kosovo Serbs have been returned to Kosovo by the Serbian authorities. The presence of Kosovo Serbs, many of whom feel betrayed by the Serbian Government, would also serve as a potent symbol of the Government's failure in Kosovo.'

The organisation's assessment was published in a report which also accused the KLA of systematically trying to clear Serbs and Roma gypsies from Kosovo, and blamed the international community for failing to prevent atrocities.

While criticising the Yugoslav Army and Serbian police for 'a decade of repression which culminated in a three-month killing spree … and the forced expulsion and displacement of more than half the ethnic Albanian population,' the main thrust of the report was on 'the wave of arson and looting of Serb and Roma homes throughout Kosovo' which followed Kfor's arrival. 'Most seriously, there has been a spate of abductions and murders of Serbs since mid-June, including the massacre of fourteen Serb farmers on July 23,' the organisation said in the report, *Abuses Against Serbs and Roma in the New Kosovo*. The farmers were shot dead as they harvested hay near the village of Gracko in central Kosovo. The killings occurred after the villagers asked Kfor to protect them from the KLA.

'The response of Kfor and the UN Mission in Kosovo to abuses against minority populations has been belated and uneven … there is little evidence of a firm commitment to a new and tolerant Kosovo in which Serb and Roma minority populations can live without discrimination,' Human Rights Watch said.

The organisation went on to say that those most at risk of killings and beatings from the returned Albanians were believed to be innocent. 'While some of those killed may have been implicated in abuses against ethnic Albanians during the armed conflict, many of the Serb victims were innocent civilians. Indeed, in many areas of Kosovo practically all military-age men have already fled. Those left behind are the oldest and most vulnerable members of the Serb community,' Human Rights Watch concluded.

In its report, the group catalogued numerous murders of ethnic Serbs in the days and weeks following Nato's arrival in Kosovo. The victims included Marica Stamenkovic, seventy-seven, and her male neighbour, Panta Filipovic, sixty-three, who had lived in the same Prizren street for decades. Their throats were cut while their spouses were out shopping on 21 June. 'Within days of Kfor's entry into Kosovo, uniformed KLA members began appearing at Serb houses demanding money and arms,' Human Rights Watch said.

Marica Stamenkovic's husband, Trifun, eighty-five, told the rights organisation that he could not find his wife when he returned from the market and his house had been broken into. 'I saw a German patrol, I told them my wife was missing, that she wasn't in the house. When I entered the house with them, I saw only my wife's knees.

Her knees were bloody. I didn't see the rest of her body; the Germans took me outside. They saw her dead; they didn't let me inside to see her.'

Crucially, Human Rights Watch also pointed out that the Serb authorities were not the only ones to have committed atrocities in Kosovo in the unrest which led to Nato's bombing campaign. 'It is important to note that the KLA has been linked to earlier abuses against Serbs, Roma and Kosovar Albanians during 1998 and during the first three months of 1999. Specifically, reports by the Humanitarian Law Centre, The International Committee of the Red Cross and Human Rights Watch's own research indicate that dozens of Serbs and a smaller number of Roma and Albanians were detained by the KLA between mid-1998 and March, 1999. At least one hundred and thirty Serbs went missing during this time and are presumed dead.'

The misery of what it means to be a refugee was fully brought home to me several weeks after my visit to the Kosovo border region. It was early September and Zoran telephoned to invite me to the flat where he was then living. He had been able to bring his wife and son to Belgrade and, at first, I thought it sounded as if life was looking up for them. Home-made biscuits were carefully laid out on a table in the basement flat and I was given beer and coffee as Zoran hesitantly asked whether I would like to see the only video he had managed to salvage from Pristina in his haste to leave.

The amateur film showed laughing and smiling men and women in their finest clothes and wearing flowers in their hair and lapels. They were clamouring around a happy Zoran on his wedding day in Pristina. 'It is our anniversary tomorrow,' said Zoran as he watched with a sad nostalgia that was almost palpable. 'Look, here are all our friends and that was our apartment. It was such a happy day.' Zoran's wife seemed to ignore the video images as they progressed from the Pristina apartment to the church and then on to the Grand Hotel for the reception. Whether she did not want to watch because the pain of remembrance would be too great, or because she was immune after viewing it so many times was impossible to say.

Zoran was transfixed by the images even though he had obviously watched the video countless times; it was as if he could not or did not want to believe what had happened to him, his family, his friends and homeland. 'All the people in this film are now refugees,' he said. 'But thank God they are all alive.' The former lawyer's situation was still perilous because he would soon have to look for somewhere else to live; the owner was to let the flat to someone else for a more realistic rent. The basement apartment was damp and the only sign that a child lived there was a pedal-car. It was the sort of flat that an impoverished British student might have rented in the early Seventies, with scraps of carpet, mismatched curtains and minimal kitchen equipment.

Zoran's son was becoming withdrawn because he had no other children to play with. However, the flat did provide a roof over the family's heads and it had a wood-burning stove which Zoran looked at wistfully: 'This would have been very useful in the winter because, wherever we end up, I am sure there will be electricity cuts.' Zoran was clinging to the hope that he would be able to sell his cherished former home in Pristina. The chances would be slim, however, since a family of strangers, ethnic Albanians, had taken it over. Zoran's neighbour in the Kosovo capital, an ethnic Albanian whom he counted among his friends, had vainly tried to protect the apartment from the invaders.

Hostile neighbours in Belgrade were meanwhile adding to Zoran's problems. Rusty needles and biscuits with human hair baked into them had been placed on his car a few days earlier. 'People here don't like people from Kosovo,' he said. 'These witchcraft symbols are part of old Serbian superstitions and are meant to wish us harm. It is really horrible.'

Zoran offered to drive me home that evening but I declined, knowing he could ill afford the black market petrol needed to drive even a couple of miles. As I left, Zoran's son was gazing mutely from behind his mother's skirt. He was unnaturally quiet for a five-year-old and I wondered about the effects on all the children who had faced the aggression of Nato's bombardment followed by violent expulsion from their homes. 'When he asks where his toys are, we try to change the subject,' said Zoran. 'I am afraid we are spoiling him a bit now, but what else can you do?'

# Chapter Fifteen

# Resign: June–September 1999

A sign by one of the bridges linking Old and New Belgrade proudly announces the presence of a restaurant called The Argument. It seemed to symbolise all that was happening in Yugoslavia as the long, hot summer progressed, although rational dialogue was almost absent among the myriad pro- and anti-government groups squabbling among themselves. Two months after the end of the Nato bombing campaign, Yugoslavia felt politically and economically as if it were on the edge of a precipice, yet Slobodan Milosevic was still at the helm and there were few signs of revolutionary fervour among ordinary people.

They were mainly just trying to survive. Schoolteachers in Belgrade were being forced to rummage through dust-bins, sell fruit on market stalls or take cleaning jobs in their spare time, because they could not survive on their state salaries. Their pay had fallen by two-thirds in ten years, from an average of DM300 (£100) a month to DM100 (£33). To make matters worse, by August they were owed almost three months' back pay. 'It will be a miracle if I survive the winter,' said Slobodanka Bozovic, a Belgrade biology teacher. 'I am really beginning to panic.'

A strike in one hundred of Serbia's two thousand primary and secondary schools was called when the new school year began on 1 September, but it collapsed within a week because of government threats to dismiss head-teachers in schools taking industrial action. Some teachers and equally cash-strapped university professors took jobs as bus and tram drivers in Belgrade, work which paid about the same as an average teacher. 'A favourite pastime is to spot the philosophy professors driving trams, because of their cultured-looking faces,' a Belgrade hairdresser said.

Concern about declining pay, unemployment and fuel shortages tightened their grip as the days shortened and the first leaves on the trees began to curl and turn brown. Hundreds of thousands of workers were still laid off because factories bombed by Nato had not been repaired or rebuilt and the knock-on effect on other industries meant that many were on part-time wages. The International Committee of the Red Cross and the Yugoslav Red Cross announced an increase in the number of soup kitchens it ran; 100,000 free meals were distributed every day in August, compared with 30,000 before the air strikes. Mothers with young children sometimes came to blows as they fought for a dwindling supply of milk at market-places each morning, and a consumer basket of the sixty-five most important foods for a family of four cost DM290 (£99) in August, 6.1 per cent more than in July, according to the Federal Bureau of Statistics. The price of tomatoes was 54.8 per cent higher, fresh cucumbers rose by 49.3 per cent, green beans 42.6 per cent, eggs 32.1 per cent and cabbage 26.2 per cent. The price of chicken was 27.3 per cent higher, and bread rose by 26.5 per cent. On one weekend alone, in late September, some food prices doubled and the black market rate for the Deutschmark – which had been the same all year – rose from ten to thirteen dinars. However, despite all the problems, there were still some wealthy Serbs in Belgrade. While some teachers were reduced to scavenging for food or scrap to sell, a plush new private school opened at the beginning of the new school year. The Milutin Milankovic academy charged parents DM7,000 (£2,330) a year to send their children there, 'to be paid in cash and in advance'. Teachers at the school earned DM1,000 (£330) a month – ten times more than their state-employed colleagues.

The West repeatedly said that Serbs should somehow remove Milosevic from power before any money for reconstruction would be forthcoming. However, the mood seemed to be one of resigned misery rather than revolutionary fervour, despite opposition attempts to marshal a concerted attempt to unseat the Yugoslav leader. Demonstrations had been organised by the two main opposition parties from the end of June. But far more startling were two protest movements started by ordinary Serbs with no political backgrounds – one in the southern town of Leskovac, the other in Valjevo in central Serbia.

The first involved what must have been one of the most heart-stopping moments ever for Serbia's party appa-ratchiks. At 8.45 on the evening of Thursday, 1 July, half-way through the broadcast of a basketball match, the unthinkable happened. A fresh-faced young man, who usually prepared the weather forecasts, appeared unex-pectedly on screen – and called on his fellow townspeople to rise up against the regime. It would have been a brave act in any part of the world, but the courage required by Ivan Novkovic to stand in lone defiance against the regime was awesome. He knew he would be arrested; he also knew he risked being beaten up and that he risked years in jail.

This was Serbia less than three weeks after Nato troops had entered Kosovo, when disgruntled troops were returning from the front and tentative protests were springing up in towns across the country. However, miser-able as they were, most people seemed to be waiting for someone else to take the lead; no one knew how the police would react to protests – police with guns who formed a force even more fiercely loyal to Milosevic than the army.

Inside the state television studio in Leskovac, horri-fied colleagues begged Novkovic to stop the videotape in which he called on Milosevic to resign, fearful that they would be implicated in this brazen act of rebellion. The young man ignored their entreaties, continued through the rest of his broadcast, stood up, blew kisses to his workmates, and calmly walked downstairs and away from the studio. In the broadcast, the quietly-spoken rebel appealed to the people of Leskovac to gather for a protest meeting on the following Monday.

Four days later, answering Novkovic's call to take to the streets, around 25,000 people came together for one of the biggest and most spontaneous protests so far. Novkovic, the hero of the hour, was not present. The day after his broadcast he was sentenced to thirty days in jail as the penalty for his defiance.

In mid-August, a week after his release, I visited the meteorologist in his home town. The thirty-four-year-old was staying in a friend's apartment and he explained why and how he planned five minutes which shook the Balkan world.

He and his wife had a six-year-old daughter, Ivana, and the family said they could no longer afford the rent on their old apartment. By now, Novkovic had been suspended from the Leskovac television station and it seemed unlikely he would ever return to his old job: he wore a badge which proclaimed: 'Turn off state television – turn on your brains'. He also had further charges hanging over his head which could lead to years in jail.

A quirk of fate had given Novkovic an uncanny resemblance both physically and in the timbre of his voice to the young Slobodan Milosevic. He had joined the military after leaving school in 1983 and trained as a meteorologist in the Yugoslav Air Force. In 1993 he left the forces and, in 1994, became a television technician and weather forecaster after a year of taking odd jobs while he decided what to do next with his life. His parents had retired after a lifetime as factory workers and his wife was a biochemist at a pharmaceutical factory in Leskovac.

'Everyone has a childhood dream,' he said as we sat drinking coffee and beer in his friend's flat, 'but people keep stealing our dreams.' Novkovic was clearly an avid reader and chose his words carefully, like a man who spent much time with his own thoughts. For a would-be revolutionary, he had drawn inspiration from particularly banal sources. 'What always excited me were books about the world of business, especially management practices in Europe, Japan and America,' he said. 'Just before the Kosovo war, I read the autobiography of Lee Iacocca [former Ford and Chrysler chief in America]) – I grew up when I read that book.' He was particularly inspired by a passage which claims that freedom is possible for anyone who wants it badly enough.

Between fifteen and twenty thousand men from Leskovac had been called up and marched off to fight in Kosovo and the town was 'almost deserted' during the war, Novkovic said. There was no particular moment or event which prompted his action; for months he had felt a growing need to make a stand against the regime. The toll in injuries, deaths and lost production for local businesses caused by the Kosovo conflict was enormous, he said, and for this he blamed Zivojin Stefanovic, the ruling Socialist Party chief in the Leskovac area. Novkovic had been spared military service because he was needed by the television station, but the Nato bombing campaign had been grim for everyone in Yugoslavia. He and his family spent the first few days of the bombing in a cellar beneath their building but, in common with many in Serbia, they eventually decided to risk staying above ground. 'My work in the Air Force meant that I was usually accurate in predicting what Nato aircraft would do,' he said. In the event, Leskovac escaped relatively unscathed from Nato attacks. Some of Novkovic's friends from the town were killed or injured while fighting in Kosovo, but he was reluctant to be drawn on this subject.

Drinking treacle-thick black coffee in his friend's neat apartment in an ugly, wasp-infested building, he explained how he overcame his fear of taking on the regime single-handed. 'Most of my colleagues lived from day to day, then all of a sudden ideas started flowing in my head,' he said. 'I started searching for my weak points and I realised they were fear and indecisiveness about my desire for freedom. I also learned to listen and to realise how important that is. Once I had conquered the fear, I said that enough is enough.'

Ivan had the idea of making a film of himself calling for the resignation of Stefanovic and Milosevic at the beginning of the Nato campaign. He seized his chance when he realised that a new sound technician, only recently returned from the front in Kosovo, might not be able to stop him. The new man's inexperience would make it easier for Novkovic to substitute videotapes at the crucial moment. Once he had decided to act, 'fear disappeared' and he moved fast. 'I was at peace with myself. It is quite incredible that I felt no fear.' On Monday, 28 June, he travelled to the nearby city of Nis and revealed his plan to the Mayor, Zoran Zivkovic, a member of the opposition Democratic Party. Novkovic had briefly met the Mayor a couple of years before, but they barely knew one another and the rebel was not sure whether he would be able to see the city's leading official. 'I wanted some reassurance, some advice from someone distant from the regime. He said it was my decision and asked whether I was fully aware of the consequences, pointing out that everything has its price.'

Travelling back to Leskovac, he decided to act almost immediately. Rising in the middle of the night, he tried not to wake his wife and daughter as he set off to the studios. 'Once I had come to my decision, everything was very easy,' he said. 'I went to the studios at 3 a.m. on Thursday morning. There was no night watchman and I had the keys and the security code to get in. I was totally alone.'

He set up a camera, sat in front of it and made a one-minute speech to see whether it was recording him. 'I replayed that and thought, "That's it!" I had my speech prepared calling for the resignation of Stefanovic and a change of government, but I am not a professional speaker and it took me five minutes to read it instead of three so I had to edit it down. Then I thought about what my bosses might do to stop me. I knew they would be shocked but I thought they might disconnect the current. In the end, they just didn't have time to react.'

After making his video, Novkovic returned home and told his wife what he was planning to do, but not when. 'I had wanted to do it during the war but my wife was crying and afraid at that time. By the time I went ahead with my plan, she fully realised she could not stop me. I am very proud of her, she has been a stabilising force for my emotions and in the end everything was very clear in our minds, clean and honest.'

That evening, while his wife and daughter sat at home watching the basketball match on television, the meteorologist set to work switching the videotapes during the half-time break. 'I could only see the reaction of some of my colleagues and they begged me to interrupt the tape. Then the station director phoned in, very angry. I said, "Don't worry, I will take full responsibility."

'All the time there was this incredible feeling. Everyone was in a state of shock. After I walked out into the street, the church bells were ringing and I felt at peace.'

The following morning, the police arrived at his home and he was arrested. 'I had no intention of hiding. The police were very correct and I told them how strongly I felt.' Novkovic said he was never ill-treated by the police or when in jail, but he was angry because 'they did not tell me my rights, that I had a right to a lawyer'. He was not allowed to see his wife for the first two weeks of his thirty-day sentence, which was pronounced by a woman judge within hours of his arrest. 'Conditions in prison were not of the best but I was always treated correctly and life in jail did not really touch me. I expected to be beaten up but I am happy to say that this didn't happen.'

After the rally on 1 July, some of the crowd went to Stefanovic's home and all but demolished it, an act condemned by Novkovic and his wife. 'I would like to come face to face with Stefanovic,' he said. 'I would like to get to know him because the fact is that he doesn't understand people. I have no hatred, I feel great pity for people in power. There is no secret. The answer to all our problems is simple. It is not just a matter of knowing what to do – but of actually doing it.' And what was his big ambition now, I asked. 'To open an independent TV station,' he replied.

A week after the people of Leskovac took to the streets, an artist in the central Serbian town of Valjevo also put his head above the parapet and led several thousand protesters in a wave of spontaneous, apolitical gatherings. Valjevo is noted for being the birthplace of a large number of soldiers who were decorated for bravery during the Great War, and for having suffered a catastrophic typhoid epidemic in the nineteenth century. In July it became synonymous with demonstrations called by Bogoljub Arsenijevic. Known by the nickname, Maki, this small, thin artist with flowing hair and beard called on people to gather in the town's main square on 12 July and to then move on and storm the nearby town hall. It looked like being a dangerous moment; it was hard to believe that the police would merely stand by if a government building were threatened.

Zoran drove me to Valjevo in the bone-jolting Golf and we arrived in the afternoon, several hours before the protest was due to get under way. A mile or so from Valjevo, police had set up road-blocks and were checking vehicles heading into the town. Journalists from Reuters news agency and CNN who arrived later in the day were briefly arrested and had their equipment seized; it may be that Zoran and I were barely given a second glance because the geriatric Golf seemed unlikely transport for a Western journalist.

We parked the car well away from the main square and the town hall for fear of unrest there later in the day. As Zoran and I walked around the town centre, we noticed large numbers of big, fit-looking young men dressed in black with shaven heads, sitting at various pavement cafés within sight of the town hall. 'They are undercover police,' Zoran murmured close to my ear. 'Try not to speak English.' Seconds later, my mobile phone rang: it was Denis Taylor from the Foreign Desk at *The Times*. I scuttled across the street and into a squat-style open-drain lavatory in a café down a side-street, where I tried to explain to London my reluctance to speak above a stage whisper.

About an hour before the protest meeting was due to start, the townsfolk began to gather. Posters advertising the event had been plastered all over Valjevo and most journalists in Belgrade had been alerted. Soon the square near the town hall was filling up with grandmothers pushing babies in prams, young mothers with toddlers, fathers carrying youngsters on their shoulders, as well as the more usual banner-carrying men in their prime.

I felt the urge to warn those who seemed to be treating the event as a family outing to stay well back from what might turn into a violent confrontation between the protesters and police. The scene was similar to protests I had seen in other towns in Serbia in the past two weeks, where a hardcore of banner-waving and whistle-blowing demonstrators cheered the speakers and jeered the names of Milosevic and his ministers, while the vast majority of the crowd seemed to be there out of a sense of curiosity. This did not seem to be the stuff of which revolutions were made and it may be the reason the police seemed to be under orders to tread softly.

Minutes before Maki stood up to address the crowd of about five thousand, Jacky Rowland arrived with a BBC camera crew, saying she had managed to get past the police road-block by smiling sweetly; they seemed to be the only other Western journalists there.

'I am not a violent man,' Maki proclaimed, 'in fact I have been in prison for refusing to undertake my National Service. But I am asking people now to raise their hands if they are willing to come with me now and take over the town hall.' About five hundred volunteered. Zoran, who had moved closer to the loudspeakers, came rushing back to me and suggested that we move quickly down the street. 'People might begin to stampede,' he said, nervously glancing around at the crowd.

Within seconds of reaching the next street corner, waves of jeering voices were drowned by the sound of breaking glass, followed by pistol shots. Police cars and vans suddenly appeared from every direction, screeching to a halt along the stretch of road outside the town hall. Dozens of blue-uniformed officers leapt out, pulling truncheons and pistols from their belts as they headed for the fray. Night was falling and it was hard to distinguish police from demonstrators as the pandemonium of breaking glass, splintering wood and occasional gunshots pierced the still, summer evening. At one point a police car came speeding away from the mêlée, straight past Zoran and me. Inside, we could see a policeman in the passenger seat, bent forwards and clutching a stomach-wound. The protesters continued kicking and battering at the door and windows of the town hall until they forced their way into the reception area.

At this point, the demonstration began to descend into the realms of farce, for no one had any idea what to do next. Bemused, the score or so who ventured into the breached building merely upturned a few chairs and scattered papers on the floor. They then shrugged – and left. The only casualties appeared to be a small number of police who had put themselves in the way of kicking feet and lashing out fists. None of the protesters was seriously hurt and, miraculously, none had been shot. The police seemed to be using a minimum of force and I became convinced that they were under orders from on high to use restraint.

Nonetheless, Maki was not to escape with impunity. The next day, he fled to Bosnia from where he telephoned me to say the police had visited his flat and threatened him and his family. He returned a couple of weeks later and organised a further round of protest gatherings in Valjevo. In August, however, he was arrested and badly beaten up. Supporters said his jaw was broken.

Yet, even as Novkovic and Arsenijevic were risking the wrath of the Milosevic regime, the flames of protest which they had hoped to fan seemed to be dying. Novkovic had managed to spur a vast number of Leskovac's 170,000 people into action in early July. But by mid-August, the main opposition parties in Belgrade had become so squabblesome that long-held plans for a massive rally in Belgrade on 19 August had fallen into disarray. Forty-eight hours before what was supposed to be Belgrade's ground-breaking demonstration, Vuk Draskovic, leader of the Serbian Renewal Movement, announced that he would not even speak at the gathering. Those who still planned to take part, including the other main opposition leader, Zoran Djindjic, were still arguing about who would address the crowd and in what order.

By now, the numbers turning up at the regular anti-government protests sparked by Ivan Novkovic in Leskovac had dwindled to about three hundred. The decline set in as soon as the main opposition parties tried to jump on Novkovic's bandwagon and take over the organisation of protest rallies there.

People throughout Serbia were miserable about the outcome of the Kosovo conflict and fearful of facing the coming winter with declining pay and increasing prices. Hundreds of thousands of people were signing petitions in towns and cities across the country calling for Milosevic's resignation. However, these were still in a minority; the majority seemed to be watching and waiting to see if an opposition figure would emerge who could

222 One Woman's War

unite the entire country. Novkovic had made it plain that he wanted to motivate people, but that he did not harbour political ambitions of his own. Many of the farmers and villagers who underpinned Milosevic's power base were also wary of change. 'If there was an election tomorrow, people in the countryside round here would almost certainly vote for Milosevic,' said Novkovic's wife.

Many of those who did want a change, meanwhile, despaired as they saw the rift between the two main opposition leaders widen. Draskovic, of the Serbian Renewal Movement, and Djindjic, leader of the Democratic Party, had been allies in 1996. They had led massive street demonstrations in protest at the annulment of local elections which had resulted in victory for the opposition. The two men and their *Zajedno* – or Together – movement had eventually forced the Government to recognise the results.

It is not clear how and why they argued and neither has given a coherent reason for the rift. The Kosovo conflict only deepened their enmity. Djindjic left Belgrade for Montenegro half-way through the Nato bombing campaign. From there he made many trips abroad to hold meetings with Western politicians across Europe. He said he felt he was better able to serve his country in this way, putting across his views to leaders in the West. Back in Belgrade, however, the Milosevic Government and Draskovic's Serbian Renewal Movement accused Djindjic of cowardice, a view readily accepted by those who had had no choice but to live through the bombardment.

The Democratic Party, meanwhile, accused Draskovic of consorting with the regime because he had accepted the post of Deputy Yugoslav Prime Minister in February. Draskovic said this was because he felt he could be most useful suing for peace in that position in the run-up to the bombing campaign. He was sacked in April, saying he had fallen foul of Milosevic for proposing some form of international presence in Kosovo.

Draskovic and Djindjic had little in common. The

Serbian Renewal Movement leader traditionally appealed to the masses and for years cultivated a Rasputin-like image, with flowing hair and beard. Although his locks were shorn a couple of years ago, Draskovic still chose words which appealed to Serbian gut reactions. He generally advocated change through constitutional means but this was interpreted by his opponents as sitting on the fence and being too close to the Milosevic regime.

Djindjic, on the other hand, was favoured by many entrepreneurs and some sections of the intelligentsia in Belgrade. Clean-shaven and with a penchant for suits and designer-label casual clothes, he looked the essence of a Western politician. The Democratic Party leader was the leading light of the umbrella Alliance for Change opposition movement which began holding a series of protest rallies across Serbia in July. The Alliance also encompassed a myriad smaller interest groups, such as farmers from Vojvodina and tiny political parties.

After Djindjic decamped to Montenegro during the Nato air strikes, the Milosevic regime accused him of treason and avoiding military conscription. As accusations of cowardice began to mount up in the weeks following the war, the Democratic Party knew he had to risk arrest and return to Belgrade, or abandon any hopes of a political career in Serbia. He flew into Belgrade airport on 4 July, to be met by a small but rapt crowd of whistle-blowing supporters and an equal number of the international press. Within days, he announced a series of anti-government rallies to be held in provincial towns across the country. These would be followed by the large gathering in Belgrade in August. Draskovic, however, thought the Serbian people would need longer to gather their resources for a mass demonstration of discontent and that August was too early.

By the end of July, Draskovic and Djindjic spent as much time attacking one another as they did condemning the Milosevic regime and ordinary Serbs despaired of

seeing a united opposition. Once, after yet more wran-
gling over the speaking order at the planned Belgrade
rally, a postgraduate student sighed and said to me: 'Do
they think it is Woodstock?' The young man's scepticism
proved to be well-founded; at least at Woodstock the
organisers knew which tunes they were supposed to be
playing. Those orchestrating Belgrade's anti-government
rally had not even decided on a coherent programme.

Paranoia was running high in the capital as the day of
the Belgrade protest dawned. Stories abounded of buses
full of protesters being turned back by police as they
tried to make their way from towns across the country.
Many people said they expected the Government to
foment trouble. The regime warned people to stay away
'for their own safety', after claiming to have arrested a
Montenegrin who had been plotting to cause an explosion
at the gathering.

The protest was held outside the Federal Parliament
building in the heart of the city and by early evening, well
over 150,000 people had come together to form a swirling
mass of humanity. Banners, hats and badges proclaimed
the presence of as many Draskovic supporters as there
were followers of Djindjic, even though the Serbian
Renewal Movement leader had vowed not to take part.
Speaker after speaker from the Alliance for Change rose
to denounce Milosevic and demand his resignation.
However, whereas some declared that another huge rally
would be held ten days later at the end of August, others
announced that the next big gathering in the capital
would take place in late September. Some in the crowd,
already confused by these conflicting messages, then
turned and began to push in panic to escape from the
centre of the mass – where someone had exploded
teargas canisters. Soon thereafter, the pent-up hopes of
nearly two hundred thousand people yearning for a
united opposition to lead them into a post-Milosevic
dawn were to be dashed. Draskovic, despite his earlier
refusal to participate, suddenly appeared from nowhere,

leapt onto the rostrum and seized the microphone. It seemed as if he had been surprised by the sheer numbers who had turned out and could not resist the lure of a ready-made audience. He badly misjudged the moment. Instead of receiving the rapt applause he clearly anticipated, he was greeted by a wave of hostility.

I was with Marija, my interpreter, and her fiancé, Sasa, and we had moved to the back of the gathering after getting a whiff of teargas. We could see Draskovic gesticulating as he paced across the speakers' dais with the microphone at his mouth, but all we could hear was a wall of noise as whistles, jeers and boos drowned out his words. The débâcle continued for about twenty minutes until the Serbian Renewal Movement leader stamped off stage.

Some in the crowd lurched forward to try to attack Draskovic, but he was protected by his bodyguards. Relations between the Serbian Renewal Movement and the Democratic Party not surprisingly then deteriorated from bad to worse. The following day, the thwarted opposition leader accused his old arch-rival, Djindjic, of instructing his supporters to jeer 'red bandits' and 'traitor' at him during the rally. Draskovic announced that he was breaking all contacts with the Democratic Party and that the idea of a unified opposition was dead.

'We're not seeking cooperation with Draskovic, but with all those who want Slobodan Milosevic to step down,' said Djindjic. 'Citizens were probably jeering out of anger with Draskovic, who had come to speak at an anti-Milosevic rally without demanding his resignation,' he added. The slanging match did little to hearten many who had left the Belgrade rally in misery, convinced that the opposition had barely begun to prise Milosevic's fingers from the reins of power.

Even if the Belgrade rally had not degenerated into a fiasco, it was clear that the vast majority of those who attended were from the Belgrade intelligentsia. There was no sign of support among the crowd of farmers,

workers, the poor, or refugees from Kosovo – the ordinary
people who would need to rise up if a full-blown popular
insurrection were to take place.

Djindjic had made the mistake of issuing a threat he
could not carry out. He told the crowd that Serbs from
Kosovo were to lead a march on Milosevic's residence in
the Belgrade suburb of Dedinje. None of the Kosovo
refugees I knew had been told of this and when I asked
Zoran whether he or anyone he knew would be prepared
to do so, he just looked at me as if I were mad. 'Not a
chance,' he said.

# Chapter Sixteen

# Living Proof: August 1999

It was my first taste of teargas – literally. A bitter, acidic sensation which hit my tongue and throat before it stung my eyes and which reminded me of the mixture my mother painted on my fingernails to stop me biting them when I was five years old. I was crammed, along with eighty thousand others, in the Red Star Belgrade football ground, watching a tense night-time match between arch-rivals Croatia and Yugoslavia – the first clash of these titans since before the break-up of Yugoslavia.

The balmy August night air was already electric with political as well as sporting tension when the teargas was thrown onto the stadium roof just above us. I was with Toma, the presenter of Serbia's equivalent of *Top of the Pops*, and Nada, the daughter of close friends of Dessa Trevisan. 'Pshgh … the bastards. Go! Go!' said Toma as he rose to his feet spluttering and blinking back stinging tears.

Still edgy after the bombing in Kosovo, I had been uneasy about the prospect of being trapped in the middle of a huge crowd if trouble broke out. Many in the packed terraces were expected to chant anti-government slogans at some point during the match and there was a heavy police presence in and around the massive ground. Furthermore, senior members of the ruling Socialist Party were ensconced in a private box just behind where we were sitting. Most sat stern-faced; only one showed any expression and that was Zeljko Raznatovic, the former paramilitary leader and indicted war criminal better known as Arkan. He had entered the

large box just before the kick-off, accompanied by the
traditional Serbian brass band he had brought with him.
After pausing to acknowledge the stares of the crowd, he
had dug in his pockets and thrown handfuls of paper
money into the midst of the throng. The Government,
worried that disgruntled fans would use the televised
match to chant their 'Slobo go' and 'Red bandits'
slogans, had reputedly bought up twenty thousand
tickets and filled those seats with their supporters.

It was 17 August, two days before the planned anti-
government rally in Belgrade. Only a small handful of
Croatian fans were brave enough to venture into Red
Star Belgrade's ground, and they sat forlornly in a sliver
of seats set aside for them on the far side. When the
Croatian team came out onto the pitch, an animal-like
ululation swelled in the throats of tens of thousands of
Serbs. 'U-U-Ustashe', they chanted, in taunting reference
to the Croatian fascists, the Ustashe, of the Second World
War. It sounded like a Zulu war cry.

The crucial European Championship match was originally scheduled for the week that Nato began its
bombing campaign in March and tension over the contest
had been building ever since. At that time, Yugoslav graffiti said of Croatia's chances: 'Only Nato can save you';
now the slogan had changed to: 'Nato cannot help you
now'. Suddenly, just after half-time, the entire ground was
galvanised with shock when someone turned the lights
out. A great, unified wail of protest rose from the fans
who immediately began chanting the very slogans the
Government had hoped to prevent; the po-faced party
men in the box above us stormed from their seats and left
the ground.

After about half an hour of noise, darkness and confu-
sion, lights suddenly flooded the stadium once more and
the game recommenced. It was later reported that the
Yugoslav Football Federation had plunged the ground
into blackness in protest at the Government's decision to
buy up tickets. As the match got underway again, I could

sense Toma on the brink of despair every time the ball came under Croat control. Time and again, he leapt to his feet, hands clenched and eyes bulging with fury. Now, suddenly his eyes were weeping as the teargas washed over us.

I grabbed Nada by the wrist and squeezed past her father, a keen football fan who had arranged the tickets for us, and yanked her up the steps towards the nearest exit, along with hundreds of other spluttering men and women. I was fearful of a stampede, but I need not have worried – the vast majority stayed where they were. 'Teargas is an everyday occurrence at these matches,' Toma said later when we were reunited at a café down the road. The score for the epic match was a nil-nil draw. Yet another tension-packed moment had passed both on and off the field. This was ordinary life in Serbia in late summer, 1999.

In August, I moved out of the Hyatt and into a flat on the top floor of an ugly building near the town centre, at the unfashionable end of 29 November Street. It was an area surrounded by factory chimneys, grim, fly-blown shops and dustbins overflowing with rotting garbage. The flat itself was pleasant enough though, light and airy, and blissfully quiet perched high away from the street noises below, with parquet floors, satellite television, a functioning kitchen and two bedrooms. It contained one of the most comprehensive music collections I had ever seen; a platinum Dire Straits disc hung on the wall near a modern hi-fi system. It was also clean, largely thanks to Danka, a middle-aged gypsy lady with whom I could communicate only in sign language and smiles.

The wiring in the flat would not have passed a safety inspection in Britain, with telephone sockets hanging by threads from the walls, and the green plastic lavatory was as temperamental as a vintage motor car. You had to climb on the seat and jiggle the ball-cock into precisely the right position if you wanted to coax water into the

cistern. Two lifts served the large, twelve-storey block, the
largest being prone to stop half-way between floors for
days on end. I learnt early on to have my lighter handy, as
the bulbs in the lifts were more for show than for illumi-
nation.

The apartment belonged to Srdjan Stojanovic, a
former rock concert promoter and journalist I had met
on the minibus travelling from Budapest to Belgrade in
late June. Srdjan was taking a course at the London
School of Economics and would not need his apartment
for several months. It was far cheaper than the Hyatt and,
more importantly, living there made me feel I was nearer
to the lives of ordinary people.

Belgrade was a curious mixture of outdated socialism
and state-of-the-art post-modernism. It was possible to
eat and drink at fine restaurants and theme bars until the
early hours, but try to catch a bus in the middle of the day
and the chances were, it had broken down or run out of
fuel. You could buy Italian designer shoes, handbags and
suits for less than half the amount they would cost in
London, but it could take days to get a mobile phone
connected. Fresh fruit and vegetables were in plentiful
supply, for those in work who could afford them, but
foreign books and newspapers were impossible to find.
Theatres and cinemas were usually full. Taxis, even after
a midsummer fare rise of sixty per cent, were fantastically
cheap; you could travel from one side of Belgrade to the
other for the equivalent of three pounds sterling.
However, I lost count of the times that the driver did not
know his way round town and on several occasions the
ancient Yugos which made up the heart of the fleet gave
up the struggle, juddered to a halt and refused to go any
further, breaking down in the middle of a four-lane inner-
city street.

Bombed-out buildings, meanwhile, stood as silent
monuments to the Nato campaign. No one made any
attempt to begin repairs. Curtains and blinds still hung
from the shattered windows and perilous lumps of

mortar and wooden beams teetered from upper floors as if the blast had happened minutes, rather than months, before.

Most Serbs were unswervingly friendly, even to those of us from countries whose governments had launched the missiles at the heart of the capital. At first, I had been wary when taxi drivers asked where I came from, followed by the inevitable 'Novinar?' – 'Journalist?' I need not have worried; I was almost invariably treated with a courtesy and politeness that would put London cabbies to shame. No one ever tried to cheat me and most just wanted to know if I needed a driver, as they were desperately short of cash.

It was Srdjan who had introduced me to Toma and his girlfriend, Dusica – meaning Little Sweet One. Toma had the look of a young Dustin Hoffman about him and had belonged to a pop group which enjoyed a couple of hits in Serbia. He spoke near-perfect English, had a biting wit and produced his weekly music charts show on TV Pink, the station run by Mira Markovic's Jul Party. Dusica was tall, raven-haired, slender and intelligent. She was studying to be an economist and together she and Toma were high on the list of the beautiful people of Belgrade. In most other places in the world, their success would have catapulted them into a high-earnings bracket; in post air-strike Belgrade, by Western standards they were broke. In common with most other people in their late twenties, Toma and Dusica had to live with their parents because they could not afford an apartment of their own.

Together, they showed me the night life in Belgrade, from gentle jazz at the Radovic Club opposite the bomb-blasted State Television Centre, to a night-club in an old synagogue near the river in the Zemun area, and live music on boats moored along the River Sava. One of the favoured haunts of the young was the Cinema Club on the ramparts of the old city wall, overlooking the zoo. Here, rock groups who performed amazing imitations of Western bands would entertain young women in glitzy,

minuscule dresses and leather trouser suits, and young
men in designer jeans and T-shirts. Immediately below
the club, at the base of the old city wall, tigers would
prowl up and down, or lie with giant paws over their ears
as if in silent pleading for peace and quiet.

All across the city, and in towns across the country,
bars would be open until two, three or four in the
morning. There was far more late night-life than in
London. It always amazed me that there never seemed to
be any violence or other unrest caused by drunkenness.
At the end of even the longest bout of drinking, singing
and dancing, everyone would quietly go home afterwards. There are drink-drive laws in Serbia, as in Britain,
and most people seemed to respect them.

On the last weekend of August, I was taken to hear
music of a different kind. Traditional brass bands from all
over the country descended on the village of Guca, near
Cacak, south of Belgrade, to take part in an annual
contest to discover the best band in the land. It was also
an excuse for the village to indulge in three days and
nights of feasting on roast suckling pig, drinking and
dancing in the street. It was a rare opportunity for me to
see Serbs of all ages at an organised gathering which was
totally apolitical, and a chance to get together in an
atmosphere of fun rather than fear.

The visit was organised by Nenad, who had been one
of my drivers in Kosovo, and I was driven there by
Goran, the demobilised soldier-doctor who had pulled us
from the rubble. Guca was set in a bowl of land high on
Mount Jelica overlooking Nenad's home town of Cacak,
and hundreds of thousands of people were already
thronging the streets and surrounding fields as we
arrived. Nenad's wife, Mira, and Dessa Trevisan were also
among our party for the rousing final day of the festival,
along with a photographer. I wanted to send pictures and
a report back to *The Times*.

As we took the mountain road out of Cacak, we
climbed past the town's bombed Sloboda factory which

used to make vacuum cleaners and other domestic appliances. I had seen the mangled ruin many times from the road alongside the plant but it was only from here, on high, that you could see the extent of the damage and begin to appreciate the ferocity of the bombardment that must have taken place.

When we reached Guca, it was like a scene from another age: dancing bears; men, women and children in elaborate folk costumes; horse-drawn carriages; hawkers selling heart-shaped sugar necklaces, pies, fruit, nuts and slices of roast meat wrapped in pancakes. The cacophony of trumpets, tubas, drums and trombones was deafening as dozens of traditional brass bands vied with one another for the attention of revellers in scores of tents and kiosks selling food and drink. The serious business of judging the nineteen bands that had made it to the finals of the contest was meanwhile under way on the village's football pitch. Young and old danced robustly around picnic baskets and hoards of beer cans as the competing bands performed on a stage decorated with pictures of Serbian soldiers. It struck me that the festival, known as a 'sabor' or 'gathering', brought far more people together than any of the opposition politicians had been able to garner for their anti-government protests.

Serbian brass bands can be difficult for outsiders to appreciate; I was astonished to see many grown men grow misty-eyed as they listened to the primaeval beat of the drums along with the booming oompah and shrill notes of the wind instruments. The music seemed to fall into two categories, both with martial undertones – mournful tunes redolent of the Last Post, and rousing marching music. I asked Goran about the words of one particularly plaintive piece. 'If I translate this old and beautiful song for you it will mean nothing,' he said. Nenad stepped in to try to help: 'It says "The song kept us going, thank God for the song."'

The photographer, Nenad and I had to race back to Cacak towards the end of the afternoon, to find a computer from which we could e-mail the pictures and report for next day's edition of *The Times*. Just before setting out, I was to realise how jittery I still was after my experience in the Kosovo bombing. I was happily surveying the scenes of revelry on the football field when a loud explosion sent me crouching instinctively behind a parked car. I began shaking as more loud explosions followed, only to see Nenad and Goran rocking with laughter – the deafening noise was from a cannon firing a celebratory salute.

By the time we returned to the gathering after sending my report to *The Times*, darkness had fallen, as had the temperature. The tempo of the festivities was more furious than ever, though. In the village square, a statue of a golden trumpeter was surrounded by swaying dancers while countless thousands were eating and drinking at myriad restaurants set up in tents. Nenad shepherded us to one of the grander marquees where we found ourselves at a table next to a grim-faced government delegation. About twenty party members sat either side of a long trestle table, as stiff and formal as if they were at a state funeral rather than a national jamboree. It was hard not to contrast their demeanour with the relaxed and smiling Yugoslav officials I had met during my first visit to the country back in 1986. It was as if the intervening years of isolation, war and the Milosevic regime had plunged the nation backwards, stamping an old-fashioned Communist joylessness on its dignitaries. The party officials' presence did not, however, deter a group of hedonists nearby from dancing with abandon on their table.

The winning band, made up of gypsies, was brought along to play to the party members. The victors, seemingly taking their cue from the government officials, played the more dirge-like songs from their repertoire. Among their number was a musician with a solid gold trumpet – the privilege of award-winning bandsmen from previous years.

The more sombre the music played by the winners, the more frenetic and outrageous became the drums and trumpets of the band playing to the dancers on the adjacent table. Sitting between the two, I became fascinated by the contrast. At one point, the drummer in the winning band struck up what was obviously considered rather too jaunty a beat, for the band-leader put out a warning hand, unseen by the officials but clearly visible to the drummer, indicating that he should curb his zeal. Soon afterwards, a middle-aged woman at the official table began to tap her feet and one hand in time with the wildly energetic music entertaining the hedonists. A grim-looking member of her group shot her a dark look and she turned her attention back to the funereal tones of the victorious band.

Earlier in the day, I had seen Djindjic, leader of the opposition Democratic Party, sitting equally dourly in front of the rostrum on the football pitch. The festival seemed to give yet another insight into the Serbian character; ordinary people were determined to enjoy themselves with abandon, uncowed by the presence of officialdom. There was also a sense of wanting to eat, drink and be merry today for tomorrow ... well, tomorrow was tomorrow. Serbs can make the Spanish *mañana* ethos seem positively hurried.

The night ended with the seventy-four-year-old Dessa gyrating wildly without the aid of her walking-stick in front of a table on which three bandsmen, playing with gusto, were perilously balanced.

The Guca festival had been over only a few days when I experienced another facet of the Serbian cultural prism. I was sitting in the foyer of a newly-renovated theatre a few yards from the wide sweep of water which marked the confluence of the Danube and Sava Rivers. Waterfalls and pools formed a cool respite from the heat outside as I drank coffee in the greenhouse-style foyer filled with the chirrup of songbirds in cages hung on the walls.

Opposite me was Ljubisa Ristic who did not look like most people's idea of a Serbian strongman. Small and dapper with delicate hands, he wore a black embroidered shirt and his bare feet were clad in thong-style sandals. With sharp eyes and dramatically drooping moustache, he appeared the quintessential artist.

Yet to many politicians in the world outside rump Yugoslavia, he was a symbol of the regime accused of some of the worst war crimes since the Second World War. As an eminent theatre director, Ristic had worked with Western stars, and won plaudits from New York's *Village Voice* magazine. But, in what he calls his 'parallel existence', he was President of the Jul Party run by Slobodan Milosevic's wife, Mira Markovic.

Ristic was one of the many gifted authors, artists, film and theatre directors who formed a rich cultural seam in Balkan society. Many had decided to stay in the region as the former Yugoslavia disintegrated around them. Some became leading lights in the turbulent world of Balkan politics. Besides Ristic, they included the Bosnian Serb leader and poet, Radovan Karadzic; and the author-turned-Serbian opposition leader, Draskovic.

In August, audiences in Belgrade were being treated to a surreal play, *Gallop Across Boden Lake*, written by Austrian playwright Peter Handke and directed by Ristic, at his newly-renovated KPGT theatre in a disused sugar refinery. Girls clad in PVC micro-skirts and carrying police batons performed a burlesque goose-step in the opening scenes of an allegorical tale of love and jealousy. With as much mime and dance as conventional dialogue, three nightmarish figures clad in a clown costume, a sombre suit, and Shakespearean dress looked and moved like the cast of *Cabaret* on amphetamines. Ristic had a captive audience. The auditorium, lined with ballet-school style mirrors, was reached via a trapdoor which was closed for the duration of the performance.

Two years previously, Ristic had directed Vanessa Redgrave in a production of *The Liberation of Skopje* at the Riverside Theatre in Hammersmith. Now, he was on the European Union list of more than three hundred banned from travel to most of Europe. He was scathing about the West. 'The lead in culture today comes from the Mediterranean lands, not the barbarian north which is cynical and arrogant and uses bombs in the name of human rights,' he said. He described how a Tomahawk missile exploded at a petrol refinery 'yards away' from his theatre at the height of the Nato bombing campaign as the audience was chatting and drinking coffee after a matinée performance.

Ristic, who was born in Pristina, the son of a Second World War Partisan fighter, said that, far from wanting to see an ethnically-cleansed Yugoslavia, he had been at pains to promote a multicultural society. The name of his KPGT theatre was made of the initial letters of the word 'theatre' in Croatian, Serbian, Slovenian and Macedonian. 'The most monstrous idea is to have an ethnically clean country – Serbia is the only part of the Balkans which is ethnically mixed,' he said. 'For me, Yugoslavia is not a political phenomenon, it is a cultural phenomenon; it emerged as a cultural idea in the nineteenth century.'

Ristic, who professed to be a dyed-in-the-wool Communist, was reluctant to discuss the left-wing views of Vanessa Redgrave. 'She is a great actress,' he said, 'but she is typical of those Communists who belong to that perverse European Left, which has a strange feeling of guilt about the past. We always disagreed about basic political ideas. I belong to the other Left, the Yugoslavian Left which is anti-Stalinist and anti-nationalist.'

Ristic became President of the Jul Party, which ruled Yugoslavia in coalition with the Socialist Party of Mr Milosevic and the Radical Party led by the ultra-nationalist Seselj, after being invited to take the post in 1998. 'My political life and cultural life run on different tracks,' he said. 'I regard my political life as inevitable; I have no ambitions to be a prime minister. I help where help is needed.'

Paradoxically, Ristic was in charge of the Jul Party's Foreign Affairs Committee, despite the restraints put on his travelling. The theatre director also claimed that years of sanctions against Yugoslavia had done huge harm to the country's cultural life. 'People can always buy petrol from somewhere,' he said. 'The cultural embargo has been the most damaging. For years we have been starved of magazines, plays, films. And when young artists want to go abroad, they are only welcomed in other countries if they say they hate Milosevic.'

Soon after meeting Ristic, I had a visitor from the West. My former husband, Pat, who had shared twenty-three years of adventures round the world with me, took a week off work to visit the troubled region and ended up in Belgrade. Of Irish-Geordie-Lincolnshire descent, he was not best known for ascetic living and the late-night drinking holes of Belgrade beckoned irresistibly. He was a senior sub-editor on *The Times* and had coaxed and cajoled dictation from me back in London the morning after my experience in the Kosovo bombing. Now he wanted to see the damage in Serbia for himself. He arrived laden with children's clothes for Goran's family, Irish whiskey for me and football paraphernalia for Toma. He also turned up with a ferocious thirst, which Toma and Dusica did their best to slake over the next four days and nights while I bunked off to do some work.

On his second night in town, however, I decided to join Pat and his new-found friends when they set off in search of live music to accompany their beer-drinking. Toma and Dusica had heard that one of Belgrade's finest live rock groups, Pan Band, were playing on a boat on the River Sava. I was one of the four-man band's most ardent fans; they were well-rehearsed, polished and entertaining. The lead singer was a rotund, bald-headed creature who often wore a Che Guevara T-shirt and who could imitate Louis Armstrong and Mark Knopfler with equal realism. The group could have outshone many who played on the London pub circuit.

It was raining when Toma picked us up in his venerable Sixties red leather-seated Renault and he wasted precious petrol while we vainly searched for the venue along an isolated stretch of riverside on the outskirts of the city. We were just about to abandon the venture and head for the cosy comfort of the Radovic jazz club, when Toma managed to contact Pan Band's guitarist on his mobile phone.

The Regata houseboat, when we finally found it, looked like something that Captain Pugwash would have abandoned as unseaworthy. A ramshackle wooden vessel, it looked as if it had been knocked together out of old tea-chests. Nonetheless, we all clambered down the slippery gangplank and found ourselves in a heaving throng of Belgrade's music-lovers, jostling for space near the band. Several friends of Toma and Dusica were already ensconced on seats in the covered half of the boat, while others were teetering with glasses on a deck area open to the night sky. 'Look at that water,' Dusica said to her friend as they wrinkled their noses and peered over the rickety handrail at the oily river, awash with floating cans, newspaper and other noxious flotsam. 'Wouldn't you hate to be in that?' A duck making her way upstream gave the filthy waters near the bank a wide berth.

Inside, revellers near the band made room for Dusica and me to sit while Pat and Toma stayed on their feet and concentrated on buying beer or watching the young women dance. Outside, we could see yet more people crowding down the gangplank and pressing their way onto the houseboat, where they joined others out on the deck jumping around in time to Pan Band's beat. It was only later that I was reminded of the fact that soldiers break step when they cross bridges to minimise the risk of straining the structure beyond endurance.

I thought Toma was suggesting that we move on somewhere quieter for a nightcap when he began gesticulating that we should leave. The houseboat had been bobbing up and down with the tide and the dancers, but this time the outside deck sloped towards the river and failed to rise back. Instead it suddenly accelerated its descent; there was no escaping the realisation that we were sinking.

About 150 people surged towards the deck in a scramble to escape; no one wanted to be trapped inside as the houseboat rolled alarmingly and threatened to pitch furniture, amplifiers and people headlong into the river. The stampede to escape merely accelerated the boat's demise and Pat grabbed my wrist and pulled me bodily over a table and through a downward-facing window as water gushed in. Still attached to him, I found myself chest-high in water, with the fast-sinking deck disappearing beneath my feet. I felt a sharp pain as my right leg slipped between two disintegrating planks, scraping my shin, and gulped oily water. With my left foot I managed to stand on something solid and I lost one shoe as I kicked free and floundered towards the crowded gangplank, with Pat still firmly clamped to my wrist. Dusica was right behind and the three of us floundered and finally clambered to the shore, Pat kicking away a chair wedged across the gangplank.

Once safe, but dripping on the riverbank, I realised I had lost my mobile phone and my purse. Pat had his mobile between his teeth. It was while we were checking our personal belongings that Dusica, who had also badly bruised her leg, said: 'Where's Toma?' Pat, ever the action man, was ploughing back into the crowd, stumbling down the water-logged gangplank in what was obviously a futile attempt to locate my missing belongings. He re-emerged a few minutes later, wading back with a girl on his shoulder, able to announce that he had seen Toma standing on the few dry square inches still left on the boat. The members of Pan Band, meanwhile, were challenging all the laws of electricity by trying to unplug their amplifiers and instruments below water. 'We were lucky we weren't fried,' said Pat.

It was a night which symbolised for me the insecurity and disarray of life in a Serbia shunned by the world and forced by sanctions to make do and mend as best it could.

# Chapter Seventeen

# A Controversial View

Less than three months after Nato entered Kosovo, the following report was flashed around the world by the main international news agencies: 'The UN police and Nato-led peacekeepers have improved security in Kosovo to the point where the murder rate is lower than that in Washington and Pretoria.' Bernard Kouchner, the UN chief in Kosovo, showed charts outlining Kosovo's rapidly declining murder rate and added that Moscow and Kosovo had roughly the same murder count.

The statistics were supposed to sound comforting but the murder rates in Washington and Pretoria had been notoriously high for years, and the densely populated capitals of the United States and South Africa bear little comparison with the rural, sparsely-peopled Kosovo. 'The rate of criminality is down – look at where we are and where we were just two months ago,' Kouchner said as he showed the charts to Richard Holbrooke, the new US Ambassador to the UN, who was on a three-day visit to Kosovo.

The optimistic-sounding report was small comfort to those who continued to live under the threat of death, day in and day out, in the province – most of them Serbs. The day after Kouchner produced his chart, Kfor spokesman Canadian Major Roland Lavois announced that the bodies of two women had been found in Prizren, one aged sixty and one aged about thirty-five. Both had been beaten to death. On the same day, Bishop Atanasije Rakita of the Serb Orthodox Church told *Glas Javnosti* that more than twenty Serbs had been killed in Prizren in the previous two weeks, while more than forty were abducted. These murders and kidnappings were commonplace, yet the Western press largely ignored them. This was partly because most journalists sent to the region to cover the Nato bombardment had left by August. Furthermore, most journalists who had gone into Kosovo alongside the Alliance in June had no way to compare the province then with the situation before the conflict since they had never visited the region before.

Every day through the summer and into autumn, the independent VIP news agency in Belgrade catalogued the humanitarian disaster which was by then befalling the Serbs – more Serb bodies found, more homes burned and more Serbian churches and monuments destroyed.

In August, the Serbian Orthodox Church – which had repeatedly called on Slobodan Milosevic to resign – issued an impassioned appeal for an end to the violence. 'It is distressing to learn that in the year of the greatest Christian Jubilee, at the end of two millennia of Christianity, Christian churches are still being destroyed, not in a war but in a time of peace guaranteed by the international community,' wrote the Serbian Orthodox Patriarch, Pavle, in a document showing photographs and details of the destruction of more than fifty churches. 'We hope that these photographs will awaken the conscience of those who are able to stop the crimes ... In Kosovo and Metohija [the full name of the province, in which Metohija means Land of Monasteries] there will be no victory of humanity and justice while revenge and disorder prevail. No one has the moral right to celebrate as long as one evil is being replaced with another and the freedom of one people is becoming the slavery of another.'

In the wider world, no one seemed to know or care. The West needed the public in Nato countries to be obsessed with the problems of the ethnic Albanian refugees in the run-up to the bombing campaign; the great powers were less keen to see attention focused on the human misery being meted out to Serbs after the peacekeepers went in. The failure of Nato peacekeepers to police the frontier was another aspect of post-war Kosovo which Western leaders were anxious to underplay.

The absence of customs controls at the Albanian-Kosovo border turned the region into a magnet for the world's drug barons during the summer. By July, more than forty per cent of the heroin reaching Western Europe was passing through Kosovo, according to Marko Nicovic, a director of the International Narcotics Enforcement Officers' Association. 'Kosovo is now the Colombia of Europe. For the Turkish, Russian, Italian and Albanian mafias, Kosovo has become a paradise,' said Nicovic, a former Belgrade police chief and drug squad detective who worked for years in co-operation with police in Britain and America. Speaking at his office in Belgrade, he told me: 'The criminals have found the one country in Europe which is not a member of Interpol.' Yugoslavia's membership of the international police organisation ceased with the imposition of sanctions against the Milosevic regime in 1993. Albanian arms and drugs gangs are particularly hard to crack because close blood-ties bind them together. They all tend to be related or know one another personally, making penetration by informers almost impossible. 'They have a brotherhood which gives them a far greater ability to form a Mafia,' said Nicovic. 'This is a cancer, as Western Europe will soon discover. As each day passes, the Albanian Mafia becomes richer and more powerful.'

I was opposed to the air strikes from the beginning: the use of bombs in the name of humanity seemed a contradiction in terms. I also felt it set a bad precedent; the campaign had not been sanctioned by the United Nations and was likely to alienate countries such as Russia who had their own civil wars to contend with and would not relish the thought of Nato intervention on their home grounds. The Nato campaign was also unlikely to achieve all its aims. The might of the world's major powers did manage to push the Yugoslav military machine out of Kosovo, but this took more than seventy days – ten times longer than initially predicted by the person who perhaps more than any other advocated the bombing, US Secretary of State Madelaine Albright.

Furthermore, while the bombing was crucial in persuading Milosevic to order the withdrawal of his troops from Kosovo, other pressures also helped twist his arm. In the days before the bombing ended, the Russians had let the Yugoslav leader know they were withdrawing their support, possibly in return for new, badly-needed loans to Moscow from the International Monetary Fund.

The Yugoslav withdrawal came after two little-reported but vital concessions were won by Milosevic. At the Rambouillet conference near Paris in February, a few weeks before Nato's opening salvoes were fired in Kosovo, the West had demanded the right to place troops anywhere in Yugoslavia, let alone in Kosovo. They also wanted a referendum to be held in Kosovo, to decide its future. Deep into the bombing campaign, delegations sent to talk with Milosevic by Russia and the Finnish President, Martti Ahtisaari, agreed to drop these two key demands.

I was also opposed to the bombing because it seemed to me that the Western powers garnered support for the campaign through a misleading propaganda barrage. Many taxpayers who were expected to foot the bill for the Nato bombing campaign did not know that the Kosovo crisis stemmed from a civil war which had been escalating for years. Atrocities had been committed by ethnic Albanian terrorists as well as by Serbs, although only the latter possessed the manpower and forces necessary to sweep the Albanians out of the province.

Bismarck is credited with saying that the Balkans were not worth the life of a single Pomeranian grenadier. The region has been racked by a series of civil wars for most of the last decade of the millennium and all sides seem to have been as violent as they were physically capable of being.

Both East and West have been at fault over the past ten years as Yugoslavia has imploded. The demonisation of the Serbs as a race has only alienated those Serbs who might have reacted with sense and reason to the break-up of their country. In bombing Yugoslavia, Nato has been responsible for the deaths of at least 1,200 civilians and inflicted enormous damage on the cultural and economic life of a country now left as a wounded and potentially dangerous animal in the heart of Europe.

An independent group of Yugoslav economists respected by Western diplomats concluded in July that the Nato bombing caused £18.8 billion damage to the Yugoslav economy. The G17 group forecast a 44.4 per cent fall in industrial production for 1999. The West, meanwhile, will have to foot the bill for the bombing itself and for policing Kosovo, probably for years to come. The cost to Nato countries of providing and launching the bombs and missiles has been put at £2.63 billion, according to a BBC2 documentary, *78 Days: An Audit of the War*, broadcast in October. Each cruise missile cost £830,000, the programme said, and the price of aviation fuel for the first week alone amounted to £150 million.

The British Government is unclear about the cost to UK taxpayers. The Foreign Office says: 'In financial terms, the cost of the Nato bombing campaign to Britain (over and above the armed forces normal expenditure) was £82 million at the end of July 1999. This figure includes the cost of food and accommodation for the thousands of British troops in Kosovo. It also includes the cost of transporting equipment to the region.' The statement then concludes: 'It does not, however, include the cost of replacing spent ordnance.'

The full price tag of the war, including peacekeeping in years to come, lost regional trade, and rebuilding shattered bridges and factories, is hard to calculate. The BBC2 programme put it at anything up to £46 billion.

When I voiced my opposition to the air strikes, I was constantly told by people in the West that 'we had to do something'. My answer was twofold: there are plenty of other 'good causes' in the world, but no one has been stampeding to intervene with bombs in the Kurdish areas of Turkey, or Tibet, or East Timor, or Burma. I suspect that the public would soon be agitating for action, in the way they did over Kosovo, were governments and television cameras deployed to feed a daily diet of the misery suffered by pro-democracy campaigners in Rangoon.

In answer to the 'must do something' chant, I would like to have seen the United Nations rather than the world's mightiest military machine take the leading role in trying to solve the Kosovo crisis. This might have taken years and almost certainly there would have been obfuscation and delaying tactics from the Serbs. A United Nations-led peacekeeping mission, with the full support of Russia and China as well as of the West, might have brought about the eventual partition of Kosovo. Not a perfect solution, but it was clear from my visits to Kosovo at the height of the Nato bombing campaign that Serbs and Albanians had lost any chance of living together again long before the first missile exploded in Pristina on the night of 24 March. Furthermore, a UN-led mission would probably have led to a far smaller earthquake on the Richter scale of human misery.

Instead, what started out as ostensibly a humanitarian cause to aid hapless ethnic Albanians has resulted in the 'ethnic cleansing' of almost the entire Serb population of Kosovo under the noses of Nato peacekeepers. Under the agreement to end the bombing, a small number of Yugoslav police were supposed to join an international police presence in the province to protect the Serbs from Albanian revenge attacks. Two months after Nato's arrival, not a single member of this proposed force had arrived.

Many of the KLA and their sympathisers who entered

Kosovo in June under the protection of Nato embarked on a systematic campaign of killing, terrorising and burning the homes of Serbs and other non-Albanians such as Roma gypsies. Even some fellow ethnic Albanians, especially those who had not joined the Albanian refugee exodus a few weeks earlier, were added to the KLA's hit-list after being branded as collaborators with the enemy. The ferocity of the attacks equalled anything the Serbs had meted out, yet there was barely a whimper of protest from the West, compared with the wave of horror and outrage which was orchestrated in response to Serb atrocities.

In 1876, Victor Hugo penned an essay 'For Serbia' following a Turkish massacre of Serbs near Belgrade. 'A nation is being killed,' he wrote. 'Where? In Europe. Are there any witnesses to this act? One: the whole world. Do the European governments see it? No.'

# Chapter Eighteen
# Christmas–New Year 1999–2000

It was two days before Christmas, 1999 and I was back in Kosovo for the first time since Nato had entered the province. Murder, kidnapping and gang warfare were rife, the United Nations showed little sign of being able to cope, and British and other troops were fast realising they were in for a long and gruelling stay.

Kosovo was nominally still part of Serbia, but in reality it was a separate country with an overwhelmingly ethnic Albanian population, language and culture policed by an overstretched army of foreign troops.

In the small town of Podujevo near the demilitarised zone which marked the de facto border between Kosovo and the rest of Serbia, the only two Serbs still living among forty thousand ethnic Albanians were a pair of little old ladies who had known one another since childhood. In a tale of strife which seemed to sum up the curse of the Balkans, Jelica Miljanovic, eighty-seven, and Jelena Cimburovic, eighty-two, had quarrelled with one another – and Jelena had moved out of the flat they shared. They argued because Jelica could no longer stand Jelena's nicotine habit.

The squabble would have been sad anywhere in the world; in Kosovo at the turn of the millennium, the rift was causing yet another headache for British troops trying to maintain order in the sensitive border area. The two old ladies had to be kept under twenty-four-hour guard and now twice as many soldiers were needed to protect them from almost constant harassment from their ethnic Albanian neighbours.

Children threw stones at their windows and made cut-throat signs if the pensioners ventured to their doors. More sinisterly, ethnic Albanian extremists had tried to force them to leave the town altogether before the twenty-four-hour guard was set up by members of the Queen's Dragoon Guards. 'I have lived here all my life and I am going to die here,' said Jelica. 'I have already paid for my memorial in the cemetery.' Didn't she feel lonely without the companionship of her old friend, Jelena? 'I hated her smoking,' she said.

The British troops who kept constant vigil in the bitter cold outside the old ladies' homes also shopped for them, put out rubbish, chopped firewood and occasionally played cards and dominoes with them. 'I have no children of my own and the soldiers are like sons to me,' said Jelica. 'I did have a cousin in Pristina but I don't know where she is now. I have not heard from her in months.' Across town, Jelena pulled her cardigan about her and lit candles as the electricity failed. 'The soldiers are one hundred times better than sons,' she said. 'The children came and broke down the fence but the soldiers repaired it for me. It is a pity about Jelica, because we used to play together when we were young.'

Looking after the little old ladies was frustrating, as well as expensive. The street markets seemed to have a plentiful supply of fruit and vegetables, but it was unsafe for the octogenarians to venture out alone. 'Sometimes they try to charge off shopping,' said Captain Dominic Roberts. 'They also complain about the prices or the goods we bring back for them. And, as it turns out, they hate one another.'

Podujevo has always been Albanian-dominated, but there had been two thousand Serbs in the town until Nato arrived in June. Then most of the Serbs had fled north towards Belgrade, outnumbered as they were by returning Kosovo Albanians and people from Albania itself who were bent on revenge. Six months on, in the week before Christmas, anti-Serb feeling still ran high in the town. British troops had recently reduced the guard they placed on one of the only three remaining Serb Orthodox churches in the area. 'We had barred the door and surrounded it with barbed wire but after talks with members of the Albanian community, we reduced our presence there. The church was destroyed within a week,' said Lt. Colonel Patrick Andrews, commanding officer of the Queen's Dragoon Guards. 'It was disappointing to say the least.' I could not help remembering that, even at the height of the Nato bombing campaign when Serbs still held sway in Kosovo, I had not seen a single mosque destroyed.

Now, on the brink of a new century, life for the remaining Serbs in Kosovo was precarious. In the southern town of Vitina, blood-spattered pavements bore testimony to scenes of carnage at a shopping centre on 20 December, when a home-made bomb was thrown into a crowd of Serbs as they drank coffee. Ten people were hurt in the attack, which occurred despite the presence of nearby American Nato peacekeeping troops. Four ethnic Albanians were later arrested in connection with the bombing.

That attack was just one of the many flashpoints which the Nato peacekeeping troops had to deal with as they struggled to restore order in a land still teetering on the edge of anarchy. The United Nations had not yet set up a judicial system or tackled an acute housing shortage. They had even failed to ensure that enough snowploughs were deployed in the right places to keep vital supply lines open during predictable Christmas-week blizzards.

Many British soldiers serving with Nato were privately scathing about the UN Mission in Kosovo (known by its abbreviation, Unmik), but they were anxious to support it publicly, fearing that Nato would be left holding the fort if morale within the UN – already low – declined even further. The delay in setting up a system of courts meant that there was still no way to try those arrested, such as the shopping-centre bomb suspects. The result was that ninety per cent of those detained were released within forty-eight to seventy-two hours.

Three days before Christmas, a fourteen-year-old girl abducted in northern Pristina was rescued within one hour by members of the Royal Green Jackets, who sealed off exit routes and sprang a 'rat-trap', catching the three kidnappers as they tried to leave the city with their hostage. Not only was there no system to try the girl's kidnappers, the peacekeepers were running out of space to hold those they had arrested.

In December, the UN mission said that it would begin appointing four hundred judges within a month. However, it was clear that some officers in the British contingent serving in Nato, which policed Pristina and territory in the north-east near the boundary with Serbia proper, believed that the UN was working far too slowly. 'Anarchy is the only way to describe the situation here now, complete anarchy,' said one. 'Unmik needs to pull its finger out – and fast.'

Before the Nato bombing campaign, Pristina had a population of 240,000, including about 47,000 Serbs. By 1 January 2000, this had swollen to 500,000, with a tiny, embattled Serb minority estimated at between 800 and 1,200. Almost all the Serbs' apartments had been taken over by ethnic Albanians and there was little chance they would voluntarily hand these back to any Serbs who felt brave enough to want to return from self-imposed exile in Serbia proper.

Few British troops went on leave over the Christmas and New Year holiday and almost all the 5,500 serving in Kosovo slept in tents. Their living conditions were in stark contrast to the 5,000 UN and other international aid agency workers in Pristina who had taken over apartments and hotel rooms while the local population fought for accommodation. In Pristina, the atmosphere was tense and the British soldiers had to keep a constant vigil over the few remaining Serbs, who rarely ventured from their homes for fear of attacks by ethnic Albanians. Many

Serbs praised the UK troops serving with Nato, saying they were doing more than any other country's soldiers to be even-handed. However, many in the British contingent privately said they needed more help from the United Nations.

Pristina was unrecognisable compared with the city before the Kosovo conflict. Street names had been changed to honour Albanian-born notables such as Mother Teresa, and every shop bore an Albanian name, often adorned with the red Albanian flag. Anyone who even inadvertently spoke Serbian was at best greeted with hostile looks; a Bulgarian soldier in Nato's peace-keeping force had been set upon and killed in the autumn after saying the Serb word for 'thank you' when stopped and asked for the time by an ethnic Albanian who then wished him 'good luck' in Serbian.

With so few Serbs left in the UK-patrolled sector of Kosovo, violent attacks on them had statistically dropped by the end of 1999. However, there were signs that inter-Albanian strife was on the rise as moderate and extremist Albanians fought for supremacy. During even the darkest days of Serb administration of Pristina, Ibrahim Rugova, the moderate leader of the Democratic League of Kosovo, could be found in his office with just two or three assistants alongside. On the day before Christmas Eve, 1999, he arrived for talks at one of the Nato buildings in Pristina with a convoy of cars surrounded by about fifty bodyguards.

During the Kosovo conflict, Nato spokesman Jamie Shea described Slobodan Milosevic as 'the organiser of the greatest human catastrophe since 1945' and as 'the instigator of a flight similar to the evacuation of Phnom Penh by the Khmer Rouge'. At the close of the old millennium, embarrassing statistics began to emerge about the atrocities that were supposed to justify the bombing of Yugoslavia. After six months of investigation and exhumation of the dead in Kosovo, United Nations war crimes investigators had found 2,108 bodies. Before the bombing, President Clinton and his Defence Secretary, William Cohen, spoke of 100,000 victims – dead and missing – of Serb atrocities. Clinton claimed that the Nato bombing prevented Milosevic from 'deliberate, systematic efforts at ethnic cleansing and genocide'.

The chief prosecutor for the UN war crimes tribunal, Carla Del Ponte, could confirm only the 2,108 figure when she reported to the UN Security Council just before the end of 1999. A pathologist, Emilio Perez Pujol, who led a Spanish forensic team looking for bodies, found only 187, mostly in individual graves. He calculated that 'the final figure of dead in Kosovo will be 2,500 at the most. This includes lots of strange deaths that can't be blamed on anyone in particular.'

So what was achieved in the bombing? According to Serbian Government and independent Yugoslav sources, at least 1,800 civilians – Serbs, Albanians and Roma gypsies – were killed by Nato and 5,000 were wounded – mostly women, children, and the elderly. About 2,000 of the injured were disabled for life.

Nearly 150 health care institutions were demolished or damaged along with their equipment, medicines and medical supplies. Among those affected were about 4,500 patients with chronic kidney failure, whose access to dialysis treatment was cut off or curtailed, 90,000 cancer patients, and 200,000 diabetes-sufferers.

Two days before Christmas, Amnesty International issued a report which painted a damning picture of Kosovo six months after Nato's entry. 'Violence against Serbs, Roma, Muslim Slavs and moderate Albanians in Kosovo has increased dramatically over the past month, pointing to a failure by the United Nations mission to protect human rights,' the rights group said. 'Murder, abductions, violent attacks, intimidation, and house-burning are being perpetrated on a daily basis.

Amnesty also warned about the rise of inter-Albanian conflict: 'Identity-based human rights abuses are coupled with abuses which appear to be part of an organised campaign to silence moderate voices in ethnic Albanian society,' it said. 'Last month, Kontakt, a multi-ethnic radio station based in Pristina, had its offices ransacked and equipment stolen. Members of the Democratic League of Kosovo Party have also increasingly become the target of attacks and intimidation.'

Amnesty concluded: 'The campaign for human rights in Kosovo is far from over. In the spring of this year the international community intervened in Kosovo with the declared aim of preventing a human rights catastrophe. However, at the closing of the year human rights abuses continue to be perpetrated on a daily basis.'

Throughout my visit to Kosovo at Christmas, I was accompanied by one or two armed British soldiers who seemed extremely edgy about venturing into certain parts of Pristina where Albanian extremists were believed to be concentrated. One snapped round, hand on his rifle, when a car backfired: 'It is almost like being in Northern Ireland – and there we were supposed to be the enemy,' he said ruefully. Here in Kosovo, the foreign troops were supposed to be the heroes and saviours of the ethnic Albanians. After all, the Nato bombing campaign had been launched on their behalf.

As I left Kosovo to head north, back to Belgrade, a Canadian soldier hugged himself and stamped his feet on a blizzard-swept hill on the de facto frontier. After checking my passport, he said: 'I am obliged to advise you, ma'am, that you are entering hostile territory.' He was referring to the Serbia still ruled by Slobodan Milosevic. Behind him stretched the mountains and plains of Kosovo which I had just visited for the first time since Nato's arrival and which the Canadian was implying was now a haven of stability in comparison. The Canadian cast wary glances down the snow-covered track towards Serbia proper. Three weeks earlier, at the beginning of December, ethnic Albanian extremists had sneaked across the boundary in the dead of night and killed two Serb policemen, so Nato troops were put on high alert over the holiday period in an attempt to prevent a repeat attack. This was, indeed, hostile territory, whichever way you looked at it.

In Britain at the turn of the year, Kosovo was fast fading from the public consciousness and the new fixation was over whether Tony Blair's spin doctors had misled the public over another expensive project – the Millennium Dome in Greenwich.

A new year message from the UN chief in Kosovo, Bernard Kouchner, was relegated to small print: 'It's all too easy to say Kosovo's over. It's not over at all, it's ahead of us.'

# Chapter Nineteen

# Postscript: Serbian Orthodox New Year, 2001

On the face of it, Yugoslavia had many reasons to be cheerful when I returned in January, 2001: the West's bogey man, federal President Slobodan Milosevic, had been overthrown three months earlier on 5 October, 2000. The Yugoslav leader miscalculated badly by calling elections in late September which he thought even if he could not win outright, would be inconclusive enough for him to claim victory. In the event, discontent among his people had spread so far and deep that an overwhelming majority voted for an alliance of opposition parties led by a relatively new challenger to the leadership, Vojislav Kostunica. Desperate to cling to power at any cost, Milosevic called for a second round of voting. But before that poll could take place, the people voted with their feet in a frenzy of strikes at coal mines, factories and finally with the storming of Parliament on 5 October. Unlike periodic protests of the previous decade, this time the unrest spread from the masses upwards.

The miracle was that the heavily-armed police and army disobeyed orders, apparently from the top, to fire on the malcontents.

But my old friend Toma knew the Milosevic era was doomed. Toma, who had accompanied me to the tear-gassed football match between Yugoslavia and Croatia in the summer of 1999, was now married to Dusica and together they helped run a nightclub in Belgrade's November 29th Street. Just after the first round of the elections, two members of the secret police had dropped in for a drink at the club and confessed that they had voted for Kostunica.

On Serbian Orthodox New Year's Eve, 13 January, I watched as tens of thousands of Serbs danced, sang and cheered their way into the year 2001 at huge open air rock concerts in the southern city of Nis. Five days later, on his last day as President of the US, Bill Clinton lifted many of the economic sanctions which had eroded the Yugoslavian economy on and off for the past decade. The new regime was busy appointing ambassadors across Europe in the countries that had shunned Yugoslavia for so long.

Yet … I still could not feel unalloyed satisfaction. Goran Zdravkovic, the soldier who helped save my life, is still a refugee from his old home in Kosovo; Zoran, the former reception manager at the Grand Hotel in the Kosovo capital, Pristina, still has no work after 18 months living in near penury in Belgrade. Kosovo is almost as lawless as it was the day Nato troops entered the province.

A far more widespread problem for ordinary Yugoslavs has been the environmental damage caused by the bombing. While Western newspapers gave lengthy coverage in early January to ever-increasing concerns about the effects of depleted uranium on Nato peace-keepers, little was said about the risk to civilians.

One man who did not live to celebrate Orthodox New Year was Milenko Zarkovic. He rarely suffered a day's illness in his life until he began work helping to clear debris from bomb sites in Serbia following the Nato air strikes.

The fifty-two-year-old father of three from the central town of Priboj was given the task of gathering and carting away rubble from bomb-blasted sites at Nis airport in southern Serbia and around Vranje near the border with Kosovo. In early January 2000 he began to feel unwell. By April he was in intensive care in a Belgrade hospital, and by the end of May he was dead.

Doctors treating Zarkovic initially asked whether he had been exposed to depleted uranium, and tests were carried out; but the results never passed to his family, despite repeated requests. Today, his widow, Milena, forty-seven, is convinced he was killed by exposure to the radioactive material which is used in Nato's anti-tank bombs. Some former colleagues of the dead man have also begun to feel unwell, says his daughter, Sanja, aged twenty-five.

In the Serbian capital, meanwhile, doctors who treat people from all over the country have begun to see a steep rise in cancers and birth defects among the newborn. Vets have also noticed an alarming increase in the number of deformed animals being born.

British and other Nato troops now serving in Kosovo may also be being affected by exposure to depleted uranium and other toxins, according to Professor Malcolm Hooper, the chief scientific adviser to Gulf War veterans in Britain. 'I would have thought that anyone in that environment would be exposed,' he told me just before I left for my New Year visit to Belgrade. 'You can't keep yourself out of the situation.'

Peacekeepers in Kosovo were ordered in the summer of 2000 to stay away from some areas in the province and French, Danish and Belgian soldiers around the province's northern town of Kosovska Mitrovica were advised not to have children for several years. Nato said that this is because some sites were contaminated by toxins from dilapidated mines and factories which were badly run by the former Serbian rulers in the province.

Kfor spokesman, Major Scott Slaten, told me in the summer of 2000, just over a year after the Nato bombing: 'DU, as far as we know, is not a significant factor. I can't say there is no effect from the bombing, but by and large it is factors such as unexploded cluster bombs that make some places out of bounds.'

Major Slaten said that he was unaware of any troops reporting depleted-uranium-related health problems.

However, in April 2000, eleven soldiers who served in the former Yugoslavia said that they were planning to sue the Ministry of Defence after suffering chronic health problems that they believe were caused by 'Balkan war syndrome'. Doctors had linked their symptoms to exposure to depleted uranium used during the Kosovo conflict, they say.

About 10,500 British soldiers were initially sent to Kosovo and many were exposed to the fine, poisonous dust, which remains in the atmosphere and pollutes water supplies. Belgium meanwhile began a systematic review of the health of the 14,000 troops it sent to the region. Tests have already reportedly identified cases of men suffering the effects of exposure to uranium, even though they were not deployed in high-risk areas such as the heavily-blasted region around Prizren near the Albanian border.

Today Serbia as a whole is a sick country. Nearly everyone you speak to – young or old – says they or a relative have suffered repeated, unexplained respiratory or digestive infections since the bombing ended last June. Now worries about depleted uranium are compounded by fears that the food chain may have been affected by toxins from bombed chemical plants and oil refineries which poured into the Danube.

The chemical spills were especially severe at Pancevo, an industrial town on the outskirts of Belgrade, where a petrochemical plant and fertiliser factory were repeatedly bombed, and over which an ominous yellow-green cloud hung for days after vast tanks of chemicals were first blasted open during the air strikes, in April 1999.

I visited Pancevo in the height of summer that year, when leaves on the trees lining the cobbled streets in the centre of the town had the decaying brown colour they should have assumed in mid-autumn. A few weeks later, the group of us who were unlucky enough to find ourselves on the rickety Regata house-boat which sank in the nearby River Sava found what looked like chemical burn marks on our clothes after we hung them out to dry. That was the evening Toma, Dusica, my ex-husband and I had gone to hear Pan Band playing and the boat had disintegrated beneath the dancers' stomping feet.

The Regional Environmental Centre for Central and Eastern Europe, an independent organisation funded by the European Union, America and Hungary, has been monitoring the toxic effects of the Alliance campaign since the bombing ended. It has identified four 'hot spots' where contamination linked to the bombing is particularly heavy – Pancevo, Bor, Novi Sad and Kragujevac.

'All these toxins have been going deeper and deeper in the ground for the past year,' said Milutin Milosevic, who runs the centre's Belgrade office. 'Five million Ecus are needed very, very quickly but we still don't know when a single Ecu will be forthcoming even though it has long been promised by the EU. The key problem is bringing help to Yugoslavia; some people seem to think you can stop the environment at the border, but this affects all countries in the region. People in the Government here are also not giving all the information they have. The Pancevo contamination was very bad but they now find they cannot tell people not to eat food grown here, or what will people eat?'

Doctors and scientists say it is too soon after the end of the bombing for a proper statistical analysis of its health effects. However, all those I spoke to said they had noticed marked increases in health problems.

Doctors say that the number of babies being born with heart defects at the Institute for Gynaecology in Belgrade, which deals with cases from all over the country, trebled in the year after the bombing campaign.

'There have been many more miscarriages – about a 30 per cent increase – since the air strikes,' says Dr Aleksandar Ljubic, who works at the Institute. 'We have also noticed an increase in abnormal births, children with problems in the central nervous system, the spine and brain, again in the range of a 30 per cent rise compared with before the bombing. We don't know yet if it is caused by radiation, bad food or viruses.'

Dr Ljubic believes that stress caused by living under the bombing campaign and lack of money in the war-ravaged nation may also be to blame for the increase in pre- and post-natal problems.

'We consider all pregnancies now to be high-risk,' he told me in his office at the Institute in the autumn of 2000. 'Many women cannot afford to travel to see a doctor so they get no ante-natal care. Many just show up here when they are actually giving birth.'

Spasoje Petkovic, Director of the Institute for Gynaecology, insists that he and his staff have noticed a 25 per cent increase in ovarian cancer since the bombing, although he points out that this is probably not a national trend as only the most severe cases are sent to the institute for treatment.

'There are increases also in virus infections and mutations in foetuses,' he told me, 'though this may be caused by stress and poor food as well as by toxicants from the bombing.' Next I spoke to Professor Branimir Nestorovic of Belgrade University Children's Hospital

'So far we have registered the increase of respiratory diseases, mostly asthma cases which have doubled,' he said. Increases in diabetes, viral infections and immune system problems have also been noticed, especially among children from heavily-bombed areas such as Pancevo.

'We have two or three times the number of cancer patients; before the bombing we had mostly leukaemia but now the number of leukaemia cases is stagnating and the number of solid tumours is rising. These tumours are attacking nerve cells, kidneys, and the liver. Children from Pancevo are coming and all of them are hissing with asthma.

'The connection with the air strikes is obvious. The

effects are going to be felt more and more in the future as heavy metals usually stay forever once they are in the body,' Professor Nestorovic warned.

Among the poisons released into Serbia's air, soil and water by the Nato bombing were mercury, polychlorinated biphenyls (PCBs) and vinyl chloride monomers (VCMs). PCBs have been linked to cancer and other illnesses and have been banned in the US since 1977. The Regional Environmental Centre says that the amount of PCBs and dioxins unleashed at Kragujevac when the Zastava car and munitions plant was bombed was one thousand times the level that would prompt a declaration of an environmental emergency in Germany. VCMs, meanwhile, have 'the potential to cause neurological and liver damage, as well as damage to foetuses, causing serious birth defects,' the centre says.

Sanja Zarkovic, meanwhile, mourns her father who died after transporting the bomb debris in southern Serbia. 'When he first became ill he said he thought he was suffering some sort of radiation illness, but everyone in the family laughed at him,' she says. 'But he became sicker and sicker and from April could no longer work. He was sent to the Emergency Medical Centre in Belgrade where the doctor asked if he had been in contact with depleted uranium. His immune system had been weakened and he caught many infections.

'Then the doctors started to refuse to talk about DU and my mother was asked not to talk about it. My father died on 22 May and the death certificate said he had had a heart attack, which we all think is nonsense. We asked for a post mortem to be carried out but they said they could only do that a week later. Then they said they could not do that because there was no cold storage to keep his body for a week and we had to bury him.'

One of Milenko Zarkovic's colleagues continues to work, clearing bomb damage debris, even though he, too is feeling more and more unwell, she says.

It was after a day pondering all these ills still besetting

the country that I had one of those nightmares which jolt you awake.

I was walking down a street in a small town in Serbia and realised that pedestrians on the pavements were staring skyward. Following their gaze, I looked up to see a beautiful, impossibly white horse with flowing mane and peering over the parapet from the roof of a high-rise building about ten storeys tall. The townspeople began whistling softly and holding out their hands, encouraging the wild-eyed creature to step forward. I watched as the fairy-tale-pretty horse edged closer and closer to the edge – until it finally plunged headlong into the void.

I remember comforting myself with the thought that the beast would have died instantly after such a fall. But the horror continued: the horse began trying to stand on obviously shattered legs, its hoofs making dreadful scraping sounds on the cobbled street as a now silent crowd gathered round. The fate of the dream-horse seemed to symbolise Yugoslavia past, present and to come.

Kosovo, the heart of the reason for the Nato bombing, continues to be a political as well as an environmental minefield. There have also been skirmishes between armed ethnic Albanians and Macedonians in the Former Yugoslav Republic of Macedonia, where so many Albanian refugees had been filmed by the world's television cameras during the Nato bombing campaign.

In the Presevo Valley, a buffer zone between Kosovo and the rest of Serbia, a joint patrol of US and Russian soldiers came under fire from a group of Albanian gunmen in December.

Why should Albanians fire on their allies? One Serbian news agency reported in January 2001: 'Now that Nato has helped Albanians cleanse Kosovo of nearly 300,000 Serbs, they don't want Kfor there, either. After all, Ibrahim Rugova, the Albanian leader, has said that, "in the future we will share responsibility and also develop an army of our own as a protective power." '

So, as the Serbian news agency put it so well, firing at the American and Russian troops may have been an Albanian way of saying 'thank you and goodbye'.

# Other available Duckbacks

## Diary of a Man in Despair

Friedrich Reck-Malleczewen    £6.99 Paperback    0 7156 3100 4

A forgotten literary masterpiece by a Prussian aristocrat whose fascinating journal and indictment of Hitler's regime, written between 1936 and 1944, has astonished and delighted readers and critics alike.

'very, very rarely one comes across a book so remarkable and so unexpectedly convincing that it deserves more to be quoted than to be reviewed ...I beg you to read this bitterly courageous book'
Frederic Raphael, *The Sunday Times*

'a vivid and extremely personal evocation of the Nazi era – a small masterpiece'

Ben Rogers, *Financial Times*

'an indisputable humanist masterpiece'

Walter Ellis, *The Times*

## Cleopatra's Wedding Present
### Travels through Syria

Robert Tewdwr Moss    £6.99 Paperback    0 7156 3099 7

Robert Tewdwr Moss describes his travel experiences with rare charm and aplomb.

'it would be hard to find a more archly entertaining, slyly informative, or poignant travel book than this'
Philip Hoare, *Independent*

'Tewdwr Moss's intense, evocative account of his travels through Syria is a perfect book of its kind. Its author demonstrates intelligence, curiosity, humour, compassion, and commendable powers of observation: everything that is required of a travel writer'

Lucretia Stewart, *Times Literary Supplement*

## The Way of Hermes

Translated by Clement Salaman, Dorine van Oyen, William D. Wharton, Jean-Pierre Mahé   £6.99 Paperback   0 7156 3093 8

The *Corpus Hermeticum* is a collection of short philosophical treatises, a powerful fusion of Greek and Egyptian thought, written in Greek in Alexandria between the first and third centuries AD. They are still read as inspirational spiritual writings today.

These translations of Hermetic writings and aphorisms provide both general reader and scholar with new English versions, based on reliable texts and faithful to the spirit and beauty of the original.

## The Pig: A British History

Julian Wiseman   £6.99 Paperback   0 7156 3092 X

A history of one of Britain's best-loved creatures, including the development of its husbandry.

'elegantly slender ... full of delightful pictures of the different breeds. Gripping'

*Independent*

'brings home to one what splendid creatures pigs are and what a contribution they have made to good living and even to survival'

Lord Blake, *Financial Times*

'a fine and well-told morality tale, whose basic message applies not only to pigs but to all livestock in all ages, the world over'

Colin Tudge, *New Scientist*

## White Stains
Aleister Crowley    £6.99 Paperback    0 7156 3103 9

Branded 'the most terrible man in England' in the 1920s,
Aleister Crowley enjoyed a measure of notoriety in his lifetime
that few would be able to match. *White Stains*, a collection of
Crowley's poetry praised by W.B. Yeats, published in paperback
for the first time, has been called 'the filthiest book of verse
ever written' and of the first edition of 100 numbered copies, 83
were pulped and burned by Her Majesty's Customs in 1924.

This edition includes an introduction by John Symonds,
Crowley's literary executor and biographer.

## An Intelligent Person's Guide to Ethics
Mary Warnock    £6.99 Paperback    0 7156 3089 X

'one of the best guides to ethics available'
Ray Monk, *Sunday Telegraph*

'this admirable book fully lives up to its title'
Robert Grant, *The Times*

## An Intelligent Person's Guide to History
John Vincent    £6.99 Paperback    0 7156 3090 3

'not only is Vincent one of the great historians of 19th-century
British politics, he is also that rarest of things in academic
history: a witty prose stylist'
Niall Ferguson, *Daily Telegraph*

## An Intelligent Person's Guide to Dickens
Michael Slater    £6.99 Paperback    0 7156 3088 1

'Michael Slater has an encyclopaedic knowledge of Dickens's
writings'
*Times Literary Supplement*

## An Intelligent Person's Guide to Modern Ireland
John Waters   £6.99 Paperback   0 7156 3091 1

'John Waters skilfully attacks those who decry any sense of nationalism or belittle any aspiration that the two parts of Ireland should be united'

Michael O'Toole, *Irish News* (Belfast)


## Boogie-Woogie
Danny Moynihan   £5.99 Paperback   0 7156 3102 0

Much-praised hilarious satire of the incestuous world of New York's contemporary art scene.

'Moynihan's first novel is spectacular stuff'

Harriet Lane, *Observer*

'a filthy corker of a book'                                      Jilly Cooper

'subversive, darkly funny'                                    *The Times*

'a highly amusing first novel'                                   *Tatler*

'witty satire ... an excellent first novel'              *Daily Mail*


## Intimate Cartographies
Lynne Alexander   £5.99 Paperback   0 7156 3095 4

A beautifully-constructed tale of a mapmaker who comes to terms with loss through the discipline of her work.

'Alexander has chosen the most difficult of subjects, the death of a child. She has treated it with sensitivity and wit, manic levity and the utmost respect, and has created something quite haunting'

Carol Birch, *Independent*

**Too Fast To Live**
Bidisha   £5.99 Paperback   0 7156 3098 9

A modern-day story of misdirected passions and amoral ambitions in a subversive rewriting of the Arthurian saga.

'Bidisha is clearly a dazzlingly creative writer'
Anthea Lawson, *The Times*

'a dark violent tale that gets under your nails like the London grime it describes'
Francesca Gavin, *Dazed and Confused*

'an inventive addition to the current school of cockney cool'
*Independent on Sunday*


**Charlotte**
The Final Journey of Jane Eyre
D.M. Thomas   £5.99 Paperback   0 7156 3094 6

An extraordinary, imaginative deconstruction of Charlotte Brontë's *Jane Eyre*, set partly in modern-day Martinique.

'a wickedly irreverent antidote to earnest study'
Charlotte Cory, *Independent*

'the test of a text like this is whether you can put it down. I couldn't. I hurtled on, gripped by the simplest desire any reader ever has. I wanted to find out what happened'
Patricia Duncker, *New Statesman*

## Never Trust A Rabbit

Jeremy Dyson   £5.99 Paperback   0 7156 3097 0

Twelve enchantingly surreal stories, recently serialised on BBC Radio Four, by Jeremy Dyson, one of *The League of Gentlemen*.

'*Never Trust a Rabbit* is ...expertly told and structured, being filled with such utterly surreal and fantastic twists and turns as one might expect of a member of BBC2's *The League of Gentlemen*'

Dominic Bradbury, *Times Metro*

'A stunning debut. His stories nestle in the little chink between Roald Dahl and Borges'

Adam Mars-Jones, *Observer*

## Layer Cake

J.J. Connolly   £5.99 Paperback   0 7156 3096 2

The critically-acclaimed contemporary gangland thriller set in London's underworld, described by Bruce Reynolds as 'the best crime novel I've ever read'.

'*Layer Cake* is a storming piece of work, funny and serious by turns with an abiding sense of conviction'

*Guardian*

'this year's crime read should be J.J. Connolly's *Layer Cake*'

Mike Pattenden, *Times Metro*

'mission accomplished. One novel in and Connolly has hit the jackpot'

*****, *Uncut*

www.ducknet.co.uk

# ORDER FORM (BLOCK CAPITALS PLEASE)

SURNAME _____ FIRST NAME _____

ADDRESS _____

_____

_____ POSTCODE _____

## METHOD OF PAYMENT (PLEASE TICK AS APPROPRIATE)

☐ Invoice to my Grantham Book Services account
☐ By cheque (payable to Duckworth Publishers)
☐ Please send account opening details (trade customers only)
☐ By credit card (Access/ Visa / Mastercard / Amex)

Card no: ☐ ☐ ☐ ☐ ☐ ☐ ☐ ☐ ☐ ☐ ☐ ☐ ☐ ☐ ☐ ☐

Expiry date: __ / __ / __   Authorising Signature: _____

**POSTAGE** (Private customers) Please note that the following postage and packing charges should be added to your order:

UK deliveries:   £3 on orders up to £16; £4 on orders over £16
Export surface:   £3.50 for first book + £0.50 for each additional book
Export airmail:   £7 for the first book + £2 for each additional book

| QTY | ISBN | TITLE | PRICE | TOTAL |
|-----|------|-------|-------|-------|
| ____ | 0 7156 3102 0 | Boogie-Woogie | £5.99 | _____ |
| ____ | 0 7156 3094 6 | Charlotte | £5.99 | _____ |
| ____ | 0 7156 3099 7 | Cleopatra's Wedding Present | £6.99 | _____ |
| ____ | 0 7156 3100 4 | Diary of a Man in Despair | £6.99 | _____ |
| ____ | 0 7156 3095 4 | Intimate Cartographies | £5.99 | _____ |
| ____ | 0 7156 3088 1 | IPG to Dickens | £6.99 | _____ |
| ____ | 0 7156 3089 X | IPG to Ethics | £6.99 | _____ |
| ____ | 0 7156 3090 3 | IPG to History | £6.99 | _____ |
| ____ | 0 7156 3091 1 | IPG to Modern Ireland | £6.99 | _____ |
| ____ | 0 7156 3096 2 | Layer Cake | £5.99 | _____ |
| ____ | 0 7156 3097 0 | Never Trust a Rabbit | £5.99 | _____ |
| ____ | 0 7156 3104 7 | One Woman's War | £6.99 | _____ |
| ____ | 0 7156 3092 X | The Pig: A British History | £6.99 | _____ |
| ____ | 0 7156 3098 9 | Too Fast to Live | £5.99 | _____ |
| ____ | 0 7156 3093 8 | The Way of Hermes | £6.99 | _____ |
| ____ | 0 7156 3103 9 | White Stains | £6.99 | _____ |
| | | | TOTAL £ | _____ |

**To: Sales Dept, Duckworth, 61 Frith Street, London W1D 3JL**
**Tel:+44 (0) 20 7434 4242 Fax: +44 (0) 20 7434 4420**
**Heidi@duckworth-publishers.co.uk**